Praise for Kory Stamper's

Word by Word

"An unlikely page-turner. . . . Stamper displays a contagious enthusiasm for words and a considerable talent for putting them together."
—*The New Yorker*

"*Word by Word* cherishes the dexterity involved in making dictionaries and . . . proves refreshingly attentive to its human stories. Part of its quirky charm is a delight in the idiosyncrasies of others—not least Merriam-Webster's many correspondents."
—*The Wall Street Journal*

"Packed with the kind of word-lore that keeps readers and writers up late at night: Where do our words come from? How and why do their meanings change year to year, century to century?"
—*The Dallas Morning News*

"Great fun. . . . [Stamper] brings both zest and style. . . . An exuberant mash note to language."
—*The Times Literary Supplement* (London)

"[*Word by Word*] mixes memoiristic meditations on the lexicographic life along with a detailed description of the brain-twisting work of writing dictionaries."   —*The New York Times*

"Anyone who loves words or has opinions about them will have fun in this sandbox of a book."   —*The Washington Times*

"A delectable feast. . . . [Stamper] declaims elegantly on the beauty and necessity of dialect, how to evaluate emerging words, and many other topics. [She] is at her best when entertaining the reader with amusing etymologies, celebrating the contentiousness of grammar, and quoting annoying emails from an opinionated public."
—*Publishers Weekly* (starred review)

"Fascinating. . . . Part memoir, part workplace chronicle and part history lesson." —*New York Post*

"A lexicographical bildungsroman. . . . [Stamper] presents passionate, precise, good-humored (and bad-humored) descriptions of every stage of the process that goes into making an entry."
—*The Chronicle of Higher Education*

"[*Word by Word*] entertains as much as it instructs."
—*The Baltimore Sun*

"A captivating book." —*Lincoln Journal Star* (Nebraska)

"Idiosyncratic and engaging." —*The Gazette* (Cedar Rapids, IA)

"A smart, sparkling and often hilarious valentine to the content and keepers of dictionaries. . . . A paean to the craft of lexicography."
—*Shelf Awareness*

"A funny inside look at how new words make their way into dictionaries, an irreverent take on the history of English itself, and a memoir of [Stamper's] own journey."
—*Daily Hampshire Gazette* (Northampton, MA)

"[A] marvelous insight into the messy world behind the tidy definitions on the page. . . . By turns amusing, frustrating, surprising, and, above all, engrossing. It is perhaps unsurprising, given her line of work, that Stamper employs words with delightful precision in her writing." —*Booklist*

Kory Stamper

Word by Word

Kory Stamper is a lexicographer who spent almost two decades writing dictionaries at Merriam-Webster. Her writing has appeared in *The Guardian*, *The New York Times, New York* magazine, and *The Washington Post*, and she blogs regularly on language and lexicography at www.korystamper.com.

Word by Word

Word by Word

The Secret Life of Dictionaries

Kory Stamper

Vintage Books
A Division of Penguin Random House LLC
New York

FIRST VINTAGE BOOKS EDITION, MARCH 2018

Copyright © 2017, 2018 by Kory Stamper

All rights reserved. Published in the United States by Vintage Books, a division of Penguin Random House LLC, New York, and distributed in Canada by Random House of Canada, a division of Penguin Random House Canada Limited, Toronto. Originally published in hardcover in the United States by Pantheon Books, a division of Penguin Random House LLC, New York, in 2017.

Vintage and colophon are registered trademarks of Penguin Random House LLC.

The Library of Congress has cataloged the Pantheon edition as follows:
Name: Stamper, Kory, author.
Title: Word by word : the secret life of dictionaries / Kory Stamper.
Description: New York : Pantheon Books, [2017].
Includes bibliographical references and index.
Identifiers: LCCN 2016024253 (print). LCCN 2016037824 (ebook).
Subjects: LCSH: Lexicography—History. Encyclopedias and dictionaries—History and criticism. Lexicographers—Biography. BISAC: REFERENCE / Dictionaries. BIOGRAPHY & AUTOBIOGRAPHY / Personal Memoirs.
Classification: LCC P327.S695 2017 (print). LCC P327 (ebook).
DDC 413.028—dc23.
LC record available at lccn.loc.gov/2016024253

Vintage Books Trade Paperback ISBN: 978-1-101-97026-3
eBook ISBN: 978-1-101-87095-2

Author photograph © Michael Lionstar
Book design by Iris Weinstein

www.vintagebooks.com

Printed in the United States of America
10 9 8 7 6 5 4 3 2

FOR MY PARENTS, ALLEN AND DIANE,
WHO BOUGHT ME BOOKS AND LOVED ME WELL

It may be observed that the English language is not a system of logic, that its vocabulary has not developed in correlation with generations of straight thinkers, that we cannot impose upon it something preconceived as an ideal of scientific method and expect to come out with anything more systematic and more clarifying than what we start with: what we start with is an inchoate heterogeneous conglomerate that retains the indestructible bones of innumerable tries at orderly communication, and our definitions as a body are bound to reflect this situation.

—PHILIP BABCOCK GOVE,
Merriam-Webster in-house "Defining Techniques" memo, May 22, 1958

Contents

Preface xi

HRAFNKELL: *On Falling in Love* 3

BUT: *On Grammar* 23

IT'S: *On "Grammar"* 38

IRREGARDLESS: *On Wrong Words* 52

CORPUS: *On Collecting the Bones* 68

SURFBOARD: *On Defining* 94

PRAGMATIC: *On Examples* 125

TAKE: *On Small Words* 136

BITCH: *On Bad Words* 149

POSH: *On Etymology and Linguistic Originalism* 169

AMERICAN DREAM: *On Dates* 189

NUCLEAR: *On Pronunciation* 199

NUDE: *On Correspondence* 216

MARRIAGE: *On Authority and the Dictionary* 230

EPILOGUE: *The Damnedest Thing* 255

Author's Note 263
Acknowledgments 267
Notes 269
Bibliography 279
Index 285

Preface

Language is one of the few common experiences humanity has. Not all of us can walk; not all of us can sing; not all of us like pickles. But we all have an inborn desire to communicate why we can't walk or sing or stomach pickles. To do that, we use our language, a vast index of words and their meanings we've acquired, like linguistic hoarders, throughout our lives. We eventually come to a place where we can look another person in the eye and say, or write, or sign, "I don't do pickles."

The problem comes when the other person responds, "What do you mean by 'do,' exactly?"

What *do* you mean? It's probable that humanity has been defining in one way or another since we first showed up on the scene. We see it in children today as they acquire their native language: it begins with someone's explaining the universe around them to a rubbery blob of drooling baby, then progresses to that blob understanding the connection between the sound coming out of Mama's or Papa's mouth—"cup"—and the thing Mama or Papa is pointing to. Watching the connection happen is like watching nuclear fission in miniature: there is a flash behind the eyes, a bunch of synapses all firing at once, and then a lot of frantic pointing and data collection. The baby points; an obliging adult responds with the word that represents that object. And so we begin to define.

As we grow, we grind words into finer grist. We learn to pair the word "cat" with "meow"; we learn that lions and leopards are also called "cats," though they have as much in common with your long-haired Persian house cat as a teddy bear has with a grizzly bear. We set up a little mental index card that lists all the things that come to mind when someone says the word "cat," and then when we learn that in parts of Ireland bad weather is called "cat," our eyes widen and we start stapling little slips of addenda to that card.

At heart, we are always looking for that one statement that captures the ineffable, universal catness represented by the word "cat," the thing that encompasses the lion "cat" and the domestic-lazybones "cat" and the bad weather in Ireland, too. And so we turn to the one place where that statement is most likely to be found: the dictionary.

We read the definitions given there with little thought about how they actually make it onto the page. Yet every part of a dictionary definition is crafted by a person sitting in an office, their* eyes squeezed shut as they consider how best to describe, concisely and accurately, that weather meaning of the word "cat." These people expend enormous amounts of mental energy, day in and day out, to find just the right words to describe "ineffable," wringing every word out of their sodden brains in the hopes that the perfect words will drip to the desk. They must ignore the puddle of useless words accumulating around their feet and seeping into their shoes.

In the process of learning how to write a dictionary, lexicographers must face the Escher-esque logic of English and its speakers. What appears to be a straightforward word ends up being a linguistic fun house of doors that open into air and staircases that lead to nowhere. People's deeply held convictions about language catch at your ankles; your own prejudices are the millstone around your neck. You toil onward with steady plodding, losing yourself

---

* Throughout this book, I will be using the singular "their" in place of the gender-neutral "his" or the awkward "his or her" when the gender of the referent isn't known. I know some people think this is controversial, but this usage goes back to the fourteenth century. Better writers than I have used the singular "their" or "they," and the language has not yet fallen all to hell.

to everything but the goal of capturing and documenting this language. Up is down,* bad is good,† and the smallest words will be your downfall. You'd rather do nothing else.

We approach this raucous language the same way we approach our dictionary: word by word.

---

* **up** *adv* . . . **7 b** (I) **:** to a state of completeness or finality (*MWU;* see the bibliography for more details)
  down *adv* . . . **3 d :** to completion *(MWU)*
† **bad** *adj* . . . **10** *slang* **a :** GOOD, GREAT *(MWCII)*

Word by Word

Hrafnkell

On Falling in Love

We are in an uncomfortably small conference room. It is a cool June day, and though I am sitting stock-still on a corporate chair in heavy air-conditioning, I am sweating heavily through my dress. This is what I do in job interviews.

A month earlier, I had applied for a position at Merriam-Webster, America's oldest dictionary company. The posting was for an editorial assistant, a bottom-of-the-barrel position, but I lit up like a penny arcade when I saw that the primary duty would be to write and edit English dictionaries. I cobbled together a résumé; I was invited to interview. I found the best interview outfit I could and applied extra antiperspirant (to no avail).

Steve Perrault, the man who sat opposite me, was (and still is) the director of defining at Merriam-Webster and the person I hoped would be my boss. He was very tall and very quiet, a sloucher like me, and seemed almost as shyly awkward as I was, even while he gave me a tour of the modest, nearly silent editorial floor. Apparently, neither of us enjoyed job interviews. I, however, was the only one perspiring lavishly.

"So tell me," he ventured, "why you are interested in lexicography."

I took a deep breath and clamped my jaw shut so I did not start blabbing. This was a complicated answer.

I grew up the eldest, book-loving child of a blue-collar family that was not particularly literary. According to the hagiography, I

3

started reading at three, rattling off the names of road signs on car trips and pulling salad-dressing bottles out of the fridge to roll their tangy names around on my tongue: *Blue Chee-see, Eye-tal-eye-un, Thouse-and Eyes-land.* My parents cooed over my precociousness but thought little of it.

I chawed my way through board books, hoarded catalogs, decimated the two monthly magazines we subscribed to (*National Geographic* and *Reader's Digest*) by reading them over and over until they fell into tatters. One day my father came home from his job at the local power plant, exhausted, and dropped down onto the couch next to me. He stretched, groaning, and plopped his hard hat on my head. "Whatcha reading, kiddo?" I held the book up for him to see: *Taber's Cyclopedic Medical Dictionary,* a book from my mother's nursing days of yore. "I'm reading about scleroderma," I told him. "It's a disease that affects skin." I was about nine years old.

When I turned sixteen, I discovered more adult delights: Austen, Dickens, Malory, Stoker, a handful of Brontës. I'd sneak them into my room and read until I couldn't see straight.

It wasn't story (good or bad) that pulled me in; it was English itself, the way it felt in my braces-caged mouth and rattled around my adolescent head. As I grew older, words became choice weapons: What else does a dopey, short, socially awkward teenage girl have? I was a capital-*n* Nerd and treated accordingly. "Never give them the dignity of a response" was the advice of my grandmother, echoed by my mother's terser "Just ignore them." But why play dumb when I could outsmart them, if only for my own satisfaction? I snuck our old bargain-bin *Roget's Thesaurus* from the bookshelf and tucked it under my shirt, next to my heart, before scurrying off to my room with it. "Troglodyte," I'd mutter when one of the obnoxious guys in the hall would make a rude comment about another girl's body. "Cacafuego," I seethed when a classmate would brag about the raging kegger the previous weekend. Other teens settled for "brownnoser"; I put my heart into it with "pathetic, lick-spittling ass."

But lexophile that I was, I never considered spending a career on words. I was a practical blue-collar girl. Words were a hobby: they were not going to make me a comfortable living. Or rather, I wasn't going to squander a college education—something no one else in my family had—just to lock myself in a different room a few thousand miles away and read for fourteen hours a day (though I felt wobbly with infatuation at the very idea). I went off to college with every intention of becoming a doctor. Medicine was a safe profession, and I would certainly have plenty of time to read when I had made it as a neurosurgeon.[*]

Fortunately for my future patients, I didn't survive organic chemistry—a course that exists solely to weed slobs like me out of the doctoring pool. I wandered into my sophomore year of college rudderless, a handful of humanities classes on my schedule. One of the women in my dorm quizzed me about my classes over Raisin Bran. "Latin," I droned, "philosophy of religion, a colloq on medieval Icelandic family sagas—"

"Hold up," she said. "Medieval Icelandic family sagas. *Medieval Icelandic family sagas.*" She put her spoon down. "I'm going to repeat this to you one more time so you can hear how insane that sounds: *medieval Icelandic family sagas.*"

It did sound insane, but it sounded far more interesting than organic chemistry. If my sojourn into premed taught me anything, it was that numbers and I didn't get along. "Okay, fine," she said, resuming breakfast, "it's your college debt."

The medieval Icelandic family sagas are a collection of stories about the earliest Norse settlers of Iceland, and while a good number of them are based in historically verifiable events, they nonetheless sound like daytime soaps as written by Ingmar Bergman. Families hold grudges for centuries, men murder for political advantage, women connive to use their husbands or fathers to bring glory to the family name, people marry and divorce and remarry, and their spouses all die under mysterious circumstances. There

---

[*] No matter how book smart, we are all idiots at seventeen.

are also zombies and characters named "Thorgrim Cod-Biter" and "Ketil Flat-Nose." If there was any cure for my failed premed year, this course was it.

But the thing that hooked me was the class during which my professor (who, with his neatly trimmed red beard and Oxbridge manner, would no doubt have been called Craig the Tweedy in one of the sagas) took us through the pronunciation of the Old Norse names.

We had just begun reading a saga whose main character is named Hrafnkell. I, like the rest of my classmates, assumed this unfortunate jumble of letters was pronounced \huh-RAW-funk-ul\ or \RAW-funk-ell\. No, no, the professor said. Old Norse has a different pronunciation convention. "Hrafnkell" should be pronounced—and the sounds that came out of his mouth are not able to be rendered in the twenty-six letters available to me here. The "Hraf" is a guttural, rolled \HRAHP\, as if you stopped a sprinter who was out of breath and clearing their throat and asked them to say "crap." The -*n*- is a swallowed hum, a little break so your vocal cords are ready for the glorious flourish that is "-kell." Imagine saying "blech"—the sound kids in commercials make when presented with a plate of steamed broccoli instead of Strawberry Choco-Bomb Crunch cereal. Now replace the /bl/ with a /k/ as in "kitten." That is the pronunciation of "Hrafnkell."

No one could get that last sound right; the whole class sounded like cats disgorging hair balls. *"Ch, ch,"* our professor said, and we dutifully mimicked: *uch, uch*. "I'm spitting all over myself," one student complained, whereupon the professor brightened. "Yeah," he chirped, "yeah, you've got it!"

That final double-*l* in Old Norse, he said, was called the voiceless alveolar lateral fricative. "What?" I blurted, and he repeated: "voiceless alveolar lateral fricative." He went on to say it was used in Welsh, too, but I was lost to his explanation, instead tumbling in and over that label. *Voiceless alveolar lateral fricative*. A sound that you make, that you *give voice* to, that is nonetheless called "voiceless" and that, when issued, can be aimed like a stream of chewing tobacco, *laterally*. And "fricative"—that sounded hopelessly, gorgeously obscene.

I approached the professor after class. I wanted, I told him, to major in *this*—Icelandic family sagas and weird pronunciations and whatever else there was.

"You could do medieval studies," he suggested. "Old English is the best place to start."

The following semester, twenty other students and I sat around a large conference table of the kind you only see in liberal arts colleges or movies with war rooms in them, while the same professor introduced us to Old English. Old English is the great-granddaddy of Modern English, an ancestor language that was spoken in England between roughly A.D. 500 and 1100. It looks like drunk, sideways German with some extra letters thrown in for good measure:

Hē is his brōðor.
Þæt wæs mīn wīf.
Þis līf is sceort.
Hwī singeð ðes monn?

But speak it aloud, and the family resemblance is clear:

He is his brother.
That was my wife.
This life is short.
Why is that man singing?

We stuttered our way through the translations. My professor went on to explain the pronunciation conventions of Old English; there is a handy and completely abstruse pronunciation section in our *Bright's Old English Grammar,** and the class delved right in.

But that first translation exercise left me with an itch at the back of my brain that wouldn't go away: "Hwī singeð ðes monn?" I stared

---

* The edition of *Bright's* I used was edited by Frederic Cassidy, a lexicographer of some renown. Lexicography and medievalists go together like swords and shields.

at the sentence for a while, wondering why the other sentences seemed to match their translations so well, but this one didn't.

This was not the first of these itches: I had had them in high-school German class, when I realized how *Vater* and *Mutter* and *Schwester* looked like Amish cousins of "father" and "mother" and "sister." I had had the same mental scratch in Latin, when I mumbled through my *amo, amas, amat* and realized that "amour"—an English word that refers to love or the beloved—looked a lot like the Latin verb *amare,* "to love." I waited until after class and asked my professor about his translation of "hwī singeð ðes monn?" and he confessed that it wasn't a literal, word-for-word translation; that would be "why singeth this man?" The itching intensified. I was vaguely aware that Shakespeare used certain words that we didn't anymore—"singeth" being one of them—but I had never wondered why those earlier forms were different from the current ones. English is English, right? But English, I was fast learning, was fluid. "Singeth" wasn't just a highfalutin flourish deployed to lend a sense of elevation and elegance to Shakespeare's writings; "singeth" was a normal, boring way to say "sing" in the late sixteenth century. And it happened to be a holdover from Anglo-Saxon. We used "singeth" as the third-person form longer than we used "sings."

I had spent years hoovering up words as quickly and indiscriminately as I could, the linguistic equivalent of a dog snarfing up spilled popcorn; I gobbled up "sing" and "singeth" without much thought about why the forms were so different. My only thought was *stupid English.* But those illogical lunacies of English that we all suffer through and rage against aren't illogical at all. It's all spelled out here, in the baby pictures of English.

From that point on, I was a woman obsessed: I traced words across the rough sword and buckler of Old English, over the sibilant seesaw of Middle English, through the bawdy wink-wink-nudge-nudge of Shakespeare; I picked and chipped at words like "supercilious" until I found the cool, slow-voweled Latin and Greek under them. I discovered that "nice" used to mean "lewd" and "stew" used to mean "whorehouse." I hadn't just fallen down this rabbit hole: I saw that hole in the distance and ran full tilt at it, throwing myself headlong into it. The more I learned, the more I fell in love with this wild, vibrant whore of a language.

Hands clasped tightly together, I tried to give Steve Perrault a heavily abridged and eloquent version of this history. He sat impassive across from me as I blithered, awash in flop sweat and aware—perhaps for the first time since I answered the want ad—that I really, really wanted this job, and I was really, really rambling.

I stopped and leaned in, breathless. "I just," I began, fanning my hands in front of me as if to waft intelligence my way. But it didn't come: all I had was the naked, heartfelt truth. "I just love English," I burst. "I love it. I really, really love it."

Steve took a deep breath. "Well," he deadpanned, "there are few who share your enthusiasm for it."

I started as an editorial assistant at Merriam-Webster three weeks later.

Merriam-Webster is the oldest dictionary maker in America, dating unofficially back to 1806 with the publication of Noah Webster's first dictionary, *A Compendious Dictionary of the English Language,* and officially back to 1844, when the Merriam brothers bought the rights to Webster's dictionary after his death. The company has been around longer than Ford Motors, Betty Crocker, NASCAR, and thirty-three of the fifty American states. It's more American than football (a British invention) and apple pie (ditto). According to the lore, the flagship product of the company, *Merriam-Webster's Collegiate Dictionary,* is one of the best-selling books in American history and may be second in sales only to the Bible.*

---

*   The company lore is difficult to substantiate: the methodology behind many
    best-seller lists is murky and opaque. It's safe to say that the *Collegiate* is
    probably America's best-selling desk dictionary just by dint of being one of

You might expect such an august American institution to be housed in lofty Georgian or neoclassical digs, something in marble with a goodly number of columns, and a pristine lawn. Think of the architectural equivalent of the word "dictionary," and what springs to mind is stained glass, vaulted ceilings, dark wood paneling, majestic draperies.

The reality is quite different. Merriam-Webster is housed in a modest two-story brick building located in what is euphemistically known as a "transitional neighborhood" in Springfield, Massachusetts. Drug deals occasionally happen in the parking lot, and there are bullet holes in the safety glass at the back of the building. The front door, framed with some moderately interesting brickwork and a lovely oriel window, is always locked; ring the bell and no one will answer it. Employees enter through the back of the building, hunched and hurried, like they're sneaking into one of the strip clubs around the corner. The interior is full of odd juxtapositions, with historic ephemera sprinkled throughout a building whose aesthetic is best described as Office Bland. One side of the basement is a nonfunctioning cafeteria from the 1950s, which was converted to a lunchroom with stout wooden tables and vast echoic linoleum surfaces, with a small office tucked in the corner at "garden level." The other side of the basement is wire-caged, dimly lit clutter that houses oddities like old grade-school dioramas of important moments in American history that have been donated to the company, crates of Urdu-language printings of our dictionaries, and the fusty glut of old papers bunged hastily into metal bookshelves. Wandering through the tight aisles, you can feel the heebie-jeebies brushing the back of your neck; it is the storage room of David Lynch's dreams.

It's not all Lovecraftian unease: two stately conference rooms bookend the building, done up with painted wood paneling and long drapes, dominated by massive, dark conference tables that are

---

the oldest continuously published desk dictionaries around. No list I consulted placed it at number two, however.

always polished to a mirror shine and upon which *no one* is allowed to place anything except special felt-backed desk pads. But those are the only rooms of grandeur in the place. The rest of the building is a rabbit warren of cubicles in varying shades of that noncolor, taupe. Even the coffee seems anachronistic: it's anonymous stuff that comes in oversized orange foil packets—packets whose vintage seems to match the industrial coffeemaker we use that dates back to the Johnson administration. The grit in the foil packets produces coffee that tastes like wet cardboard, but it is our coffee and we will not change it. Recently, the editorial floor finally acquired one of those new one-cup jobbies that hiss like an angry lizard. People nonetheless make and drink the vile orange-foil stuff.

There's an odd juxtaposition of people, too. Downstairs you'll find the employees who enjoy talking: customer service, marketing, IT. It's not a loud office, but there's conversation, laughter, the electronic burble of phone calls, the whump of boxes being hefted and dumped. People prairie-dog over the tops of their cubicles and call to their co-workers: "Hey, you going for a walk at lunch today?" It is perfectly, blandly normal. Head up the echoey stairwell to the second floor, and the happy din damps into silence. You come to a landing with two heavy fire doors facing each other, closed. Listen; it sounds empty, abandoned, perhaps a little haunted. It doesn't help that it's also much darker in the stairwell than you anticipated. The tableau gets you wondering what weirdnesses they've squirreled away up here—more unsettling dioramas, perhaps, or Miss Havisham languishing in a dusty chaise longue—when one of the doors suddenly swings open. The person on the other side starts, eyes like dinner plates, then ducks their head, whispers, "Sorry," and scurries around you. The door is open: beyond are more cubicles, lots of books, and the *feel* of people, though not the *sound* of people. Welcome to the editorial floor.

The vast majority of people give no thought to the dictionary they use: it merely *is,* like the universe. To one group of people, the dictionary was handed to humanity *ex coeli,* a hallowed leather-clad tome of truth and wisdom as infallible as God. To another group of people, the dictionary is a thing you picked up in the bargain bin, paperback and on sale for a dollar, because you felt that an adult should own a dictionary. Neither group realizes that their dictionary is a human document, constantly being compiled, proofread, and updated by actual, living, awkward people. In that unassuming brick building in Springfield, there are a couple dozen people who spend their workweek doing nothing but making dictionaries—sifting the language, categorizing it, describing it, alphabetizing it. They are word nerds who spend the better parts of their lives writing and editing dictionary definitions, thinking deeply about adverbs, and slowly, inexorably going blind. They are lexicographers.

To be fair, most lexicographers didn't think much about the people behind dictionaries before they applied for their jobs. For all of my love of English, I gave scant thought to the dictionary and never even realized that there was more than one dictionary; there is no "*the* dictionary" but rather "*a* dictionary" or "*one of several* dictionaries." The red Webster's dictionary that we all used is just one of many "Webster's" dictionaries, published by different publishers; "Webster's" is not a proprietary name, and so any publisher can slap it on any reference they like. And they do: nearly every American reference publisher since the nineteenth century has put out a reference and called it a "Webster's."* But I knew none of this until I started working at Merriam-Webster. If I gave dictionaries so little thought, then I gave lexicography itself bugger all.

This is the song of my people. Most lexicographers had no clue that such a career path existed until they were smack in the middle of it.

---

* The company now called Merriam-Webster lost exclusive rights to the name "Webster" in 1908 when the First Circuit Court of Appeals averred that the name "Webster" had passed into the public domain when the copyright on *Webster's Unabridged Dictionary* expired in 1889. Easy come, easy go.

Neil Serven, an editor at Merriam-Webster, is an outlier. He sums up his brief childhood musings on how dictionaries came to be thusly: "I imagined dark halls and angry people."

There are not many of us plying our trade these days; language may be a growth industry, but dictionaries are not. (When's the last time *you* bought a new dictionary? I thought so.) And yet whenever I tell people what I do—and after they make me repeat it, because the statement "I write dictionaries" is so unexpected—one of the first things they ask is if we're hiring. Sit in a room all day, read, ponder the meanings of words—to anyone who even remotely likes words, it sounds like the ideal job.

At Merriam-Webster, there are only two formal requirements to be a lexicographer: you must have a degree in any field from an accredited four-year college or university, and you must be a native speaker of English.

People are surprised (and perhaps slightly appalled) to hear that we don't require lexicographers to be linguists or English majors. The reality is that a diverse group of drudges will yield better definitions. Most lexicographers are "general definers"; that is, they define all sorts of words from all subject areas, from knitting to military history to queer theory to hot-rodding. And while you don't need expertise in every field conceivable in order to define the vocabulary used in that field, there are some fields whose lexicon is a little more opaque than others:

When P* is less than P, the Fed can ease its credit policies, allowing bank credit and the money supply to grow at a faster rate. The P* formula is:

$$P^* = M2 \times V^*/Q^*$$

where M2 is an official measure of the money supply (checks plus checkable deposits, savings, and time deposit accounts), V* is the velocity of M2, or the number of times that money turns over, and Q* is the estimated value of Gross National Product at a nominal growth rate of 2.5% a year.

To someone like me who has an antagonistic relationship with math, this is a nightmare. What's P? Checkable deposits are different from checks? Money has *velocity* (and not just away from me)? If there's someone on staff, however, who has taken economics courses, they are likely equipped to navigate this sea of jargon. Consequently, we have a minyan of English and linguistics majors on staff, but we also have economists, scientists of every stripe, historians, philosophers, poets, artists, mathematicians, international business majors, and enough medievalists to staff a Renaissance Faire.

We also require that our lexicographers be native speakers of English, for a very practical reason: that's the language we focus on, and you need mastery over all its idioms and expressions. It is a sad reality that in your daily work as a lexicographer, you will read some good writing and a lot of mediocre and terrible writing. You need to be able to know, without being told, that "the cat are yowling" is not grammatically correct whereas "the crowd are loving it" is just very British.

Your status as a native speaker of English also becomes a place of comfort you can return to throughout your career. There will come a point when you are deep in the weeds of a word, hunched over your desk in bone-crushing, head-in-hands concentration. You will have been staring at this entry for days, unsure of how to proceed, and that filament of sanity inside you will suddenly fizzle and snap. It will become clear to you, in the space between heartbeats, why you are having a hard time with this entry: it is because you realize now that you do not, in fact, actually speak English—that the words you are reading are in some Low German dialect and you are no longer certain that they mean anything. It will be 3:00 p.m. on a Wednesday in April; you will glimpse preternaturally sunny weather through the sliver of window near your desk; the shouts of children walking home from school will sound both alien and familiar; cool, metallic panic will slide down your gullet and wave up at you from your stomach. Don't be alarmed: this is normal when you spend all day alone with nothing but the English language. Simply stand, walk briskly downstairs, and ask the first marketing or customer service person you see, "Am I speaking English?" They will assure you that you are. They might remind you that we hire only people who speak it natively.

There are some additional unmeasurable and unstated requirements to be a lexicographer. First and foremost, you must be possessed of something called "sprachgefühl," a German word we've stolen into English that means "a feeling for language." Sprachgefühl is a slippery eel, the odd buzzing in your brain that tells you that "planting the lettuce" and "planting misinformation" are different uses of "plant," the eye twitch that tells you that "plans to demo the store" refers not to a friendly instructional stroll on how to shop but to a little exuberance with a sledgehammer. Not everyone has sprachgefühl, and you don't know if you are possessed of it until you are knee-deep in the English language, trying your best to navigate the mucky swamp of it. I use "possessed of" advisedly: *You* will never *have* sprachgefühl, but rather sprachgefühl will have *you,* like a Teutonic imp that settles itself at the base of your skull and hammers at your head every time you read something like "crispy-fried rice" on a menu. The imp will dig its nails into your brain, and instead of ordering take-out Chinese, you will be frozen at the take-out counter, wondering if "crispy-fried rice" refers to plain rice that has been flash fried or to the dish known as "fried rice" but perhaps prepared in a new and exciting way. *That hyphen,* you think, *could just be slapdash misuse, or* . . . And your Teutonic imp giggles and squeezes its claws a little harder.

If you don't have sprachgefühl, it will become very apparent about six months into your tenure as a lexicographer. Don't be disappointed. This just means you can leave for a more lucrative job, like take-out delivery driver.

You must also be temperamentally suited to sitting in near silence for eight hours a day and working entirely alone. There will be other people in the office—you will hear them shuffling papers and muttering to themselves—but you will have almost no contact with them. In fact, you are warned of this over and over again. The first part of my interview at Merriam-Webster was a tour of the sepulchrally quiet editorial floor. Steve pointed out that there were no phones at most desks; if you needed to make or take a phone call, for whatever horrible reason, there are two phone booths on the editorial floor available for your use. The phone booths are still there. They are rarely used, tiny, unventilated, and not soundproofed; they are not rarely used *because* they are tiny, unventilated, and not soundproofed, however. They are rarely used because editors don't talk on the phone if they can help it. I marveled aloud at the phone booths, and Steve looked askance. Was I expecting to have a phone at my desk? he wondered. I assured him I was not. My previous job as an assistant in a busy office left me drained and bone shaken, and I nearly wept for joy at hearing I wouldn't have a phone at my desk.

The second part of my interview was conducted with Fred Mish, Merriam-Webster's then editor in chief, who sat in one of the small conference rooms like a spider in his lair, waiting for the fly in her nice interview clothes to come twitching in. He cast an eye over my résumé and asked with some incredulity if I *enjoyed* interacting with people, because if I did, then I should understand this job promised nothing of the sort. "Office chitchat of the sort you're likely used to," he grumped, "is not conducive to good lexicography and doesn't happen." He wasn't lying: I began work at Merriam-Webster in July; it took me about a month to exchange hellos (and in some cases just hellos) with the other forty editors on the floor. One of my co-workers told me that there had been a formal Rule of Silence—and you could hear the capitalization as he said it—on the editorial floor until the early 1990s. I was recently told that was a fiction, but one of the editors who was hired in the '50s to work on *Webster's Third New International Dictionary* claims it was true. "The silence of the lambs was a fact," says E. Ward Gilman, one of the greats of lexicography and an editor emeritus at Merriam-

Webster, "although I don't remember who would have kept telling newbies about it."

Emily Brewster, who has been an editor at Merriam-Webster for over fifteen years, sums up the secret longing of every lexicographer: "Yes, this is what I want to do. I want to sit alone in a cubicle all day and think about words and not really talk to anybody else. That sounds great!"

There's a good reason for the quiet. Lexicography is an intermingling of science and art, and both require a commitment to silent concentration. Your job as a definer is to find the exact right words to describe a word's meaning, and that takes some serious brain wringing. "Measly," for example, is often used to mean "small," and you could get away with simply defining it as such and moving on. But there's a particular kind of smallness to "measly" that isn't the same sort of smallness associated with the word "teeny"— "measly" implies a sort of grudging, grubbing smallness, a miserly meagerness, and so as a definer you begin wandering the highways and byways of English looking for the right word to describe the peculiar smallness of "measly." There is nothing worse than being just a syllable's length away from the perfect, Platonic ideal of the definition for "measly," being able to see it crouching in the shadows of your mind, only to have it skitter away when your co-worker begins a long and loud conversation that touches on the new coffee filters, his colonoscopy, and the chances that the Sox will go all the way this year.[*]

Of course, we do need to occasionally communicate with each other in order to function. We now use e-mail, but until computers were common on the floor, there was a system of interoffice communication called "the pink."

At Merriam-Webster, every editor has the same set of tools at

---

[*] "Measly" is defined in the *Collegiate Dictionary, Eleventh Edition,* as "contemptibly small." Emily Brewster thinks it might be the best definition in the whole book.

their desk: a personalized date stamp, with your last name and the date, which is how you sign and date any physical thing that crosses your desk; a fistful of pens and pencils (including a few stubby old Stabilo pencils, formerly used to mark insertions and deletions on shiny-papered galleys and now hoarded against the coming Pencil Apocalypse); and a box of three-by-five index cards in pink, yellow, white, and blue. The colors are not to make your tan-gray cubicle festive; they have a purpose. White cards are for citations, any little slip of English usage that you want to make note of. Blue cards are for production reference. Yellow cards, or buffs, as we call them, are for drafted definitions only. Pink cards, or pinks, are for any miscellaneous notes for the file: typo reports, questions about how to handle an entry, comments on existing definitions.* Pinks also ended up being used for personal communications.

It worked like this. Say you have a group of editors who typically go out to lunch together on Friday. You don't want to bother each editor by sauntering over to their cubicle to blab about whether it's Indian or Thai this week, so you write a pink. The initials of each editor go in the upper-right corner of the card; the question goes in the middle. You sign the note and throw it in your out-box for the first morning interoffice mail pickup. The note goes to the first editor on the list; they answer, then cross their initials off and drop the note in the next editor's in-box.

Circuitous and less efficient than a conversation? Absolutely. But risk walking to a colleague's desk only to see them startle and freeze like a rabbit as the hawk swoops in? No, thank you.

Because gabbing around the watercooler isn't encouraged, lexicographers are perhaps a little awkward when it comes to the niceties of casual human interaction. When I was being given my tour of the building after joining the staff, we came up to one editor's desk

---

* Even though everything has been electronic for some time, the word "pink" has stuck. When we annotate a production spreadsheet, we still refer to it as "sending a pink to the file."

to find it was chock-full of historical Merriam-Webster ephemera: old advertising posters and giant prints of historical illustrations and, above them all, a black-and-white portrait of a man. The editor happily explained what all the pictures and posters were, then pointed at the portrait. "And that," he said, "is an editor who used to work here, and one day he went home and shot himself." My eyes widened; he merely crossed his arms and asked us where we had all gone to college.

Nowhere else is our institutional introversion borne out than at the Merriam-Webster holiday parties. The parties are usually held in the afternoon, and in the basement of the building, which in some years is literally spruced up for the occasion. Traditionally, the editors ring the cafeteria in groups of twos and threes, clutching our wine and murmuring quietly among ourselves while the marketing and customer service folks whoop it up in the center of the room near the shrimp cocktail, having quantifiable, voluble amounts of loud fun. It's not that editors don't like fun; it's that we like our fun to be a little less whoop-y.[*] "We're not antisocial," says Emily Vezina, a cross-reference editor. "We're just social in our own way."

Lexicographers spend a lifetime swimming through the English language in a way that no one else does; the very nature of lexicography demands it. English is a beautiful, bewildering language, and the deeper you dive into it, the more effort it takes to come up to the surface for air. To be a lexicographer, you must be able to sit with a word and all its many, complex uses and whittle those down into a two-line definition that is both broad enough to encompass the vast majority of the word's written use and narrow enough that

---

[*] The editorial floor has its own holiday potluck that is much more our speed. The long galley tables are cleared off for the food, and editors congregate around the citation files, the tall banks of drawers holding our plates while we all practice talking in a normal tone of voice. The editorial potlucks have gone on for over twenty years and will probably go on for another twenty, along with that damned coffeemaker.

it actually communicates something specific about this word—that "teeny" and "measly," for instance, don't refer to the same kind of smallness. You must set aside your own linguistic and lexical prejudices about what makes a word worthy, beautiful, or right, to tell the truth about language. Each word must be given equal treatment, even when you think the word that has come under your consideration is a foul turd that should be flushed from English. Lexicographers set themselves apart from the world in a weird sort of monastic way and devote themselves wholly to the language.

Which leads to the third, and possibly most slippery, personality quirk required to do lexicography: the ability to quietly do the same task on the same book until the universe collapses in on itself like a soufflé in a windstorm. It's not just that defining itself is repetitive; it's that the project timelines in lexicography are traditionally so long they could reasonably be measured in geologic epochs. A new edition of the *Collegiate Dictionary* takes anywhere from three to five years to complete, and that's assuming that most of the editors on staff are working only on the *Collegiate*. Our last printed unabridged dictionary, *Webster's Third New International,* took a staff of almost 100 editors and 202 outside consultants twelve years to write. We began work on its successor in 2010; because of attrition, there are, as of this writing, 25 editors on staff. If we hold to the schedule, the new *Unabridged* should be finished a few weeks before Christ returns in majesty to judge the quick and the dead.

Lexicography moves so slowly that scientists classify it as a solid. When you finish defining, you must copyedit; when you finish copyediting, you must proofread; when you finish proofreading, you must proofread again, because there were changes and we need to double-check. When the dictionary finally hits the market, there is no grand party or celebration. (Too loud, too social.) We're already working on the next update to that dictionary, because language has moved on. There will never be a break. A dictionary is out of date the minute that it's done.

It is this slog through the fens of English that led Samuel John-

son, the unofficial patron saint of English lexicography, to define
"lexicographer" in his 1755 *Dictionary of the English Language* as
"a writer of dictionaries, a harmless drudge." It's a definition people
chuckle over, but it is in earnest. In a 1747 letter to the Earl of Chesterfield, Johnson writes,

> I knew that the work in which I engaged is generally considered as
> drudgery for the blind, as the proper toil of artless industry; a task
> that requires neither the light of learning, nor the activity of genius,
> but may be successfully performed without any higher quality than
> that of bearing burthens with dull patience, and beating the track
> of the alphabet with sluggish resolution. . . . It appeared that the
> province allotted me was of all the regions of learning generally
> confessed to be the least delightful, that it was believed to produce
> neither fruits nor flowers, and that after a long and laborious culti-
> vation, not even the barren laurel had been found upon it.

Bearing burdens with patience, beating the track of the alphabet
with sluggish resolution, the least delightful, the long and fruitlessly
laborious—and that was how Samuel Johnson felt about lexicography *before* he started writing his famous *Dictionary*.

He didn't lighten up any once he had finished, either. The preface
to his magnum opus begins,

> It is the fate of those who toil at the lower employments of life, to
> be rather driven by the fear of evil, than attracted by the prospect
> of good; to be exposed to censure, without hope of praise; to be
> disgraced by miscarriage, or punished for neglect, where success
> would have been without applause, and diligence without reward.
> Among these unhappy mortals is the writer of dictionaries.

And yet these unhappy mortals continue their work. An academic friend who studies old dictionaries remarked that it seemed
less like a job and more like a calling, and so, in some ways, it is.

Every day, lexicographers plunge into the roiling mess of English, up to the elbows, to fumble and grasp at the right words to describe ennui, love, or chairs. They rassle with them, haul them out of the muck, and slap them flopping on the page, exhausted and exhilarated by the effort, then do it again. They do this work for no fame, because all their work is published anonymously under a company rubric, and certainly not for fortune, because the profit margins in lexicography are so narrow they're measured in cents. The process of creating a dictionary is magical, frustrating, brain wrenching, mundane, transcendent. It is ultimately a show of love for a language that has been called unlovely and unlovable.

Here's how it happens.

But

On Grammar

My husband is a musician, which means that I occasionally get invited to swank parties full of cool people with interesting hair. I go along for spousal support and mostly as a dorky foil; I plant myself near the food and start shoving as much of it in my mouth as I can in the hopes that no one will engage me in conversation.

Inevitably, someone with better social skills comes over and asks, "What do you do?"

"I write dictionaries," I will say, and then sometimes the inquisitor will brighten. "Oh, dictionaries!" they'll respond. "I love words! I love grammar!"

This is the point at which I will begin eyeing the room for exits and sending strong telepathic messages to my husband, who is deep in conversation across the room, talking about Schoenberg or electronica. I know what's coming, and here it is, uttered between sips of cheap box wine: "You must be great at grammar."

I will grab a handful of whatever snack is closest and cram it into my maw so all I can do in response is nod in a noncommittal sort of way. I hope that the head waggle does it and I am not required to say what I am actually thinking: one of the first things you encounter as a working lexicographer is the stark reality that you only *think* you're good at grammar, and the kind of grammar you are good at is—sorry—useless.

You might have been the sort of student who loved diagramming sentences, or the one who could theoretically hold forth at raging parties on the difference between the disjuncts and conjuncts (if people invited lexicographers to raging parties, that is). Maybe you're a polyglot, collecting languages like lucky pennies, cherishing their differences and similarities until you can evoke an entire language's feel and weight by running your thumb over the face of one word. People who become lexicographers are naturally interested in the clockwork of English, but years of studying those little wheels and cogs can make you myopic. You don't realize how myopic until you back away from the bench and take a look around.

Your first training as a lexicographer, the Style and Defining classes, is that chance to push back from English and get your grammatical bearings. The Style and Defining classes I took as part of my orientation were held in a small conference room at the back of the editorial floor. The editorial conference room is really nothing more than a glorified storage space, a little nook left over after the freight elevator and the stairwell were built, but it has a window and so was deemed too nice to fill with cleaning supplies. It's currently stuffed with old dictionaries and a small table, around which four editors can sit comfortably and six in introverted terror, warily holding their elbows to their sides and breathing shallowly so as not to make unintentional physical contact with anyone else in the room.

The editor training us was E. Ward Gilman, or Gil as we called him. By the time I came around, he had been at Merriam-Webster for forty years and had trained at least two generations of definers. He was the editor who wrote most of our *Dictionary of English Usage* and was a regular sparring partner with *The New York Times*'s On Language columnist, William Safire. On paper, Gil was intellectually imposing, though in person he was amiable: ample of gut and with an unaffected, folksy manner, a bit like a nineteenth-century sea captain gone to seed. None of us knew that at the time, though, and so we sat across from him, eager and slightly cowed in the over-warm editorial conference room. Our Style and Defining notebooks were open to the section called "A Quirky Little Grammar for Definers" (third edition, fourth printing). The sun dawdled through the window, and the musty, vanilla fug of old dictionaries hung around us. Gil leaned back and sucked his teeth. "Grammar. Some of you," he warned, "are not going to like what I am about to tell you."

A lexicographer's view of grammar begins with the parts of speech, eight tidy categories we shunt words into based on their function within a sentence. If you survived the American educational system, you can probably rattle off at least four parts of speech—noun, verb, adjective, adverb—and here the nerds among us chime in with the remainder: conjunction, interjection, pronoun, and preposition. Most people think of the parts of speech as discrete categories, drawers with their own identifying labels, and when you peek inside, there's the English language, neatly folded like a retiree's socks: Person, Place, Thing (Noun); Describes Action (Verb); Modifies Nouns (Adjective); Answers the *W* Questions (Adverb); Joins Words Together (Conjunction); Things We Say When We Are Happy, Surprised, or Pissed Off (Interjection).

Your first disconcerting realization as a lexicographer is that you are the person who is responsible for sifting the language and placing individual words in those drawers. This is a sharp whack against your naive assumptions about how words come into being and exist. You mean words don't just appear ex nihilo in the drawer they're supposed to be in? Some slob in a beige office in Massachusetts is the one who decides what a word *is*?

Not quite. Your job as a lexicographer, and part of the reason why Gil is looking doubtfully in your general direction this afternoon, is to learn how to carefully parse English as it is used, sentence by sentence, and correctly classify the words within that sentence by their function. You don't decide what part of speech a word is—the general speaking, writing public does. You merely discern what its part of speech is and then accurately report it in the dictionary entry.

This should be a comfort, but it is not. English is a remarkably flexible language, and its grammar is not nearly as tidy as we have been led to believe. Those parts of speech are not discrete boxes keeping everything dust-free and separate but more like a jumble of fishing nets. Randolph Quirk, lead author of *A Comprehensive Grammar of the English Language,* calls this "gradience." Many words are caught easily in those individual nets: In the sentence "dictionaries are great," we can tell that "dictionaries" is a noun because it fits into the common, oversimplified paradigm we are all taught to identify nouns: person, place, thing. There are, however, plenty of words that live on the periphery of a part of speech, and they can get tangled between those fishing nets. Nouns can act like adjectives ("*chocolate* cake"); adjectives can act like nouns ("grammarians are the *damned*"); verbs can look like verbs ("she's *running* down the street") or adjectives ("a *running* engine") or nouns ("her favorite hobby is *running*"). Adverbs look like everything else; they are the junk drawer of the English language (*"like so"*).

Even within one net, the catch is still eel slick: a lexicographer can look at the sentence "The young editors were bent to Webster's will" and, after some mental finagling, decide that "bent" is actually a verb here (the past tense of "bend"). Very good. Is this use of "bend" transitive (that is, it requires an object, as in "I bend steel") or intransitive (that is, it doesn't require an object, as in "reeds bend")? "Were bent" could be a passive use of "bend," where the force doing the bending is hidden from lexical view, and transitive verbs are generally used in passive constructions—but who is the actor? Webster's disembodied will? Older editors who were not going to take any young-upstart bullshit? It is all muddling in your mind. You put the end of your pencil in your mouth to keep yourself from muttering in exasperation and wonder if you're nonetheless wrong: that "bent" here is actually the adjective we've formed from the past participle of "bend"—the adjective that appears in "go to hell and get *bent*."[*] You have pulled your notepad toward you and

---

[*] **bent** *adj* . . . —**get bent** *slang*—used as an angry or contemptuous way of dismissing someone's statement, suggestion, etc. <I try to call him the next

are scrawling all sorts of unintentionally creepy sentences on it—
"the young editors were *subdued,*" "[someone] *subdued* the young
editors"—trying to figure out whether this use is transitive or not,
and the more you write, the less you know.

You're not alone. Peter Sokolowski of Merriam-Webster now
keeps a rare editorial artifact, passed down from editor to editor:
the Transitivity Tester. The Transitizer, as some of us call it, is a
pink with a sentence on it and a hole cut out where the verb of the
sentence is so you can lay the card over your problem verb and read
the resulting sentence to see if that verb is, in fact, transitive. The
Transitizer reads, "I'ma _____ ya ass." I'ma <u>bend</u> ya ass (to Webster's will). There you go: this sense of "bend" must be transitive.

This mayhem is possible in part because those hallowed parts of
speech we hew to aren't inherent to English. In the West,[*] they were
first hinted at in the fourth century B.C. by Plato in *Cratylus,* where
he names verbs and nouns as two parts of a sentence. Aristotle,
never one to be left out of an opining party, added "conjunction" to
Plato's two parts of speech but defines it in his *Poetics* as "a sound
without meaning" (English teachers who have encountered one too
many "and . . . and . . . and . . ." run-on sentences would heartily
agree). The parts of speech we use today were established in the
second century B.C. in a treatise called *The Art of Grammar,* which
gives us our first incarnation of the eight parts of speech: noun,
verb, participle, article, pronoun, preposition, adverb, and conjunction. This system has been futzed with over the centuries: article
was dropped, interjection was added, participle was later considered a flavor of verb, and adjective was pried out of the noun class
and became its own thing. By the time English lexicographers came

---

morning to apologize, but he tells me to *get bent.*—Chuck Klosterman, *Sex,
Drugs, and Cocoa Puffs,* 2003> (*MWU*)

[*]   Like many things that are claimed as Western inventions, grammar was first
practiced in the East. According to scholars, there is a rich tradition of grammatical typology in Sanskrit that dates back to at least the sixth century B.C.
and probably the eighth century B.C.

on the scene in the late Middle Ages, our parts of speech were fixed and based entirely on Latin and Greek.

This occasionally presents problems, because English is not Latin or Greek. In Latin, for instance, there are no indefinite or definite articles, no "a," "an," or "the." Articles are generally implicitly understood from the context. The main literary dialect of ancient Greek, just to keep things spicy, has a definite article but no indefinite article. This seems as foreign as outer space to native English speakers—you're able to say "the lexicographer" but not "a lexicographer"? In Attic Greek, no, that's not possible. The indefinite article, as in Latin, was implied by context. However, if we go a little further back to Homeric Greek, then there are no articles at all, like in Latin. This is not particularly helpful for English grammarians, because our language is lousy with articles.

Given that our parts of speech are modeled on Latin and Greek, and neither Latin nor Greek has the articles that English has, what part of speech should a lexicographer give "a"?

Gil's "Quirky Little Grammar" provides a cheat sheet with quick paradigms to help clarify common uses. These paradigms are often dotted liberally with warnings about the many pitfalls awaiting lexicographers as they begin pulling this sticky mess of a language apart to peer at its entrails. Here is the paragraph on articles in the "Quirky Little Grammar":

> 4.2 Article. There are three: the indefinite articles *a* and *an* and the definite article *the*. Not much room for confusion here, right? All three are also prepositions (six cents *a* mile; 35 miles *an* hour; $10 *the* bottle), and *the* is an adverb (*the* sooner *the* better). In more sophisticated grammars, articles are one kind of determiner.

The entirety of Gil's grammar is like this: here is a part of speech, and here are all the ways that this particular part of speech will drive you crazy as you attempt to parse its uses. The main sections explain the basic attributes of one part of speech, and the subsections list all the possible deviations from those basic attributes.

The reality is that your high-school English teachers lied to you about what words can do because doing so makes English much, much simpler. Yes, conjunctions connect two clauses ("this is stupid *and* I'm not listening anymore"), but certain types of conjunctions show a subordinate relationship between the clauses, and those conjunctions look a lot like adverbs ("she acts *as if* I care"). Prepositions, you learned, always introduce a noun or a noun phrase ("he let the cat *inside* the house"). But your teacher didn't tell you that sometimes prepositions don't introduce a noun or a noun phrase, because that noun or noun phrase is understood ("he let the cat *inside*"). Everyone knows that adverbs answer the questions "who?" "what?" "when?" "where?" "why?" and "how?" but few people realize that conjunctions and prepositions can do the same thing. Gil notes that no one has bothered to provide a compendious description of what a noun is because everyone is supposed to know what a noun is. "Person, place, thing" is wholly inadequate: "hope" is a noun, as is "murder." Are those people, places, or things?

The hardest words to sort grammatically are the ones that no one ever notices—the small ubiquities of English. Ask any lexicographer who has been at this gig for a while what word had them hunched over their cubicle at 6:00 p.m. on a Friday, hands clutched to their temples, the office copy of Quirk open on their desk while the night janitor loudly scrummed with the big recycling bin, and the answer will not be a polysyllabic hummer like "sesquipedalian." The answer will be "but," "like," "as." They are sly shape-shifters that often live between parts of speech; they are the ones you will keep coming back to throughout your career to parse and re-parse, the ones that will give you a handful of uses that you stare at for days and days before muttering "to hell with it" and labeling them as adverbs. And because English is so flexible, two lexicographers with the same training can look at the same sentence, refer to the same grammars, tear out the same amount of hair, and yet place the target word in two different parts of speech. What can they do *but try*?

That damned "but." What is it? As I read that sentence, Quirk to hand, this "but" must be a conjunction. Admittedly, I've backed into this decision: in order to know what "but" is, I first have to figure out what "try" is. I do all manner of nerd pyrotechnics to figure this out: I diagram the sentence, I substitute other verbs after "but" to see if they substantially change the grammatical feel of the word, I stare into the middle distance and give my sprachgefühl time to rattle the bones of "but try." In the end, I decide that this "try" is the verb of a clause ("they try") which has an implied subject. If this "try" is a clause, then "but" is a conjunction, because in function that "but" is joining two clauses—even if that second clause is just one stated word and one implied word. This is not an easy determination. It comes after another cup of coffee and thirty minutes of flipping through all 1,779 pages of Quirk, muttering curses.

I e-mail my colleague Emily Brewster and ask her to weigh in. Emily is one of our current grammar mavens; after Gil's retirement in 2009, Emily was tapped to help write the usage notes and paragraphs for our dictionaries. She has a degree in linguistics and is whip smart, the sort of woman who can give you an offhand, spot-on grammatical analysis of just about anything and do it in plain English. If anyone could confirm this "but" was a conjunction, it'd be Emily.

She wrote back fairly quickly. She called "but" a preposition.

But, but, but, I responded, look at that "try," doesn't it make sense if you read it as a clause with an implied subject? (This was less a challenge and more a cri du coeur: I spent thirty minutes in Quirk, isn't that worth something?) If that "but" is a preposition, then explain why "try," a verb—one of the parts of speech that isn't supposed to be the object of a preposition—is there?

Emily was happy to give me a fuller answer; she needed a break from her current defining batch anyway, as she'd been staring at citations for "ball gag" since lunch.

After doing some of her own nerd pyrotechnics on that sentence, Emily decided that there's not so much an implied subject in that stupid "try" as there is a hidden infinitive: "What can they do but

[to] try?" Emily and I both knew how that shakes out: infinitives don't need the "to" to be an infinitive; infinitives *can* be taken as noun substitutes, which are one of the things that *can* be the object of a preposition; that means the "but" here is a preposition if you tilt your head and squint a bit.

There's a lot of squinting going on, I complain. Is there anything in that sentence that hints that "try" is a noun substitute except for its appearing at the ass end of "but"?

It took Emily a bit of time to respond. Her verdict: "Ack."

We were both sure of our decisions until we began talking to each other, and now we're dabbling with grammatical agnosticism, not sure of anything anymore. Now you know why we like to shorten "part of speech" to "POS." The abbreviation also stands for "piece of shit," and we find it a fitting, oddly comforting double entendre.

If lexicographers and linguists had their way, English would have twenty-eight parts of speech, enough that we could shoehorn most of those grammatical outliers into some tidier containers. (Linguists have proposed even more complicated systems, and they tend to use them within their publications.) But there's enough grammatical variation in English that it's unlikely that twenty-eight parts of speech would be enough. There are roughly a dozen different types of *pronouns* in English alone. The harmless drudges can talk fluently about them, because that sort of esoteric knowledge is always the province of the eccentric. But I am unconvinced that the vast majority of English readers and speakers need to know the difference between them or would care if they did. Even lexicographers can only delve so deep.

"My feeling is," says Steve Kleinedler, executive editor of *The American Heritage Dictionary,* "it really doesn't matter what you call it. If you're defining how it's used, and you're showing what frame it's used in, whether you call it a conjunction or a preposition or an adverb—that's just a category. The parts of speech exist for categorization purposes, to make it easier to find. When it doesn't fit exactly, or when it bleeds—as long as the definition is there, you're well served."

A few years after my training, I was proofreading in the letter *T* and saw we listed "the" as an adjective. I thought it might be a mistake, so I checked the entry in our unabridged dictionary, *Webster's Third:* adjective. Setting aside the proofs, I saw Gil leave his office and cornered him at the coffeemaker to ask about it. I knew our options for parts of speech were limited, I explained, but "adjective" seemed a little random. Not entirely random, he said—"the" *did* modify nouns, like adjectives, and we had tradition on our side in case of complaints: "the" had been entered in dictionaries as an adjective since the nineteenth century. But, I said, it seemed like an imperfect fix. The point is to accurately describe how a word is used, and that includes its part of speech. If we can't get that right . . . Gil sighed. He had just come out of his office for coffee, and now someone who thought they were Webster's gift to grammar was accosting him about the English articles. "Well," he harrumphed, "given that your options are limited, where else are you going to put the damn things?"

Lexicographers and linguists claim to be peeveless—we are, after all, objective scholars of language—but that is disingenuous. Emily Brewster confesses to caring about the distinction between "lay" and "lie," and even after all these years stumbling across "impactful" in prose makes me blanch, and this is *after* I have had to goddamn define "impactful." But there's one ur-peeve, one particular and incredibly minor complaint, that lexicographers and linguists indulge in with all the zeal of a convert defending the one true faith: everyone but them uses the word "grammar" wrong.

To linguists and lexicographers, the word "grammar" has generally referred to the way that words interact with each other in a sentence or the systematic rules that govern the way those words interact. Grammar, to the lexicographer, tells us why we say "He and I went to the store" and not "Him and I went to the store," or why we stick the verb between the subject and the object (usually) and not at the end like German does (as in, "why we the verb between the subject and the object stick," which is perfectly grammatical and normal in German). Lexicographers are pretty decent with this sort of grammar, which is (ostensibly) objective and factual.

But when people who aren't linguists and lexicographers talk about "grammar," that's not what they mean. They're not talking about the systematic rules that govern where the verb goes in a standard English sentence; they're talking about a much broader view of language. To them, "grammar" is a loose conglomeration of stylistic word choices that get codified into right and wrong, misspellings that every English speaker has made at some point in their life and yet are branded as "bad grammar," half-remembered "rules" about usage shamed into them by their middle-school English teachers, and personal, sometimes irrational, dislikes. This is the grammar that shows up on Internet memes about "your" and "you're," the sort of grammar that people are referring to when they claim you can't end a sentence with a preposition, the grammar that is invoked when people complain that the "10 items or less" sign at the grocery store is "bad grammar."

This sort of grammar is likely something you, dear reader, value highly, because it takes work to master and you've likely devoted a measurable chunk of your waking hours to mastering it (as have we all). Think of this sort of grammar like building blocks. The earliest stuff we learn is laid unconsciously and underground: when there's more than one of a noun, we generally mark that by adding an -s to the end of the word; verbs go in the middle of a sentence, between a subject and an object; verbs can change their form when they refer to different speakers; and so on. This becomes the foundation that we start with.

As we go through life (and particularly through school), we collect more blocks to stack on our foundation: don't end sentences with prepositions; don't use the passive voice; use "were" for "was" in conditional clauses (though not always, and the exceptions are more blocks to collect later). The blocks become smaller, able to be wedged into any noticeable gaps in our walls. "Lay" is used with a stated object ("lay the book on the table") and "lie" is used without a stated object ("I'm going to lie down on the sofa"); "who" is only used in reference to people and "that" only in reference to things; definitely do not ever, under any circumstances, use "ain't." We scrabble at these and mortar them into place, building our towers higher and higher and always comparing ourselves with people who have found fewer bricks or have built their towers sloppily. It's all reckoned as "grammar" to us, by which we inevitably mean "good grammar" and by which we measure ourselves against others.

This is also the sort of grammar that young lexicographers are steeped in, and so when Steve Perrault asks if we have a "good grasp of English grammar" in the interview, we puff and preen a bit. Of course, we say, we have a *great* grasp of grammar; we have spent an entire life fortifying this tower with as many bricks as we could find.

Alas for us. One of the first things every lexicographer must do in their Style and Defining class is face their own linguistic prejudices and be willing to suspend or revise them in light of evidence to the contrary.

For me, this came down to the word "good." In one of our early Style and Defining classes, Gil bellowed the word at us. "Adjective or adverb?" he asked.

There was a pause—*everyone knows the answer to this,* I thought; *is this a trick question?*—and I stepped into the breach. "It's an adjective," I said, memories of some language arts teacher from years past barking *"Well! Well!"* at me every time I said, "I don't feel good." You feel *well,* because "well" is an adverb; you don't feel *good,* despite what James Brown proclaims, because "good" is an adjective.

"What about 'I'm doing good'?" he asked. "Isn't that adverbial?"

I felt not so good: that *was* adverbial. "But," I reasoned, "you're not supposed to say that. You should say 'I'm doing well.'"

He smacked his lips. "And do you say 'I'm doing well,' or do you say 'I'm doing good'?" He looked pointedly at me. We both knew that I had—just five minutes earlier!—answered his question about how I was doing with the grammar practice with "I'm doing good." I was fairly certain he was about to fire me, or perhaps unhinge his jaw and swallow me whole, and so I tried my level best to melt into the floor. He ignored my discomfort and went on. "Good" has been used for almost a thousand years as an adverb, even though usage commentators and peevers have condemned this use. Dictionaries, he explained, were records of the language as it is used, and so we must set aside our disdain for the adverb "good" (and here he looked over his glasses at me) and record its long use in our dictionaries in spite of the rather pointless foofaraw around its existence.

Then Gil sat back and smiled broadly. And my tower—bricks began falling all over the goddamned place.

Gil made his speech in part because the whole notion that the dictionary merely records the language as people use it grates against what we generally think dictionaries do. Many people—and many people who think they'd be good at this lexicography gig—believe that the dictionary is some great guardian of the English language, that its job is to set boundaries of decorum around this profligate language like a great linguistic housemother setting curfew. Words that have made it into the dictionary are Official with a capital *O*, sanctioned, part of Real and Proper English. The corollary is that if certain words are bad, uncouth, unlovely, or distasteful, then folks think that the dictionary will make sure they are never entered into its hallowed pages, and thus are such words banished from Real, Official, Proper English. The language is thus protected, kept right, pure, *good*. This is commonly called "prescriptivism," and it is unfortunately not how dictionaries work at all. We don't just enter the good stuff; we enter the bad and the ugly stuff, too. We are just observers, and the goal is to describe, as accurately as possible, as much of the language as we can. This approach is "descriptivism," and it is the philosophical basis for almost all modern dictionaries. All a word needs to merit entry into most professionally written dictionaries is widespread and sustained use in written English prose. You'd be surprised how many "bad" and "unlovely" words make it into written English prose on a consistent basis.

You'll notice all the scare quotes I'm throwing around, but I throw them around advisedly: uses that fall outside what we think of as Standard English are given a moral charge. Well-meaning parents tell kids that "ain't" is bad English; people sneer at those who use "irregardless"; we've each survived that one high-school teacher who has, throughout your paper, circled every preposition that appears at the end of a sentence and commented at the top of your essay "an A+ idea corrupted by C- grammar."* There are tons (literal imperial tons) of books about improving yourself through better grammar, books with titles like *When Bad Grammar Happens to Good People* and the honest-to-a-fault *I Judge You When You Use Poor Grammar* (and note the use of "poor" here instead of the slightly more informal but more common "bad." The idea that "poor" marks quality whereas "bad" marks morality is truly a peeve beyond all other peeves—a real peever's peeve. Well done). This attitude goes to extremes: an acquaintance recently shared with me his belief that when words gain new meanings, it is not just linguistic and educational degradation but an active work of Evil (with a capital *E*) in our world.

Prescriptivism and descriptivism have been shoehorned into this moral dualism as well. The former purportedly champions the "best practices" of English and eschews the newfangled linguistic relativism of descriptivism.† Prescriptivism, then, must be good—how can the "best practices" of English be anything but good? And

---

* I had that teacher, and that comment still chaps my hide.

† Modern linguistic relativism goes back at least two thousand years: "Multa renascentur quae iam cecidere, cadentque / quae nunc sunt in honore vocabula, si volet usus, / quem penes arbitrium est et ius et norma loquendi." (Many words shall revive, which now have fallen off; / and many which are now in esteem shall fall off, if it be the will of usage, / in whose power is the decision and right and standard of language.) Horace, *Ars Poetica*, A.D. 18. What a commie hippie liberal.

if prescriptivism is good, then descriptivism, its principles, and its practitioners must perforce be bad. In a letter to his publisher, E. B. White, the second half of the famous Strunk and White responsible for the best-selling writing guide *The Elements of Style,* beautifully expresses the modern complaint against descriptivism:

> I have been sympathetic all along with your qualms about "The Elements of Style," but I know that I cannot, and will-shall not, attempt to adjust the unadjustable Mr. Strunk to the modern liberal of the English Department, the anything-goes fellow. Your letter expresses contempt for this fellow, but on the other hand you seem to want his vote. I am against him, temperamentally and because I have seen the work of *his* disciples, and I say the hell with him.

Descriptivists, those anything-goes hippies: we have seen their work, and right-thinking people everywhere say to hell with them. Now, as a lexicographer, you are one.

It's

On "Grammar"

The bloody battle to defend English and champion "good grammar" hasn't always been in existence; in fact, prior to about the middle of the fifteenth century, there was very, very little thought given to English as a language of discourse, officialdom, and permanence. Prior to that, most official documents were recorded in Latin (the gold standard for Languages of Record) or French.* Sure, there had always been anonymous writers (and a few onymous† ones, too, like Geoffrey Chaucer) who chose to preserve their wisdom—or fart jokes, in the case of Chaucer—in English, but it wasn't taken seriously as a literary language until Henry V suddenly began using it in his official correspondence in 1417. Within a few decades, English had become the language of the English bureaucracy, replacing French and Latin almost completely.

The problem with this shift was that both French and Latin, having been used as languages of record for a while, were already comparatively standardized, and English was not. Latin and French

---

* Plenty of the monarchs that we think of as fair, ruddy Englishmen and Englishwomen were actually French. King Richard the Lionheart (rule, 1189–1199), the absent monarch during Robin Hood's fictional reign and brother to the rotten prince John, couldn't speak a lick of English and spent most of his time in the Duchy of Aquitaine when he wasn't smashing the Holy Land to bits or being locked up in an Austrian prison. The first truly "English" king to take the throne after the Norman Conquest was Henry VII, and he was really Welsh.

† **on·y·mous** \'änəməs\ *adj* : bearing a name; *especially* : giving or bearing the author's name <an *onymous* article in a magazine> *(MWU)*

had written forms that stood independent of their pronunciation; English, on the other hand, was entirely phonetically spelled. That meant that while Medieval Latin had one way to spell the word that we know as "right" (*rectus*) and Old French as used in English laws and literature had six (*drait, dres, drez, drettes, dreyt,* and *droit*), Middle English, the form of English in use when it became an official language of record, had a whopping *seventy-seven* recorded ways to spell "right."* The *Merriam-Webster's Concise Dictionary of English Usage* puts it best: "English now had to serve the functions formerly served by Latin and French . . . and this new reality was a powerful spur to the formation of a standard in written English that could be quite independent of variable speech."

The key words here are "in written English." The pronunciation of English continued to be wildly variable, but starting in the fifteenth century, a standard written form began to emerge. (It should be noted that though this movement began in the middle of the fifteenth century, English spelling wasn't fully standardized for at least another five hundred years, give or take.) The focus was on making English a suitable language of record; you couldn't have official court and legal documents written in whatever form of the language the local scribe had at hand. The type of English used among the clerks of the chancery† (called, appropriately, Chancery English or

---

* reȝt, reght, reghte, reht, reit, rethe, reyȝt, reyght, reyt, reyte, rȝt (which was likely a transmission error because there's no vowel where there should be), rich, richt, ricth, riȝ, riȝght, riȝht, riȝhte, riȝt, riȝte, riȝth, riȝtt, riȝtte, riȝty (another transmission error with that extra *y*), righte, rigt, rigth, rigthe, rih, rihct, rihht, rihst, riht, rihte, rihtt, rihtte, rijȝt, rist, rit, rite, rith, rithe, ritht, ritth, rothes (plural, another transmission error with that whopper of an *o*), rycht, ryde, ryȝ, ryȝght, ryȝht, ryȝhte, ryȝt, ryȝte, ryȝth, ryȝthe, ryȝtt, ryȝtte, ryȝtth, ryȝtthe, ryg, rygh, ryghe, ryght, ryghte, ryghtȝ, rygt, rygth, ryht, ryhte, ryt, ryte, ryth, rythe, rytht, wryght (*w-,* probably another transmission error), ziȝt (*z-,* definitely a transmission error), and, of course, right.

† ¹**chan·cery** \ˈchan(t)-s(ə-)rē, ˈchän(t)-\ *n -ies . . .* **2 :** a record office originally for issuance and preservation of a sovereign's diplomas, charters, and bulls and later for the collection, arrangement, and safekeeping of public archives and ecclesiastical, legal, or diplomatic proceedings *(MWU)*

Chancery Standard) became the seed around which Early Modern English was able to form.

It wasn't all the law clerks. The printing press came to England in the fifteenth century, which helped speed along the standardization process. William Caxton and Richard Pynson, the two most well-known British printers at that time, adopted the Chancery Standard.

While Chancery Standard was spreading throughout the realm in the form of books and printed pamphlets, trying its level best to regularize English spelling, English itself was growing like gangbusters. In the sixteenth century, English was established as a language of record; now it was time to make it a fully literary language.

The problem was that plenty of England's best writers thought English wasn't quite up to the task. This wasn't anything new: complaints about the fitness of English have practically been a national pastime since at least the twelfth century, and if the written record were more complete, I'm sure we'd find scrawled in the corner of some Old English manuscript a complaint that English is horrible and Latin is way better. John Skelton wrote a poem that most likely dates to the early sixteenth century in which he claims that "our naturall tong is rude" and really not up to the task of poetry, and he was the *damned poet laureate of England*. If English was going to be a literary language, it had a lot of work to do.

Vocabulary boomed in the sixteenth century, and many of those new words were words borrowed from lovely, literary languages on the Continent—Latin, Italian, and French. The Romance-language borrowings weren't without controversy—Shakespeare himself made fun of people who piled on the highfalutin foreignisms just to sound smart*—and by the end of the century the language was

---

* MOTH [aside]: They have been at a great feast of languages, and stolen the scraps.
COSTARD: O! they have lived long on the alms-basket of words. I marvel thy master hath not eaten thee for a word, for thou art not so long by the head as "honorificabilitudinitatibus": thou art easier swallowed than a flap-dragon. (*Love's Labour's Lost*, 5.1.36–42)

growing so quickly, both with borrowed words from other languages and with foreign speakers attempting to get their mouths around this burgeoning language, that a handful of native speakers stepped in to provide order. In 1586, William Bullokar, a man who was interested in regularizing and reforming English, published the first English grammar (appropriately titled *Bref Grammar for English*); in 1604, Robert Cawdrey published what is held to be the first monolingual English dictionary.

The concern was that English was becoming terribly unruly, and it needed some reining in. Some called for a large-scale remedy—an academy of English that would not only prescribe good usage but proscribe bad stuff out of English. By "bad stuff," they meant not just words that people thought were uncouth but all forms of the language—styles, uses, poetic meters, the whole kit and caboodle—that were deemed inelegant and unlovely. Daniel Defoe loved the idea of an English academy: he thought it would be best not only for English but for English identity and interests. The job of the academy would be "to encourage Polite Learning, to polish and refine the English tongue, and advance the so much neglected faculty of correct language; also, to establish purity and propriety of style, and to purge it from all the irregular additions that ignorance and affectation have introduced; and all those innovations of speech, if I may call them such, which some dogmatic writers have the confidence to foster upon their native language, as if their authority were sufficient to make their own fancy legitimate."

Don't think Defoe didn't like English. He goes on to say, "By such a society I daresay the true glory of our English style would appear; and among all the learned part of the world be esteemed, as it really is, the noblest and most comprehensive of all the vulgar languages in the world."

This desire to see English exalted wasn't Defoe's alone: Jonathan Swift longed for it; John Dryden strove for it. A grammar was no longer a book used to teach foreigners how to speak English but a book used to teach native English speakers how to speak English.

If that seems presumptuous, realize this: literacy (particularly formal education) was booming in the eighteenth century, and it wasn't too long before "good grammar" became the dividing line between the educated, well poised, polite, and morally upright and the ignorant, vulgar, and morally compromised. English, the grammarians claimed, was a system that could be reduced to a set of logical rules and expectations, and these logical rules expressed right thinking. This weird connection between morality and English usage didn't just appear ex nihilo: England and its colonies were beginning to undergo a huge social shift in which middle-class merchants (many of whom traditionally had a rudimentary education but nothing beyond) were making enough money to buy their way into polite society, and members of the aristocracy (most of whom had an exemplary education) were losing lands, money, and therefore influence. People moving up the social ladder have always aspired to the manners and education of the rank above them, but they need help in doing so; the eighteenth century was no exception. Merchants who were suddenly flush with cash were expected to behave as if they had always been so, particularly when it came to business.

Help came in the form of letter-writing guides written specifically for the benefit of the rising middle class. Daniel Defoe released one such guide, *The Complete English Tradesman in Familiar Letters,* in 1725. The book is filled with all manner of business advice for the middle-class merchant, along with some solid moralizing: "I cannot allow any pleasures to be innocent, when they turn away either the body or the mind of a tradesman from the one needful thing which his calling makes necessary, and that necessity makes his duty."

The eighteenth-century English grammars were thus the linguistic complements to the etiquette books. Robert Lowth, the bishop of London, wrote *A Short Introduction to English Grammar: With Critical Notes* in 1762 and explains in the preface,

It is with reason expected of every person of a liberal education, and it is indispensably required of every one who undertakes to inform or entertain the public, that he should be able to express himself with propriety and accuracy. It will evidently appear from these notes, that our best authors have committed gross mistakes, for want of a due knowledge of English grammar, or at least of a proper attention to the rules of it.

In Lowth's grammar, we have the beginnings of our popular notion of what constitutes "grammar." The first line of his book reads, "Grammar is the art of rightly expressing our thoughts by words," and his grammar doesn't just cover actual grammar, like the difference between a preposition and an adverb, but also what we moderns call "usage," like when to use "will" and when to use "shall" ("*Will,* in the first person singular and plural, promises or threatens; in the second and third persons, only foretells; *shall* on the contrary, in the first person, simply foretells; in the second and third persons, promises, commands, or threatens") and how important it is to use "who" and "whom" correctly, because confusion between the two means that you have not mastered the subjective and objective cases yet.[*]

This is not grammar for grammar's sake, however. To Lowth's mind, propriety and accuracy of expression become the hallmarks of a gentleman. Good manners, good morality, and good grammar all go hand in hand.

The moralizing continues to this day, in no small part because we like to be correct and because bombast sells. Lynne Truss released her book *Eats, Shoots & Leaves: The Zero Tolerance Approach to Punctuation* in 2003, and it was full of outsized, near-biblical smiting of people who misused punctuation:

The confusion of the possessive "its" (no apostrophe) with the contractive "it's" (with apostrophe) is an unequivocal signal of

---

[*] Lowth hammers this home by noting that even translators of the Bible can't get this right: for "Whom do men say that I am?" (Matt. 16:13, Mark 8:27, Luke 9:18), Lowth sighs, "It ought in all these places to be who."

illiteracy and sets off a simple Pavlovian "kill" response in the average stickler. The rule is: the word "it's" (with apostrophe) stands for "it is" or "it has." If the word does not stand for "it is" or "it has" then what you require is "its." *This is extremely easy to grasp.* Getting your itses mixed up is the greatest solecism in the world of punctuation. No matter that you have a PhD and have read all of Henry James twice. If you still persist in writing, "Good food at it's best," you deserve to be struck by lightning, hacked up on the spot and buried in an unmarked grave.

Though Truss must certainly be joking regarding the unhappy fates of those who use the wrong "its," some of her readers seem to have missed the joke. One online review begins, "I proudly consider myself a punctuation martyr." Truss's book was a runaway hit in spite of the fact that I'd wager every person who read that paragraph has, at some point in their life, misused "its" and "it's." And it's not as though the genre reached its hand-waving apotheosis in Truss. In 2013, N. M. Gwynne released a book called *Gwynne's Grammar: The Ultimate Introduction to Grammar and the Writing of Good English,* in which Gwynne (a businessman turned autodidactic schoolmarm) begins his grammar with a logical proof that one cannot be truly happy unless one uses what he considers "good grammar": "In summary of the proof: grammar is the science of using words rightly, leading to thinking rightly, leading to deciding rightly, without which—as both common sense and experience show—happiness is impossible. Therefore, happiness depends at least partly on good grammar."

So what is the grammar that leads us to true happiness? It's consistent with the grammar we find in other books: avoid splitting infinitives because some of your readers may find them inelegant; ending a sentence with a preposition is wrong because the word "preposition" literally means "to position before something"; get your "its" and "it's" straight because it's not that difficult.

The biggest problem with this sort of grammar, however, is that it sounds logical but it's based on a faulty logic. Take the oft-repeated injunction to get "its" and "it's" straight. Everyone claims it's remarkably easy to remember that "its" is possessive and "it's" is a contraction. But logic tells us that in English, 's attached to a noun signals possession: the dog's dish, the cat's toy, the lexicographer's cry. So if English is logical, and there are simple rules to follow, why doesn't "it's" signal possession? We know that 's also signals a contraction, but we don't have any problems with differentiating between "the dog's dish" and "the dog's sleeping"—why should we suddenly have problems with "it's dish" and "it's sleeping"?

This type of grammar often completely ignores hundreds (and, in some cases, well over a thousand) years of established use in English. For "it's," the rule is certainly easy to memorize, but it also ignores the history of "its" and "it's." At one point in time, "it" was its own possessive pronoun: the 1611 King James Bible reads, "That which groweth of it owne accord . . . thou shalt not reape"; Shakespeare wrote in *King Lear*, "It had it head bit off by it young." They weren't the first: the possessive "it" goes back to the fifteenth century.

But around the time that Shakespeare was shuffling off this mortal coil, the possessive "it" began appearing as "it's." We're not sure why the change happened, but some commentators guess that it was because "it" didn't appear to be its own possessive pronoun, like "his" and "her," but rather a bare pronoun in need of that possessive marker given to nouns: 's. Sometimes this possessive appeared without punctuation as "its." But the possessive "it's" grew in popularity through the seventeenth and eighteenth centuries until it was the dominant form of the word. It even survived into the nineteenth century: you'll find it in the letters of Thomas Jefferson and Jane Austen and the speechwriting notes of Abraham Lincoln.

This would be relatively simple were it not for the fact that "it's" was also occasionally used as a contraction for "it is" or "it has" ("and it's come to pass," Shakespeare wrote in *Henry VIII*, 1.2.63). Some grammarians noticed and complained—not that the possessive "it's" and the contractive "it's" were confusing, but that the contractive "it's" was a misuse and mistake for the contraction "'tis," which was the more standard contraction of "it is." This was a war that the pedants lost: "'tis" waned while "it's" waxed.

"Its" and "it's" began to diverge in the nineteenth century, likely as a way to distinguish the possessive form from the contraction. But old habits die hard: The possessive "it's" still shows up with regularity in print, and not just in hand-lettered flyers for local garage sales. Our files have recent evidence of the possessive "it's" in everything from *Vogue* to *The New York Times Magazine* to *Gourmet* to *Time* magazine (which is quoting Ronald Reagan), and then some. They are, of course, typos, but the fact remains that each "it's" was unobtrusive enough that it slipped slyly by the two people most invested in an error-free article: writer and editor.

So where do these rules come from, if not from actual use? Most of them are the personal peeves, codified into law, of dead white men of yore.

Take, for example, the rule that we're not to end sentences with prepositions. It's one that is drummed into most young writers at some point in their careers, and failing to heed it will result in some teacherly knuckle smacking (literal or figurative). If you ask a modern adherent to this rule why, exactly, you aren't supposed to end a sentence with a preposition, they merely goggle at you as if you had just asked why you aren't supposed to lick electrical sockets. Because it's *objectively better* not to, that's why.

The rule itself was first articulated by the seventeenth-century poet and literary critic John Dryden. He had used the terminal preposition in his early works, but as he aged and gave himself wholly over to the glories of Latin, he decided against its use:

> I cast my eyes but by chance on Catiline; and in the three or four last pages, found enough to conclude that [Ben] Jonson writ not correctly. . . . The preposition in the end of the sentence; a com-

mon fault with him, and which I have but lately observed in my own writings.

When his works were reprinted later in his life, he took the opportunity to tidy up some of the follies of youth, and the terminal preposition was one such folly. Later editions of his work are carefully scrubbed of terminal prepositions: "the age which I live in" became "the age in which I live" and so on.

Why the fuss? Dryden was a son of the Renaissance, and as such was a fan of all things classical: a classical liberal arts education, which placed an emphasis on grammar and rhetoric; the classical (and mostly Latin) authors; the elegance, concision, and precision of Latin itself. It wasn't just a passing fancy: Dryden often translated his sentences into Latin to see how concise and elegant they were, then translated them back into English with Latin's lovely grammar in mind. This is likely what led Dryden to deplore the terminal preposition—in Latin, prepositions can't come at the end of sentences, and Latin is the ne plus ultra of elegance, refinement, and—most important—longevity. Dryden's distaste for the terminal preposition was repeated and reinforced by usage writers of the eighteenth and nineteenth centuries until it became a rule.

The problem with this rule is a familiar one: English grammar is not Latin grammar. The languages are cousins, but not close ones, because they come from different branches of the Indo-European language tree. English has a grammatical structure similar to other Germanic languages, and Latin has a grammatical structure similar to other Italic languages. Blending grammatical systems from two languages on different branches of the Indo-European language tree is a bit like mixing orange juice and milk: you can do it, but it's going to be nasty.

One of the grammatical hallmarks of English is that you can stick a preposition at the end of a sentence without any deleterious effect whatsoever. In fact, the terminal preposition isn't just possible, but is and has been standard operating procedure for prepositions from the very beginnings of English. The terminal preposition had been in continuous, easy use seven hundred years before John Dryden was in short pants, and it continues in easy, idiomatic use. You can, of course, choose not to end your sentence with a preposition, but that is a stylistic choice, not a grammatical diktat from on high.

The fact is that many of the things that are presented to us as rules are really just the of-the-moment preferences of people who have had the opportunity to get their opinions published and whose opinions end up being reinforced and repeated down the ages as Truth. Many of the rules that make up the sort of grammar that Gwynne and others care about actually go against a long and established track record of use by the very authors who are championed as the practitioners (and, yea, defenders) of Proper English. In plain language, even peevers mess it up.

David Foster Wallace, modern literary titan, described himself in a famous *Harper's* essay as a "snoot," a "really extreme usage fanatic, the sort of person whose idea of Sunday fun is to look for mistakes in Safire's column's prose itself." He was a prolific writer and a very careful one, too; he used "nauseated" instead of "nauseous" to mean "to feel sick," for instance, an old grammatical peccadillo to be sure, and one that even the most prescriptivist usage commentators today merely shrug over. Bryan Garner, one of Wallace's prescriptivist heroes, has even almost given up on this one: in his *Garner's Modern American Usage,* he rates this a Stage 4 on his Language-Change Index: "The form becomes virtually universal but is opposed on cogent grounds by a few linguistic stalwarts." Be that as it may, good usage mattered to Wallace. So it is a surprise to see, in one of his stories published in *Harper's,* an instance of the oft-bemoaned object of snooty scorn, the figurative "literally":

> The moment hung there between us, borderless and distendent, my impulse to clear my own throat blocked only by a fear of appearing impertinent; and it was in that literally endless expectant interval that I came to see that I deferred to the infant, respected it, granted it full authority, and therefore waited, abiding, both of us in that

small and shadowless father's office, in the knowledge that I was, thenceforth, this tiny white frightening thing's to command, its instrument or tool.

Did he mean to use it in an ironic way? Were we supposed to divine some sort of smirk in it? It's impossible to say: all we have is this instance of the figurative "literally" in the work of an author who is known for his self-professed snoothood and his lexical precision. Another piece of evidence for the figurative "literally," supplied by someone who would probably deplore such a hyperbolic use in anyone else's prose.

And thus it ever was: Jonathan Swift disparages the use of contractions as evidence of "the deplorable Ignorance that for some Years hath reigned among our English Writers; the great Depravity of our Taste; and the continual Corruption of our Style," then turns around and uses them all over the place in his *Journal to Stella*. E. B. White says in *The Elements of Style* that "certainly" is "used indiscriminately by some speakers, much as others use very, to intensify any and every statement. A mannerism of this kind, bad in speech, is even worse in writing"; it shows up in his *Second Tree from the Corner* ("You certainly don't have to be a humorist to taste the sadness of situation and mood"). Lynne Truss's book "eloquently speaks to the value of punctuation in preserving the nuances of language," slobbers one adoring reviewer—one among many—and yet Truss commits oodles of punctuation errors throughout her own usage book on punctuation, including one on the cover: there should be a hyphen between "Zero" and "Tolerance." Humanity sets up rules to govern English, but English rolls onward, a juggernaut crushing all in its path.[*]

---

[*] "Juggernaut" is an adaptation of one of the Hindi names for Vishnu, Jagannāth, "lord of the world." Supposedly, a giant avatar of Jagannāth would be drawn through the streets on a cart during a festival, and some devotees would allow themselves to be crushed by the cart's wheels as it passed by them. "Supposedly" is the key word in the previous sentence. For more etymological dubiosities, see the chapter "Posh."

•

This is what you, the lexicographer, must contend with as you go through your Style and Defining classes with Gil: the realization that most of these little bits of information that you've hoarded to fortify your defenses against linguistic and moral attack are rubbish. It is a betrayal—*I wasted how many years of my life trying to master the difference between "between" and "among" when I could have been dating exciting people instead?*—but one you must get over quickly. The lexicographer's job is to tell the truth about how language is used and, in doing so, set down their own poniards. As you go through the written record, you'll find that Shakespeare used double negatives and Jane Austen used "ain't." You'll find that new and disputed coinages have come in and have not taken away from the language as it was used, but added to it; that words previously considered horrendous or ugly—words like "can't"—are now unremarkable. In spite of all this apparent error, the lexicographer must conclude—indeed, must *believe*—that English is not only still alive but flourishing.

Many of the rules that have been codified into "grammar" uphold an ideal, not a reality. The grammarians of the seventeenth century onward weren't interested so much in preserving the language as it was used as in perpetuating a re-formed idea of what language should be. The first soldiers in the fight to preserve English radically changed English, not according to the best practices of the great writers of the language, but according to their own views of elegance and correctness. What they wanted to preserve and promote didn't, for the most part, actually exist: it was a convenient fiction that was painted in moral terms, thereby ensuring its own propagation. Let me say that again: *Standard English as it is presented by grammarians and pedants is a dialect that is based on a mostly fictional, static, and Platonic ideal of usage.* Under this mentality, the idea that the best practices of English change with time is anathema. It doesn't preserve English so much as pickle it. It's a circle unbroken: in every age, some learned pedant discovers all over again that English is a clunker, and they race to the rooftops to shout it to the unwashed, stupid masses and begin fomenting for a walkback. Even Samuel Johnson gets into the act:

If the changes that we fear be thus irresistible, what remains but to acquiesce with silence, as in the other insurmountable distresses of humanity? It remains that we retard what we cannot repel, that we palliate what we cannot cure. Life may be lengthened by care, though death cannot be ultimately defeated: tongues, like governments, have a natural tendency to degeneration; we have long preserved our constitution, let us make some struggles for our language.

We think of English as a fortress to be defended, but a better analogy is to think of English as a child. We love and nurture it into being, and once it gains gross motor skills, it starts going exactly where we don't want it to go: it heads right for the goddamned electrical sockets. We dress it in fancy clothes and tell it to behave, and it comes home with its underwear on its head and wearing someone else's socks. As English grows, it lives its own life, and this is right and healthy. Sometimes English does exactly what we think it should; sometimes it goes places we don't like and thrives there in spite of all our worrying. We can tell it to clean itself up and act more like Latin; we can throw tantrums and start learning French instead. But we will never really be the boss of it. And that's why it flourishes.

Irregardless

On Wrong Words

One of the tasks that every Merriam-Webster editor must do is answer editorial correspondence. Since the 1860s, dictionary users have been encouraged to write to the company with questions about its books or the English language, and some long-suffering editor will respond.

There are a few flaws in this system. The first is that the customer writing to us generally believes the prescriptivist misconception that dictionaries are gatekeepers for the language, and so when they write in, it is to froth in rage all over us at our inclusion of any word they think is unworthy. The second flaw in this system is that the person who must deal with this hysteria and give a good, calming account of why that word is in a dictionary is someone who has taken this job specifically because it promises almost no human interaction.

Unfortunately for me, I had previously held jobs where my primary duty was to be yelled at for extended periods of time by customers,* so I was often tasked with answering the angriest e-mails. Most of these e-mails expressed surprise, frustration, and doom over one dictionary entry or another, and it was my job to calmly explain the rationale behind that entry. I didn't mind too

---

* Insurance claims adjuster, alumni donations solicitor, and bakery assistant (where I once had an angry customer pick up an Elmo cake and throw it at my head).

much: we had ample evidence for all the entries in our dictionaries tucked away in our files, the research to answer these questions was often interesting, and at least no one was hollering at me over the phone.

That all changed one day when I was sorting through my correspondence and came across a forwarded e-mail from someone irate that we entered "irregardless" into our dictionary. I rolled my eyes: *obviously* "irregardless" isn't a valid word, and so it wouldn't be entered into our dictionaries. This correspondent had clearly just picked up any old crap dictionary, stumbled across an entry for the nonword "irregardless," and assumed that we were at fault. Totally frustrating.

I drafted a reply that stated it wasn't in the dictionary, and to prove it, you can visit our website and search our online dictionary for the word, where you will find the following note. ... Here I needed the language that we used at that point in time when someone looked up a word that wasn't entered in our online dictionary. I opened up the site, typed in "irregardless," and promptly lost it: *"irregardless" was entered in our dictionary.* So great was my surprise that I actually said, out loud and at a normal volume, "You have *got* to be shitting me."

Dan Brandon, one of the science editors who sat near me, answered from the depth of his cubicle, "Probably."

The spectrum of hatred against "irregardless" might be unmatched. Everyone claims to hate the word "moist," but the dislike is general and jokey: *ew, gross,* "moist," *bleh.* People's hatred of "irregardless" is specific and vehemently serious: it cannot mean "without regard to" but must mean "with regard to," so it's nonsensical and shouldn't exist; it's a double negative and therefore not allowable by anyone with sense and judgment; it's a redundant blend of "irrespective" and "regardless," and we don't need it; it is illogical and therefore not a word; it is a hallmark of uneducated speech and shouldn't be entered into the dictionary. All of these complaints point in one direction: "irregardless" is evidence that

English is going to hell, and you, Merriam-Webster, are skipping down the easy path, merrily swinging the handbasket.

The truth is I felt for the complainant. "Irregardless" was just wrong, I thought—I knew this deep down at a molecular level, and no dictionary entry was going to convince me otherwise. But sharing my personal linguistic beef with the world was not part of the job, so I buttoned my yap and answered the correspondence. Yes, it's entered, I said, but please note that it's marked "nonstandard" (which is a fancy way of saying it's not accepted by most educated speakers of English) and we have a very long usage paragraph after the one-word definition that explains you should use "regardless" instead. We are duty-bound to record the language as it is used, I concluded, gritting my teeth and mentally sprinkling scare quotes throughout the entire sentence.

I had hoped this would be an isolated letter, but no: more came in, and I had to answer each of them point for point. I regret to inform you, I would write, that "irregardless" is in fact a word: it is a "series of speech sounds that symbolizes and communicates a meaning usually without being divisible into smaller units capable of independent use,"* and not only is it a word, but it is one with a surprising amount of use in written, edited prose for reasons that are unclear to the humble drudge. Yes, "irregardless" looks like it should mean "with regard to," but that's not how people use it, and the dictionary is about the business of recording how people use words. True, it is a double negative, but that doesn't negate (*ha-ha*) the fact that people still use it in speech and writing. Redundancy in English vocabulary is commonplace—this isn't a detriment, just a fact—and we cannot strike "irregardless" from the record for being redundant, because we'd have to burn down half of the language if we start cutting redundant words out of it. You are correct that

---

*   Some people write back to tell me I am "A Idiot": "irregardless" can be broken down into "ir-" and "regardless." This is true, but "ir-" is not a unit capable of independent use, and so I am not "A Idiot" in this particular case.

"irregardless" is an illogical coinage, but so is "inflammable" to mean "able to catch fire" and "unthaw" to mean "to thaw," and yet no one disputes that those are words. And of course we understand that "irregardless" is generally thought to be incorrect; that's why the lengthy usage paragraph suggests—in spite of our being liberal commie descriptivists—that people use "regardless" instead of "irregardless." Thank you for taking the time to write.

I answered these complaints for years and in time came to an uneasy accord with myself. I had looked at the evidence, and yeah, "irregardless" is used plenty in edited print. Accordingly, it merited entry into our dictionaries. But I was never going to like "irregardless," and I was never going to think it was a good entry, and I was still going to hold the opinion that people who used "irregardless" were, at best, sloppy as hell.

That changed in 2003, when I was now a managing editor overseeing a big chunk of the editorial correspondence. An e-mail came down the transom claiming that "irregardless" was the "superlative form" of regardless—among educated Mississippians, in any event.

I took my glasses off and rubbed my eyes until I saw fireworks. It was early; perhaps I wasn't fully caffeinated, or even awake. Perhaps this was a nightmare, and when I looked again, that e-mail would say that "irregardless" was stinky and y'all are wrong.

I looked. No dice.

The superlative form of any adjective or adverb is the form that denotes an extreme or unsurpassed degree or level of adjective- or adverbness. Usually superlatives for adjectives are the "-est" form of the word: "nice" and "nicest," "warm" and "warmest." But not always: "best" is the superlative of "good," "most interesting" the superlative of "interesting."

Superlatives can be used only with adjectives or adverbs that are gradable; that is, ones that can have different degrees of themselves— "cold," for instance, can get "colder" and even "coldest"—or can be more or less of themselves: honesty can be measured as "more honest" or "less honest." Can "regardless" be gradable? I didn't think so; at least it didn't sound right. My sprachgefühl remained steadfastly quiet. Could something be "more regardless"? No. Well, this correspondent clearly didn't know what he was talking about. The part of my brain that likes to prove it's the smartest thing in the room piped up: you know that people use grammatical terms imprecisely. It may be that "irregardless" isn't the superlative form of "regardless," as my correspondent claimed, but an intensive form of "regardless," just like the infix "fucking" turns "absolutely" into the intensive "absofuckinglutely." But why in the world would a word that is supposed to be an intensive form use a prefix ("ir-") that means "not"—a prefix that is, in a way, a minimizer? Because, I reasoned, this whole line of thinking and the claim that my correspondent had made were both bullshit.

Now, I was not about to answer this e-mail, because in order to do so, I would have to investigate, and if five years of lexicography had taught me anything, it was that going through the evidence might lead to my being unswervingly wrong about a word I still deeply felt was bogus. I knew that if the evidence proved me wrong about "irregardless," then I was no better than the blustering, fustigating peevers who wrote to complain about lesser sins like the noun "above" or the existence of the word "moist."* In other words, even though I knew English didn't work this way, in my heart I wanted "irregardless" to be ugly and *morally wrong* so that I could feel smart and *morally right*. I had, in this instance, bought into the lie I just spent several pages demolishing. I passed the e-mail along to another editor for response, then pushed back from my desk and walked too casually over to our citation files.

The raw material used in writing dictionary definitions are called "citations." They're snippets of words used in the wild and usually in edited prose. Each citation contains a highlighted word, a little lexical gold nugget embedded in its context, and citations are pulled from everywhere and everything, from books to ads to personal let-

---

* A perfectly cromulent word. Sorry, world.

ters to newspapers to anything with print on it. These are the things lexicographers evaluate in order to define a word; every entry in a dictionary is justified with fistfuls of citations. At Merriam-Webster, the citation files are both paper and electronic; the paper citation files take up a solid third of the floor and date back to the mid-nineteenth century.

I dragged my finger over the drawer labels until I found the one that housed all the paper citations for "irregardless," then slid it open. It's pretty unlikely, I thought, plucking a stack of index cards from the file, that "irregardless" was an intensive form of "regardless," but I should do my due diligence.

Almost immediately, I ran across this snippet of use:

I remembered the magnitude of his problems—problems I was just beginning to truly understand—as a black man and as an artist, growing up poor, forced to endure the racist terrorism of the American South. He was unlucky in love, and no prince of a parent. *Irregardless,* as the old people said, and as Mr. Sweet himself liked to say, not only had he lived to a ripe old age . . . , but he had continued to share all his troubles and his insights with anyone who would listen, taking special care to craft them for the necessary effect. He continued to sing.

I leaned my head against the cool metal of the cabinet and let this swish around my brain. There was something peculiar about this "irregardless"—the emphasis it's given in the text, in particular. It's italicized; it's set off with that "as the old people said"; it almost seems to act as a long wave of the hand, one that will forestall any further discussion on the previous point—like a more highfalutin version of "anyhoo." You don't see this sort of emphasis with most written uses of "irregardless." Those uses are unremarkable, save for the fact that they use the word "irregardless." No italics, no setting off with "as the old people said," no nada. I checked the citation again; it had been rejected as supporting evidence for the current entry for "irregardless." In other words, this particular use of "irregardless" wasn't covered by the existing definition for "irregardless" (which is "regardless"). Another clue that this use of "irregardless" was different. I almost put the stack of citations back, but my sprachgefühl rattled my brain. *You know you want an answer to this once and for all,* it taunted.

And so I went spelunking. I found evidence of this peculiar "irregardless" dating back to the 1860s, sprinkled throughout the country, from New Orleans to New York. Several instances of "irregardless" appear in proximity to a "regardless," which sure looks like a deliberate choice that means "irregardless" isn't just a flat synonym of "regardless":

> The language of the people would be infinitely improved if all children were forced to learn Bible verses—and they ought to be regardless of religion.
>
> If one-tenth the time expended upon literature were expended upon study of the Bible as the climax of art in literature (irregardless of moral effect), how much sweeter and purer English as she is spoken, would become!

My sprachgefühl giggled and ran circles around my brain. If "irregardless" is a synonym of "regardless," and the writer felt that "regardless" was perfectly adequate for the previous paragraph, why use a word in the following paragraph that was, by the time this showed up in print, well on its way to being despised?

The early signs of disfavor show up in the late nineteenth century, when there is a spate of them set off in quotation marks in opinion pieces, a little linguistic sneer at the object of scorn. "If the Board sees proper to authorize Mr. Leland to carry on their negotiations," a writer for *The Weekly Kansas Chief* huffs in 1888 (in a typical use), "we may continue to announce that Mr. Leland has secured such and such a compromise, 'irregardless' of the displeasure of the Troy *Times,* the tool of Guthrie, the bondholders' attorney." There's also the claim that the word is new, a surefire way to get people riled up about it. The *Atchison Daily Globe* shares this bit of breaking news with its readers in 1882: "Parson Twine has a new word—irregardless."

What's remarkable about all this is that the word's earliest uses in print, from the late eighteenth century to the mid-nineteenth century, are unremarkable. There are no scare quotes, no italics, no [*sic*]s—just the word appearing in print as if it were any other word. But by the end of the nineteenth century, it's suddenly become evidence of an undernourished mind:

> The REPORTER has been given a copy of the following actual report, submitted to his trustee by a Jefferson township teacher a few days since:
>
> "I have been trying to bend all into some regular years work. The school formerly not being graded at all, and allowed to run at random in their books. I found many obstacles and difficulties to overcome. Keep the scholars in regular year's work irregardless of their desire, is my best judgment. Strive to make good citizens of the scholars in school I have. But had poor citizens to begin with. Therefore, they are not ideal citizens in a school yet by any means."
>
> The trustee suggests that it would probably be inuseless to suggest anything for these unrestless scholars who are so irregardless of their conduct.

The paper's very pointed response to this use of "irregardless" echoes the common complaint today: you can't use a prefix ("ir-") that means "not" and a suffix ("-less") that essentially means "not" and expect that the word resulting from such a jumble is going to be understandable. Though it's worth noting that this very construction—[not][word][not] meaning [word][not]—showed up much earlier in English. The written record is sprinkled with words like "unboundless" and "irrespectless," among a few dozen others, and we have evidence of this sort of tomfoolery back to the fifteenth century. Why are there so many of these stupid and illogical compounds in the written record? Logic be damned: everybody knows that the more syllables you slap onto a word, the smarter you sound. The *Logansport Reporter* is the first to also slyly touch on a major underlying irritation with "irregardless": it's dialectal and therefore sounds uneducated. This, again, appears to be an opinion created well after the fact of the word's existence, but no matter.

Think of English as a river. It looks like one cohesive ribbon of water, but any potamologist* will tell you that rivers are actually made up of many different currents—sometimes hundreds of them. The interesting thing about rivers is, alter one of those currents and you alter the whole river, from its ecosystem to its course. Each of the currents in the river English is a different kind of English: business jargon, specialized vocabulary used in the construction industry, academic English, youth slang, youth slang from 1950, and so on. Each of these currents is doing its own thing, and each is an integral part of English.

One type of current you find in the river English is dialect. Dialects are little subsets of a language, and they have their own vocabulary, syntax, phonology, and grammar that sometimes overlap with other dialects of the main language and sometimes don't. "Y'all" is a dialectal term for the second-person plural pronoun; it's completely standard in some dialects of American English, particularly the ones in the South, and while it's common to hear speakers of those dialects use it easily, it's not a normal part of the dialect we call Standard English.

We tend to think of dialects (insofar as we think of them at all) as regional—Southern English, Boston English, Texan—but different social classes, ethnicities, and age-groups can have their own dialects. That means that dialects can be polarizing; they and their speakers are often subject to stereotype and scrutiny.

---

* **pot·a·mol·o·gist** \ˌpätəˈmäləjə̇st\ *n, pl* **-s** : a specialist in potamology *(MWU)*
pot·a·mol·o·gy \ˌpätəˈmäləjē\ *n, pl* **-gies** : the study of rivers *(MWU)*

I am a passionate defender of the linguistic worth of dialects out of self-defense: I have been the subject of that sort of stereotype and scrutiny. I grew up a working-class white kid in a Mexican and black school, where the main dialects spoken were Chicano English and African-American Vernacular English. I was the odd kid out: I natively spoke a weird mishmash of North Inland, holdovers from my parents' Great Lakes upbringings, and General Western American, the big regional dialect of my home state of Colorado. But this is knowledge gained in hindsight, of course: at the time, I was just a hapless dorky kid who wanted to fit in with my peers. Like a sponge, I began soaking up bits and pieces of each culture and its dialect while at school. I listened to Gloria Estefan and El DeBarge, Tejano and R&B; I played double Dutch and Chinese jump rope; I called my friends "chica" and "muchacho" and "homey" and "girlfriend."

As we got older, the way we talked became political. I watched parents push their kids to talk "like a white person," to linguistically pass, because they had spent a lifetime calling businesses like the cable company and hearing the secretary's lips smack over their Chicano lilt or the cadence of their blackness, while she demurred that they weren't going to be able to set up an appointment for, oh, dear, quite a while, you understand. I came of age before the Great Ebonics Controversy, when white people despaired that letting black students speak Ebonics[*] (their native dialect) in the classroom would usher in the end of English and "proper education" as we know it. But long before the rest of the world was aware of the politics of sounding black, I had friends split over whether sounding white was a sellout and whether sounding black was playing into a racial stereotype. Some friends dropped "homey" in favor of "guys"; others dropped "homey" in favor of "nigga." My Mexican friends began to work on dropping their uptalk, toning down their

---

[*] A name that has, for a very long while, been a dog whistle. This dialect has several names—Black Vernacular English, Black American English, African-American Vernacular English—but linguists never call it Ebonics.

lilt; they got sick of classmates in the halls sneering "illegal" at them and telling them to go back to Mexico, a country they weren't born in and had never visited.

If they didn't make the decision on their own, they were forced into it: I had one social studies teacher who proclaimed to us on the first day of class that everyone was expected to speak "correct and proper English" in class and a failure to do so would mean marks off on participation. Among the transgressions he would mark people down for were failure to sound the *g* at the end of any "-ing" word ("*g*-dropping," a typical marker of African-American Vernacular English); substituting a long *e* for the *i* in words like "growing" and "fill" ("tensing the lax /ɪ/," a phonological quirk of Chicano English); slouching in your chair and mumbling ("mutiny," a marker of being a teenager in a class taught by a jerk). My friend Stephanie, who was black, and I lolled on her living room rug after class, knocking our tennis shoes together and fuming about the rule while doing our current events homework. "I don't need no old white man telling me how to speak 'proper English,'" she grumbled. "I *already* speak it." Her mother hollered from the kitchen, "*Some* white man, Stephanie. You don't need *some* white man telling you to speak proper English."

I was not unaffected: One day I was telling my mom about my school day, and she cut me off. "Can you *queet talkeeng like deez*?" she mimicked. "We *don' talk like deez*." I was bewildered. "I'm just talking," I said, and in the heavy silence afterward she said, "You know, your friends probably think you're making fun of them when you talk like that." Whether it was disingenuous or not, it worked: I was suddenly, keenly aware that I looked white but sounded black or Chicana and that this reflected somehow poorly on me. I was from that point onward very careful about the types of words that came out of my mouth and how they sounded. I abandoned uptalk; I stopped *g*-dropping and /ɪ/ tensing and did my level best to sound smoothly, blandly western and white.

As careful as I was, my dialect still betrayed me when I relocated to New England for college. The way I spoke sounded completely normal to my ears, but drop that dialect smack into the middle of Massachusetts and suddenly I was a big ol' hick. My roommate used to make fun of how flat and wide my vowels were; I spoke so slowly that one classmate assumed I had a speech impediment. I said "howdy" often, and in response one deeply stupid (or cruel) woman asked if I rode a horse to school and had electricity where I grew up. Each comment, no matter how it was phrased, was intended to prove one thing: I was outside, a stranger. I was not from here, and so was exoticized or ostracized accordingly.

It wasn't until much later—once I began studying English—that I realized how important dialects are to a language. They give us lots of vocabulary, and their proliferation is a sign of linguistic growth. It wouldn't be overstating it to say that without dialects there *is* no language. The more I learned about dialects, the more I respected them. Dialects that might seem "uneducated" or "low" are actually full of a complex grammar that you, a nonnative speaker of that dialect, can't understand. In African-American Vernacular English, for instance, there's a difference between "he been sick," in which "been" stands in for Standard English's present perfect "has been," and "he *been* sick," where that stressed "been" marks that the action or state came into being a long time ago. Native speakers of AAVE have no problem navigating the two "beens."

While everyone thinks that they speak Standard English, no one *natively* speaks it: Standard English is itself a dialect based on a written ideal that we learn as we gain education. If we all spoke Standard English as a native dialect, then books on "good grammar" or "proper English" would be useless; we'd already know it because it'd be our very first dialect. All the rules about terminal prepositions, the correct use of "dilemma," and not using "snuck" would be pointless: we would absorb those finer points of usage as easily as we absorb oxygen. That we have to learn Standard English proves that it is not our native dialect. But that's okay: native English speakers actually speak *multiple* dialects of English and

can usually switch between them depending on the circumstance.*
Dialects are great!

"Irregardless," though? Can't we just quietly ignore it?

Here's the other interesting thing about rivers: they flow wherever they damned well please.

I had other work to do, and so set "irregardless" aside, but whenever I had a spare moment, I'd poke around in the correspondence files to see if other people claimed that the word was standard where they were from (they did), or I'd log in to one of the databases to see if I could find more evidence of an intensive or emphatic "irregardless" (I did). Over time, something insidious happened: in all this looking at "irregardless," I began to actually *appreciate* it. Make no mistake: I wasn't going to use it or champion its use, but I admired its tenacity, its ability to hang on to the periphery of Standard English for so long. It was a totally illogical coinage, but just one among many other illogical coinages (like "unravel") that have flourished for centuries. What if, I mused one day driving home from work, "irregardless" developed a nuanced emphatic use in dialectal speech, and when the word was committed to paper and spread abroad, it was flattened into just meaning "regardless" without shape or nuance? It's hard to convey this sort of emphasis in writing, especially when few people were willing to commit to print a word that was called "uneducated." That means, I realized, that in spite of all the violent hatred leveled at "irregardless," it was not only still in use but had maybe developed a *second, emphatic* meaning sometime back in the nineteenth century

---

* My favorite example of this bouncing between dialects, called code switching, comes from the comedy duo Key and Peele. In one of their skits, two black men on cellphones approach a crosswalk. One is talking to his wife about buying her tickets to the orchestra; the second is making a call. As soon as they see each other, they both immediately and emphatically slip into speech patterns consistent with AAVE. The second man crosses the street, and as soon as he's out of earshot of the first man, he slips back into his natural voice: higher and slightly lisping. "Oh my God, Christian," he says, "I almost totally got mugged just right now."

that had just barely clung to life but spread through various speaking communities like wildfire. "Irregardless" wasn't just a static irritation: it was an active force of language growth. My eyes widened, and I giggled and slapped the steering wheel. I had broken. "Irregardless" was no longer the grammarian's bête noire and the harbinger of linguistic doom to me: it was a word with depth, with history, with some attitude.

In short order, I became America's foremost "irregardless" apologist. I recorded a short video for Merriam-Webster's website refuting the notion that "irregardless" wasn't a word; I took to Twitter and Facebook and booed naysayers who set "irregardless" up as the straw man for the demise of English. I continued to find evidence of the emphatic "irregardless" in all sorts of places—even in the oral arguments of a Supreme Court case. One incredulous e-mail response to my video continued to claim "irregardless" wasn't a real word. "It's a made-up word that made it into the dictionary through constant use!" the correspondent said, and I cackled gleefully before responding. *Of course* "irregardless" is a made-up word that was entered into the dictionary through constant use; that's pretty much how this racket works. *All* words are made-up: Do you think we find them fully formed on the ocean floor, or mine for them in some remote part of Wales? I began telling correspondents that "irregardless" was much more complex than people thought, and it deserved a little respectful respite, even if it still was not part of Standard English. My mother was duly horrified. "Oh, Kory," she tutted. "So much for that college education."

As staunch a defender of dialect as I am, I fall into the same trap that all of us do: I consider myself the center of the lexical universe. The difference is that I should know better.

My younger daughter has spent her formative years in the mid-Atlantic region of America, which means that she and I speak different dialects. You would think that this would be a source of wonder to me daily, but it started out as a source of utter frustration.

One day, she came home from school, and I wandered out of my office to chat with her. "Do you have any homework?" I asked.

"No," she said, "I'm done my homework."

This particular construction is a marker of the local dialect (and also happens to be a marker of Canadian English). It's usually used with the participles "done" (as above) and "finished" ("I'm finished my burger"), though I also hear it with the participle "going" ("I'm going Emily's house"). These are all completely normal sentences around here, and in my town this construction is used by people of all socioeconomic levels, from doctors to panhandlers. It is wholly unremarkable.

Except it was wholly remarkable to me.

"No," I corrected her. "You're done *with* your homework."

"Right," she answered. "I'm done my homework."

All my years of training, all those hours spent carefully crafting responses to people who complained about the dialectal "ain't" or "irregardless," were thoroughly defenestrated. What motivated me was fear of judgment. "I'm done my homework" is not a part of Standard English, and my beautiful little girl was going to be judged on the basis of her abilities with Standard English, and I didn't want anyone to think she wasn't smart because she says "I'm done my homework." Never mind that just about *everyone* who spent their formative linguistic years here says that. Never mind that she will eventually learn that "I'm done my homework" is not Standard English, and she will, like the rest of us, learn to switch between her native dialect and the prestige dialect. Never mind that my own dialect is "wrong" here. Maternal worry surfaced in dialect shaming.

There are times when the marginalization of a dialect, or of vocabulary from that dialect, has more dire results. John Rickford, a professor of sociolinguistics, has done an extensive analysis of the testimony given in the Trayvon Martin case by Trayvon's friend Rachel Jeantel. Jeantel was on the phone with Martin as he was being pursued, and later shot, by George Zimmerman. She was, then, really the only witness to the shooting (apart from George Zimmerman) who was present in that courtroom.

Jeantel is black, and she natively speaks Haitian Creole as well as English. Throughout her testimony, the defense kept asking her if she understood English or if she was having a difficult time understanding the questions put to her. She consistently objected: she understood the questions just fine, and she was answering them honestly and completely. The problem was that she was answering them in AAVE, a dialect whose speakers are often painted as ignorant and uneducated. The white jury interrupted proceedings several times and claimed they could not understand her, and the defense attorney questioned one part of a pretrial deposition she gave concerning what she heard during the struggle. During that interview, she said she heard someone yell, "Get off!" and when she was asked, "Could you tell who it was?" the transcript indicated that she first answered, "I couldn't know Trayvon," and later, "I couldn't hear Trayvon." But Rickford points out that, even in Haitian Creole, those answers make no sense in context. "When another linguist and I listened to the TV broadcast of the recording played in court we heard, instead, 'I could, an' it was Trayvon.'" Rickford notes that he'd need to listen to a better recording of the initial interview that was transcribed. "But," he goes on, "she definitely did not say what the transcript reports her to have said."

It's hard to jump to the conclusion that the jury would have decided differently had the interview been transcribed differently. But the "mights" weigh very heavily: had a native speaker of AAVE been on the jury or in the courtroom, Jeantel's testimony might not have been discredited, and the verdict might have been different. That is, as we say in my native dialect, worth reckoning.

Corpus

On Collecting the Bones

After I got my job at Merriam-Webster, friends would ask me what my day-to-day work looked like. It makes sense: the idea that anyone spends eight hours a day doing anything with dictionaries beyond shelving them or using them as doorstops is absurd. And yet there I was, spending eight hours a day eyeballs-deep in dictionaries. Absurd is as absurd does.

So what does absurd do? I assured my friends that the work was utterly dreamy for a nerd like me: I spent most of my day reading.

Heads would tilt; drinks would float back down to the tabletop. Sly incredulity would slide over their faces. Reading. *Really*. Not finding new words, not culling old ones. Just reading. I'd smile broadly. Oh, yes. Yes, yes.

There is a common perception about lexicographers—common insofar as there is *any* perception about lexicographers—that they are the creators, redeemers, and sustainers of the language, some nebbish Holy Trinity. This misperception leads to all sorts of odd assumptions about what my work looks like. Folks assume that I spend my day in a locked, smoky conference room, chomping on cigars and guzzling scotch, where other lexicographers and I bark out the latest, greatest additions to the language like carica-ture admen. Dartboards and blindfolds are sometimes invoked; extensive bribery setups are hinted at—how else did "Xerox" and "Kleenex" get into the dictionary?

After such a buildup, it is perhaps disappointing to find that dictionary work really is so mundane. One of my daughter's friends summed it up best: after he heard what I did, his mouth fell open and he proclaimed, "Oh my God, that is the most boring thing I have ever heard in my life." But for others, that sounds like heaven. One new acquaintance reached across the table and grasped my wrist:* "They pay you to *sit and read* for eight hours a day?" Her eyes went glassy with delight.

As a record of language in actual use, a dictionary has to be based on something outside the lexicographer's head, and that something is a representative sample of the gargantuan bulk of printed English prose. How you get this representative sample is through a long-standing tradition that begins and ends with reading.

As we have seen, English dictionaries began to proliferate in the late sixteenth century as power and wealth in England began to shift from the aristocratic class to the merchant class. London became a center for global trade and exploration, and your average merchant needed a level of literacy that he (or she) hadn't needed in previous ages. Early English dictionaries were bilingual—Latin and English, French and English, Italian and English—because English was a newly global language. Bilingual dictionaries served not only the London merchants who were doing trade in these languages but also the foreigners who did dealings with English merchants and had to wrestle with a language whose vocabulary and grammar were serpentine.

As literacy ramped up in London, and grammar schools (particularly for young men) became more common, so too did reference books that were the forerunners of modern dictionaries. By the late sixteenth century, several popular primers included word lists to help the student progress in reading and writing English: the schoolmaster Richard Mulcaster's 1582 *Elementarie* (or, more properly, *The First Part of the Elementarie Vvhich Entreateth Chefelie*

---

* Reader, I flinched.

of the Right Writing of Our English Tung, Set Furth by Richard Mul-caster) ended with a list of around 8,000 words that every learned student should know; Edmund Coote's 1596 *The English Schoole-Maister* contained a list of about 1,680 words.[*]

The first book that scholars will call a proper monolingual English dictionary is the 1604 *A Table Alphabeticall . . .*[†] by Robert Cawdrey. Cawdrey's book likely grew out of his work as a schoolmaster, and he makes it clear in the letter to the reader that opens his dictionary that his intention is to get people to use words that fit the context, to learn when to use high-flown language and when to use down-home words, and generally quit putting on lexical airs. The letter's a marvel: it not only tells people how to use a dictionary but deliciously throws shade at educated and well-traveled people who speak only to impress ("Doth any wise man think, that wit resteth in strange words . . . ? Do we not speak, because we would haue others to vnderstand vs?").

Though Cawdrey claims his dictionary is for everyone, it's not: it's a list of hard words for the educated. No gentleman trained at Cambridge needs a slob like Cawdrey to tell him what the word "say" or "dog" means; Cawdrey's book instead focuses on higher-level words like "cypher" and "elocution" and the sadly now-rare "spongeous" ("like a sponge"). But how did Cawdrey decide which hard words to cover? Certainly his work as a schoolmaster

---

[*] Coote's list offered rudimentary definitions; Mulcaster's list included none. Mulcaster foisted that on someone else—in introducing his word list, he yearns for someone to make a comprehensive dictionary of English for the native English speaker: "The want whereof, is the onelie cause why, that verie manie men, being excellentlie well learned in foren speche, can hardlie discern what theie haue at home, still shooting fair, but oft missing far" (166).

[†] *. . . conteyning and teaching the true writing, and vnderstanding of hard vsuall English wordes, borrowed from the Hebrew, Greeke, Latine, or French, &c. / With the interpretation thereof by plaine English words, gathered for the benefit & helpe of Ladies, Gentlewomen, or any other vnskilfull persons. / Whereby they may the more easilie and better vnderstand many hard English wordes, which they shall heare or read in Scriptures, Sermons, or elswhere, and also be made able to vse the same aptly themselues.* Good Lord, Cawdrey.

helped him discern which words students had trouble with, but he also borrowed liberally from specialty glossaries and primers that had already been printed, including both Mulcaster's and Coote's. So Cawdrey has two lexicographical claims to fame: first proper monolingual English dictionary, and originator of the great lexicographical tradition of plagiarism.

This is the general approach that lexicography takes for another sixty years or so: dictionaries are lists of hard words for educated, well-read people, and the words worth defining sprang generally from the mind of the lexicographer and the drudgery of others who had gone before. These early dictionaries focused sometimes on foreign words that we had kidnapped into English and sometimes on multisyllabic words we had churned out. What they did not include were simple, ordinary words, because those were already common enough that no scholar needed to know them. Early dictionaries were entirely didactic: they were meant to improve the education of those who already had some education.

That began to change in the mid-seventeenth century. A handful of dictionaries devoted to "thieves' cant," or the words used by the lower, sometimes criminal, classes in London, appeared on the scene. It may seem like an abrupt shift to go from the elevated language of the educated to the slang of pickpockets, but even this change is motivated by reading: there was a genre of writing called rogue literature that was popular during the sixteenth and seventeenth centuries in England. These books, plays, and pamphlets purported to be the true-crime pulp fiction of Elizabethan England: they were tell-all confessionals by beggars, hustlers, and thieves, and the educated class ate them up. Consequently, authors of rogue literature began to publish dictionaries of thieves' cant so their readers could better understand their works.

Books during this era were big business, and dictionaries flourished: in the hundred years after Cawdrey's *Table Alphabeticall* was published, a rough dozen new dictionaries hit the market. If books flourished, it was because of the push into literacy. The Protestant Reformation put a new emphasis on the ability to read and understand the Scriptures for oneself in one's native language, and schools popped up to aid that purpose. When the age of Enlightenment eclipsed the Protestant Reformation, the value of literacy as a byway to reason skyrocketed: we exhibit right thinking, the maxim went, by using exactly the right words. By the eighteenth century, dictionaries included ordinary words so that everyone, from scholar to slob, could express themselves properly.

Expanded literacy didn't just mean more money for booksellers. Readers needed—and wanted—more information about the words they were using: what made a particular word more meet than another, how were certain words pronounced, when was one meaning base while another elevated? Existing dictionaries didn't comprehensively answer these questions. One dictionary might include a handful of ordinary words; another might include cant; another might focus only on the words of law or botany; another might not be comprehensive enough. In short, readers wanted more bang for their buck and, in wanting, wished into existence the modern dictionary and the modern lexicographer.

First was Nathaniel Bailey, whose 1721 *An* [sic] *Universal Etymological English Dictionary** not only included everyday words

---

*   "... COMPREHENDING The Derivations of the Generality of Words in the English Tongue, either Ancient or Modern, from the Ancient British, Saxon, Danish, Norman, and Modern French, Teutonick, Dutch, Spanish, Italian; as also from the Latin, Greek, and Hebrew Languages, each in their proper Characters. AND ALSO A brief and clear Explication of all difficult Words, derived from any of the aforesaid Languages, and Terms of Art, relating to Anatomy, Botany, Physick, Pharmacy, Surgery, Chymistry, Philosophy, Divinity, Mathematicks, Grammar, Logick, Rhetorick, Musick, Heraldry, Maritime Affairs, Military Discipline, Horsemanship, Hunting, Hawking, Fowling, Fishing, Gardening, Husbandry, Handicrafts, Confectionary, Carving, Cookery, &c. TOGETHER WITH A large Collection and Explication of Words and Phrases used in our Ancient Statutes, Charters, Writs, Old Records, and Processes in Law; and the Etymology, and Interpretation of the Proper Names of Men, Women, and remarkable Places in Great-Britain: Also the Dialects of our different Countries. Containing many Thousand Words more than either Harris, Philips, Kersey, or any English Dictionary before extant. To which is added, A Collection of our most common Proverbs, with their Explication and Illustration. The whole Work compiled and methodically digested, as well for the but also gave extensive histories, notes on various uses, and stress marks so people would know where to put the emphasis on a word they might have only read. It was aimed at *everybody*—students, tradesmen, foreigners, the "curious," and the "ignorant"—and accordingly included a good number of taboo and slang words, including "cunt" and "fuck" (both coyly defined in Latin, not English). Bailey's dictionaries were wildly popular.

After Bailey came Samuel Johnson, His Cantankerousness. Son of a London bookseller, a university dropout, afflicted with depression and what modern doctors think was likely Tourette's—"a man of bizarre appearance, uncouth habits, and minimal qualifications"— Johnson was bewilderingly chosen by a group of English booksellers and authors to write *the authoritative* dictionary of English.

Because of the seriousness of the charge, and because Johnson was scholarly but not a proper scholar, he began work on his dictionary the way that all of us now do: he read. He focused on the great works of English literature—Shakespeare, Milton, Dryden, Locke, Pope—but also took in more mundane, less elevated works. Among the books that crossed his desk were research on fossils, medical texts, treatises on education, poetry, legal writing, sermons, periodicals, collections of personal letters, scientific explorations of color, books debunking common myths and superstitions of the day, abridged histories of the world, and other dictionaries.

When he saw a word that piqued his interest, he underlined it, put the first letter of that word in the margin of the book, and then passed those heavily marked texts to his assistants, who would copy the passage down on a piece of paper. The pieces of paper were filed alphabetically; they were what Johnson referred to in writing his dictionary.

Johnson's system became the basis upon which nearly every dictionary from 1755 forward was prepared. Noah Webster used heavily

Entertainment of the Curious, as the Information of the Ignorant; and for the Benefit of young Students, Artificers, Tradesmen, and Foreigners, who are desirous thoroughly to understand what they Speak, Read, or Write." They sure don't title dictionaries like they used to.

annotated copies of books (and many, many other dictionaries) in preparing his 1828 *American Dictionary of the English Language;* every managing editor at what would be called the *Oxford English Dictionary* oversaw a public reading program to gather quotations and rare words from an international cadre of readers (including at least one murderous nutbar);* dictionary companies today still underline, bracket, and extract quotations, which we call "citations," from a wide variety of sources.

It's a system that *seems* laughably easy.

Noah Webster, in an 1816 letter, wrote that "the business of a lexicographer is to collect, define, and arrange, as far as possible, *all* the words that belong to a language." All words—technical language, jargon, cant, interesting words, boring words—were, in Noah's view, ripe for harvesting.† But modern lexicographers shift the emphasis of Noah's statement a bit to the left: the business of a lexicographer is to collect, define, and arrange, *as far as possible,* all the words that belong to a language. The fruit isn't as low hanging as Noah's sound bite would lead you to believe. No dictionary in the world records all the words in any given language.

A lexicographer can't rely solely on their native knowledge of the language when evaluating a word for entry—how could I, a half-assed medievalist, know whether "EBITDA," a word used in accounting, is widespread when I have never seen it before and

---

* Said murderous nutbar is Dr. William Chester Minor, one of the most prolific and linguistically sensitive readers *OED* editor James Murray had ever employed, and also a permanent resident of the Broadmoor, England's best-known asylum for criminal lunatics. Minor was such a great reader because he got his pre-insane start doing the exact same work for the Webster's folks; his name is found in the preface of Webster's 1864 *American Dictionary of the English Language, Royal Quarto Edition, Unabridged.* He was a science editor and, from what we in the office can tell from the correspondence available to us, not a very good one.

† "Noah's view" as expressed here is some hat-waving fustian; in practice, Noah omitted quite a few "vulgar" and "low" terms from his dictionaries.

hope never to have to encounter it in my everyday life? Even the editors who are reckoned to be specialists—the science editors—aren't necessarily experts. "We don't have expertise in everything," says Christopher Connor, one of Merriam-Webster's life sciences editors. "We're just tasked at doing it." That's why many dictionary companies have some sort of reading program that gives lexicographers the raw materials they use to write a dictionary definition.

A tool is only as good as the materials used to make it (as I have heard my father holler from the depths of the garage, usually after a sudden, clarion "clang" followed by a daisy chain of expletives), and a dictionary is no exception. The aim of a general dictionary isn't to just skim the language, siphoning off the lightweight flotsam that everyone sees; nor should it dredge the bottom of the language, pulling up rare and archaic words from the depths where they have slid into the rusting muck. To have a truly representative sample of the language to define from, you need both depth and breadth.

English is a language that invites invention (whether you like it or not), and the glories of the Internet make it possible to spread that invention abroad (whether you like it or not). That means that we tend to see new coinages everywhere we go—words like "mansplain," a lovely little portmanteau* of "man" and "explain" and used broadly to refer to a man pedantically explaining something to a listener under the false assumption that the listener knows less than the speaker does on the subject. "Mansplain" stuttered into existence around 2009, and by the beginning of 2013 it was everywhere: from *The New York Times* to *The Huffington Post,* from *The Globe and Mail* of Canada to the *Sunday Tribune* in South Africa to the *Sunday Guardian* in India. And of course it was everywhere: it's

---

* A portmanteau is a word whose form and meaning are a blend of the forms and meanings of two other words. That's a stuffy explanation for a fun class of words: consider "smog," a blend of "smoke" and "fog," or "brunch," a blend of "breakfast" and "lunch." "Portmanteau" is itself a portmanteau: it's the medieval French word for a large suitcase and is a blend of *porter* ("to carry") and *manteau* ("mantle, cloak").

a *great* word. It birthed a whole brood of "-splains": an informal list I keep at my desk includes "grammarsplain," "wonksplain," "poorsplain," "catsplain," "whitesplain," "blacksplain," "lawsplain," and the inevitable "sexsplain," all found in various articles online.

A casual reader might assume that "mansplain" and the "-splain" affix were the It Words for the second decade of the twenty-first century—not just everywhere, but important *because* they were everywhere. And sure enough, everyone who knew what I did for a living asked, from 2013 onward (and with equal parts eagerness and horror), "Have you entered 'mansplain' yet?" I would assure—or disappoint—them, "No, it's not in yet," and in return they would inevitably get irked. One friend responded, "I thought you were supposed to be on the bleeding edge of language change!" I assured her that we were but that the bleeding edge of language change wasn't always the most prominent one. I had been spending, I said, a lot of time looking at uses of "bored of."

She blinked in what I can only hope was ravening interest but was more likely blank incredulity. "Bored of," she repeated.

Yes, "bored of," as in "I'm *bored of* being asked about 'mansplaining' every fifteen minutes." For hundreds of years, "bored" was always paired with "by" ("I'm *bored by* your grammarsplaining") or "with" ("I'm *bored with* your grammarsplaining"), but in recent years lexicographers began to notice that "bored" was beginning to be paired more with "of." This trend has been much more common in the U.K. than in the United States—in fact, the folks at Oxford Dictionaries say that they have more evidence nowadays of "bored of" than they do of "bored by," and the evidence shows uses of "bored with" and "bored of" are neck and neck over there—but it's creeping in on this side of the pond as well. It's a small change, just a little slip in the linguistic tectonic plates of "bored," but lexicographers can feel the shock waves ripple through the language. Because it may be that this particular use of "of" here in "bored of" is the beginning of a new meaning of "of," and that, my friends, is the sort of thing that gets lexicographers all hot and bothered. "Bored of" is a new use that few people notice, but it's far more prevalent than all the uses of "mansplain" chucked together. Skimming the surface of the language means that you skip over this small but beautiful specimen.

Skimming's out, but that doesn't mean that you should attempt to sound the bottom of the language, either. In one of my early defining batches for the *Unabridged Dictionary,* I had the word "abecedarian." It's relatively rare, one of those ten-dollar words that people whip out when trying to prove that they competed in the National Spelling Bee. Rare or not, I needed to read through the citations we had for it to determine if a change to the definition was needed. I was familiar with the first definition given, "one that is learning the rudiments of something (such as the alphabet)," but it had another definition I had never seen before: "one of a 16th century Anabaptist sect that despised human learning on the ground that the illiterate needed no more than the guidance of the Holy Spirit to interpret Scripture." I mimed an "ooh"—in the office you'd never actually articulate an "ooh," because that counts as talking and talking is frowned upon—and went diving into the citations. The history of religion in Europe is something I know a very small bit about, and this promised to be a gas. Reformation Anabaptists! Illiteracy! The Holy Spirit! Truly, my defining cup runneth over.

But "abecedarian" is a rare word, and this sense of "abecedarian" was the rarest ever. There was almost nothing in our extensive citation files for it; no one at Merriam-Webster had evidently encountered this word in print. So how did it end up in the dictionary? A pink from the early twentieth century let slip that the evidence was in a single book in the editorial library. I slid the file drawer closed and plodded down to the basement, where we kept the old editorial library books next to the rolls of packing tape and the ghost of George Merriam, doomed to moan for eternity about the price of ink and the crazy demands of the Webster family. And thus began a wild-goose chase for evidence of this odd Anabaptist sect's name—a chase that lasted almost a week, involved me tracking down earlier and earlier screeds against the Anabaptists in a variety of languages, and ended with an e-mail from a professor-friend that began, "So I read further in that *Historiae anabaptisticae* text and consulted some of Melanchthon's letters written during the period in which Storck et al., were in Wittenberg and the aftermath of that." It was all terribly exciting in that look-at-me-using-my-Latin way, but it was, lexicographically, a waste of my time. If this particular use of "abecedarian" is so rare that I can't find much evidence of it, then it is probably one of those uses that's sucked deep into the sludge of discarded words that makes up the bottom of the river English and probably shouldn't get a full week of my time. Yes, I learned a lot about the Zwickau prophets and the early beginnings of Anabaptism, but in the end, when I sat down and did a dispassionate inventory of what I had found about the word, I discovered that it didn't change the definition at all. A week of editorial time stuffed down a rabbit hole, and all I came out of it with was the knowledge that I am the world's biggest epistemophilic dork. What I learned wasn't even good cocktail-party fodder. Depth, then, isn't all it's cracked up to be.

So we aim for the even middle: a variety of resources with some depth. But here is a truth lexicographers—people who sing praises to objectivity and worship raw, unparsed data—would rather you ignore: deciding on a balanced source list is really a subjective art. How much academic writing should go in? Academic writers want you to read everything they write (because someone has to), and many fields are rife with specialty journals of one stripe or another. If we read the *Journal of Modern Literature,* should we also read *Contemporary Literature*? What about *American Literature*? If we read that, do we need to add *Early American Literature* to the mix, or can we assume that *American Literature* will also cover some early American literature? And not to be jingoistic, but do we also have to read the *Canadian Review of Comparative Literature* or the *Scottish Literary Review*? I exaggerate, of course, but just barely. Edge out into the sciences, and your list blossoms into thousands of possibilities, including nine separate journals all called *Journal of Physics*. So much whiffling deliberation over which *Journal of Physics* you should read, and yet it might not really matter, because most published writing isn't academic. Your time would be better spent agonizing over whether to read both *People* and *OK!* magazine.

The early lexicographers made very deliberate choices to omit sources they felt were not up to snuff. Samuel Johnson got very sniffy about including American sources; Noah Webster thought that some of the giants of British literature were too inflated to include in a sensible language of good English.* Modern lexicographers are (or try to be) less snooty in their selections, but they also have to make choices. Before you is the latest Margaret Atwood novel and the entirety of the Twilight book series. Twilight is wildly popular, but you suspect it's not going to yield a lot vis-à-vis new words. Margaret Atwood's book is not quite as popular as the teen vampire/werewolf/paranormal romance, but it will probably yield more new words. Do you eschew what is generally held to be popular dreck for something more literary? Doesn't dreck have a place in the world, too? One of the complaints against *Webster's Third New International Dictionary* was that it included a number of quotations—forty-five in all—from Polly Adler's book *A House Is Not a Home*. Polly Adler's name was well-known to discerning readers of the early twentieth century: she was the most celebrated brothel owner and madam in New York. Her memoir supplied some fantastic quotations, including the delightful "trying to chisel in on the beer racket." Which brings us to an important consideration: Who are you, you overeducated and myopic boob, to judge whether a book is (a) dreck and (b) probably not a gold mine of neologisms?

---

* "Whatever admiration the world may bestow on the Genius of Shakespeare, his language is full of errors, and ought not to be offered as a model for imitation."—Noah Webster, the man heralded as "America's Schoolteacher," in his 1807 pamphlet *A Letter to Dr. Ramsay . . . Respecting the Errors in Johnson's Dictionary.*

Plenty of lexicographers thought that when the Harry Potter series first debuted, it wasn't going to give us much in the way of lasting coinages, because it was a fantasy series. And now we see the word "muggle," used unironically to refer to a (usually provincial) person outside a particular culture or group, all over the place, including in an article discussing the language of a Supreme Court dissent.

Modern lexicographers have something else to contend with: the vast ball of wax that is the Internet. Reference publishers have traditionally been a little squidgy about mining the Internet for citations because most writing on the Internet isn't edited. Then again, books, news, and periodicals are reorienting themselves to be online properties. What you see in the printed version of *The New Yorker,* for instance, isn't the same content you may see on its website. As print sources have shrunk, so too have their editorial staffs, which means that some formerly reliable sources are now spottily edited (if they're edited at all).

The Internet has also posed another problem for the lexicographer: sources can be changed, edited, or disappear at will. Much was made in 2015 of Bryan Henderson, the *Wikipedia* editor whose personal mission was to delete and revise all appearances of "is comprised of" on the open-source encyclopedia. He has made—by hand—over forty-seven thousand edits to the site, most of them replacing "is comprised of" with "is composed of" or "consists of." There was a lot of hooting and hollering both in support and in detraction of Mr. Henderson, but lexicographers frowned slightly and rubbed the crease of editorial worry between our brows. We've all seen an interesting use online—perhaps a "bored of" or an "is comprised of"—that we add to the files, only to go back later and find it was edited out. Damn mutability, we mutter. Yet the record has always been mutable: John Dryden edited later editions of his works to avoid words like "wench" because he found, as he grew older, that he preferred "mistress" instead.

There is one final point to consider. In an age of dictionary contractions, where reference companies are cutting editors left and right and you're lucky to have half a dozen editors on staff, how are you going to read all this goddamned stuff?

Some dictionary companies have attempted to fix this problem by using what's called a corpus. A corpus is a curated collection of full-text sources usually dumped into a searchable database of some sort. These corpora* are online, available both publicly and by subscription. Some focus on newspapers; some on a mix of academic and nonacademic writing; some include transcripts of news broadcasts; one famously only includes the scripts of American soap operas. Most contain hundreds of millions of words, and they've been a boon to lexicographers. The best of them label and subdivide their sources so lexicographers can sort through transcribed speech or academic writing, or they tag the words in their corpus with parts of speech—a godsend when you are defining a word like "as," which has five parts of speech. And they collect things that lexicographers never had easy access to before. Sci-fi and fantasy novels; the proceedings from Britain's early modern criminal court; Usenet group posts; hand-printed zines and pamphlets from the punk 1970s and 1980s; comic books: before the advent of the Internet, lexicographers chasing down a hunch had to know that those materials existed and hope they were housed somewhere within easy commuting distance and overseen by a charitable librarian.

Corpora are also excellent for collecting dialect terms or regionalisms. These are words that are specific to a dialect or region and that don't have much national or international use. The word "finna" is an excellent example: it's common in Southern English as an alteration of "fixing to," which is itself a Southernism for "going to," and it rarely appears in edited print outside the American South. That means that the Yankee lexicographers up north would rarely encounter it in national print, but you can find it in corpora that include smaller regional newspapers and publications. Corpora lit-

---

* Never, ever "corpuses." Lexicographers and linguists call them corpora.

erally open up new lexical worlds that lexicographers might have only glimpsed before. Before corpora, lexicographers could only look at what they had personally collected. Now, with just a few keystrokes, you can get a sense of the geographical distribution of a word or get a sense as to how widespread a given word is compared with another word.

But as great as corpora are—and they really are—they can't compete with a real-life person trawling through a magazine or a web article, waiting for something to snag on their sprachgefühl. Linguists love corpora; where two or three linguists are gathered, there shall you find heavy-breathing fetishism about the size, scope, all those possibilities, all that *data*. Yet all the data in the world is useless unless you can find someone to parse and interpret it.

An online dictionary start-up called Wordnik made waves in 2015 when it announced a fund-raising campaign to document the "million missing words" of English—words that were so new or rare they weren't entered into any dictionary. The way it was going to do this was to search the Internet for any glossed word—that is, a word that is explained in running text right after its first use, like this. Wordnik was using a data analytics firm to help it find its million words by looking for trigger texts, like "also called" or "known as." One co-founder of the data firm told *The New York Times* that Wordnik's research was going to help track how quickly new words are adopted:

> "We can actually measure when words get adopted in mainstream lingo," he said, by looking at when writers stop explaining neologisms like "infotainment" and start using them as if their meanings were commonly understood. "It will be interesting to see which words will very quickly get adopted and which words remain outsiders."

There are a number of metrics that trained lexicographers look for when judging whether a word has fully settled in to the language. The disappearance of that gloss I mentioned above is one, and it works fairly well—provided that you are savvy about where you're looking. Because these days, the most productive new words—and by "productive," I don't mean "useful" but "used a lot and all over the place"—come from a few fields that are just bursting with jargon and specialized vocabulary, like computer programming, medicine, and business. Within those fields, that jargon and specialized vocabulary are well understood and so show up without the trappings we give to new words to mark them as such: quotation marks, italics, glosses. But in general-interest publications, those specialty terms will still show up in quotation marks, italics, and with glosses, because they haven't really settled in to the language of the Regular Guy. When it comes time to write a dictionary, I might enter the specialized term in an unabridged dictionary, where people expect harder terms and more specialized vocabulary, but not in an abridged dictionary, which people expect to have the words you need every day. Or I might decide that it's an important enough word that even though it's still being glossed regularly, it deserves entry right away: words like "AIDS" and "SARS" will probably get entered into a dictionary fairly quickly after they first show up on the scene, because you can reason that the syndromes they name are significant enough health events that they are not going anywhere very soon. Those sorts of decisions are made on a human level; people with experience in the trenches of language change can make those decisions far better than natural-language processing programs currently can. Computers are, however, far quicker.

Thinking about documenting language brings on a gurgle of dread deep in the editorial gut. The philosophy of citation gathering actually runs counter to how language forms. Because we live in a literate society with comparatively easy access to books and education, we tend to believe that the written word is more important and has more weight than the spoken word. It makes some sort of sense: speech is ephemeral, captured only once by the listener and sorted like mental junk mail, a little slip of information that may or may not be useful and that either gets tossed or ends up moldering underneath the grocery list, the name of your first pet, and the chorus to the Beatles' "All You Need Is Love." Writing, on the other hand, is eternal; just ask anyone who has posted anything of questionable taste on the Internet. Once it's written down, it's *real*.

But this is, to use a technical term, totally bogus. Speech is actually the primary way that language gets transmitted, and linguistic research of all stripes bears this out. Under ordinary circumstances, we learn to speak before we learn to read, and anyone who has tried to learn a foreign language knows that the gold standard of fluency isn't your reading comprehension but your ability to ask a native speaker of that language which team they favor in the World Cup and to fully understand and participate in the argument that will inevitably ensue. That means that new words and phrases are almost always coined and spoken for some time before they get written down, and that is a whole area of language creation that the lexicographer doesn't have access to.

But ah—so what? If a word is really important, you may reason, then someone will eventually write it down, and then lexicographers will eventually see it, catalog it, and define it. Alas, not always. First, not all writing is public. Letters, grocery lists, notes we've written to each other in middle school, are not typeset and put in volumes for general consumption. Even the letters of great men and women—letters that would have some sort of literary or historical significance—are published in incomplete volumes or are lost to time. That's a linguistic loss: many people are freer in these personal communiqués with the language they use. They're willing to innovate, abbreviate, create nonce words, and let their linguistic guard down, and this means that there is a whole host of new and exciting words that will never be seen by a lexicographer.

Which brings us to the second difficulty: a word has to be *seen* by a lexicographer, and while we are voracious, compulsive readers, there is no way that the world's lexicographers could possibly read everything in print. Not only are there more print sources around than ever before, but the Internet gives everyone with access the opportunity to be a well-read author. That's not hyperbole. In June 2014, a sixteen-year-old teen named Peaches Monroee made a six-second video in which she called her eyebrows "on fleek," meaning "good" or "on point." In November, just five months after Monroee posted her video, nearly 10 percent of all Google searches worldwide were for "on fleek."

My colleague Emily interviewed Monroee for a blog post and asked where "on fleek" came from. Was it family slang, a play on "on point" and "flick," some sort of blend of "fly" and "chic"? No: Monroee says she just made it up.*

Madeline Novak, our director of editorial operations, had just come by my desk to drop off the list. I was busy reading the front matter of the *Third,* a form of hazing that all new hires at Merriam-Webster are required to undergo as part of their training, but was happy to set those forty-five pages of four-point type aside for this. "Take a look," she had said, "and let me know what you want to get started on."

The list I was now scanning was the official Reading and Marking list—the catalog of sources we regularly read and marked, arranged both alphabetically (natch) and by subject area. I whumped my copy of the *Third* shut, hissed a quiet "yes," and hunched over the list like a kid who had just discovered her older sibling's stash of M&M's. My eyes flitted up and down the pages: everything from *Better Homes and Gardens* to *Today's Chemist at Work, Vibe* to *Commonweal, The New York Times* to—I squealed as quietly as I could and ended up sounding like a slow leak—the *Rocky Mountain News,* one of my hometown papers. Madeline suggested I pick

---

* There is an entry for "fleek" (no "on") at UrbanDictionary.com that dates back to 2003 and means "smooth" or "nice," but as of this writing, Peaches can still lay claim to coining "on fleek."

three or four to start out; within five minutes, I had already written out a list of about fifteen sources I'd like to read, and this was just the list of periodicals and newspapers! I hadn't even *seen* the book list yet. Forget the M&M's: this was a whole candy store.

I put my pencil down and marveled at my luck. Here I was, a woman who didn't just like to read, but who *couldn't stop* reading—a woman who read ads on the bus, then moved to receipts in my pockets, then finally to reading over strangers' shoulders because I couldn't help it, I *had* to—here I was, actually getting paid to read. *This job,* I decided, *is the shit.*

Reading and marking is* one of the core skills of a lexicographer, and like the other core skills of a lexicographer—defining, proofreading, assiduously avoiding eye contact—it takes practice. The process itself is simple: read something and be on the lookout for a word that catches your eye; when you find a word, underline it; bracket enough of the context around the word so that a future definer can determine how the word is used and what it means; put a check in the margin next to the marked word so the typists don't go blind trying to find your faint, chicken-scratch underlining in all that text. Repeat until you have nothing else to read. But it's the reading itself that requires some work. Most people assume it's the idyllic, lost-in-it-all reading that most logophiles (and prospective lexicographers) dream of. Alas, it's no relaxation fest, or it's not intended to be. "I get the sense that most people read and mark at the end of a long day," says Steve Perrault, "and I think that's the wrong approach."

For a new lexicographer, this means that in addition to unlearning and relearning grammar as a new editor, you need to unlearn and relearn reading. This is done with practice sessions. While my new-hire crew was having Gil hammer out our linguistic prejudices like a mechanic with an old bumper, Steve was teaching us how

---

* Not a mistake: "Reading and marking" looks like a compound subject, which would require a plural verb, but the two actions are taken as one. You don't read without marking; you can't mark without reading.

to read. The goal behind reading and marking is to add new and interesting words to the citation files, and to do that well, you must pay attention to what you're reading—but not too much attention. The commonest problem a lexicographer encounters in reading and marking is finding oneself interested in the content and not the language. For instance,

> At the Barbra Streisand $5000-a-head Demo fund-raiser on her Malibu spread, Hugh Hefner arrived with a scantily clad youngie who noticed Nancy Pelosi staring at her and snapped, "Don't think I'm dumb, sweetie, just because I'm not wearing anything!"

Who was the half-naked bimbo, and was she really as smart as she thought she was? What did Nancy Pelosi say in response? What did Hugh Hefner say in response? Oh God, I am *dying* to hear how this went down.

If you are too, then you are not actually reading and marking, you are just reading. You are so focused on the potential for drama that you probably missed "Demo," a great shortened form of "Democratic" that you don't see often, and "spread," a word that you usually see in reference to an array of foods, not a house. It wasn't all a wash: you likely caught "youngie" because it appears after "scantily clad." *O tempora! O mores!*

For lexicographers, skimming is just as dangerous as diving headfirst into the story behind the words. When we skim, we are looking for key words and familiar patterns in text, not reading word by word or line by line. Skimming that passage above, you can quickly latch onto a few blockbuster words: "sweetie," "scantily clad," "Barbra," "Hugh Hefner." But you will likely miss the "a" and "head" in "$5000-a-head"—both uses that are not necessarily new but certainly don't appear in print as much as they do in speech, and so are worth potentially marking. You might also mark "fund-raiser," hyphenated as it is, so that you have evidence of it moving from an open compound to a hyphenated compound. That's the sort of subtle shift that reading and marking intends to catch.

But you only catch these shifts with practice. Our practice reading and marking consisted of photocopies of articles that Steve had already read, from magazines with some narrative interest to make you work harder—trial by *Entertainment Weekly.* Steve gave you the reading; you went back to your desk and marked; and then you reviewed it together in the editorial conference room, with Steve suggesting good words you might have missed and explaining why marking other words is less helpful.

One of my colleagues, Emily Vezina, vividly remembers her reading and marking training. She was reading a page of *Entertainment Weekly,* and Steve was going paragraph by paragraph with her. "What did you mark in the first paragraph?" he'd ask, and she'd run down what she marked. If he thought it was a good mark, he'd just nod and say, "Okay, good." They went on like this until the last paragraph, which was a review for the movie *American Pie* 2. "And what did you mark here?" Steve asked.

She paused. "I had just started working here," she explains now, "and I didn't know this guy very well. And he was my boss! But he asked, so I answered." She cleared her throat and said, "Ah, I marked 'horndogs,'" and he paused a bit, and then said, "Okay, good." No word, no matter how stupid, is beneath your notice.

You may note that I keep referring to "words that catch your eye." It's true that the words that tend to catch a lexicographer's eye are words that are new in some way. But because lexicographers write definitions based on the citations they collect, you end up with a very unbalanced file if all you're marking are new words. Consequently, there have been times when the muckety-mucks at Merriam-Webster have requested that we all mark every third or fifth word in at least one source just to fill our files with words that would not usually catch our eye. Modern online corpora help us fill in those gaps, but in the pre-corpora days we did citational spackling ourselves (and with a lot of apologies and homemade cookies for the stalwart typists who had to take all those sources and turn each underlined word into a discrete citation).

Part of that spackling also involved making sure that we were reading a wide variety of sources. With the reading and marking list in front of me, I whittled my choices down to an eclectic four—*Time, Car and Driver, Popular Mechanics*, and *Christianity Today*—and, in due time, began to receive copies of them in my in-box, along with that day's lunch pink. In the top-right corner of the cover was a label with my initials on it, heralding that this copy of *Car and Driver* was *mine,* all mine, and, directly below my initials, another editor's initials. I was moderately irked: I had chosen these magazines for *me,* not for MDR or DBB or KMD or any other editor on staff. I had to *share*? This was becoming less "the shit" by the moment.

The vast majority of periodicals read at Merriam-Webster are read by more than one editor. That makes sense: to reading and marking, each editor brings their own idiolect—their own unique collection of vocabulary, grammar, dialect markers, specialized vocabulary gleaned from hobbies, and other linguistic odds and ends you pick up as you move through time and space in English. What I thought was a completely boring and well-established use of "hot rod" in *Car and Driver* was, to someone who didn't grow up with a hot-rodder,[*] new and exciting vocabulary. The flip side also applies: if I don't know anything about cars, then I may completely miss a very subtle shift in the meaning of the word "drivetrain"; perhaps now drivetrains are not merely mechanical but incorporate computers and other underhood magic that I barely understand. If the same person (me) misses the same shift long enough, then the definition will eventually be out of date because you (I) don't know jack about drivetrains.

Or, because it's all unfamiliar vocabulary, I might decide that I'm going to mark every single instance of "V-6" and "cat" for "catalytic converter" and "horses" for "horsepower" that I run across in every

---

[*] **hot·rod·der** *n, pl* **-ders** **1** : a hot-rod driver, builder, or enthusiast *(MWC11).* Now this word can be in your idiolect, and you will be a better person for it.

issue I read. This is a problem we call "overmarking." When you overmark, you accidentally and unintentionally inflate the number of times that this particular use of "cat" shows up in the citation files. Worse, it's very likely that no one has marked the feline sense of "cat" nearly as much because it's so damned common, and therefore some hapless editor down the road has to explain in the file that in spite of what the objectively collated evidence in the file suggests, "cat" is not used in written English to mean "catalytic converter" more than it's used to mean "a small domestic feline usually appearing on the Internet in widely shared videos, pictures, and memes."

The aforementioned MDR and DBB were physical science editors who would go behind me and make sure to mark those shifts in specialty vocabulary that I would inevitably miss, because I am no kind of scientist or mechanic. KMD was another editor with thirty years of experience on me, and when I would casually flip through an issue of *Time* that she had marked after I had, I would marvel at the things she found. While waiting for the coffeemaker to finish up a pot of orange-foil gack, I pulled one of the latest issues toward me and checked the page numbers she had listed next to her initials. One was a full-page ad that she had marked: "The acclaimed new Dodge Durango sport utility vehicle from the drawing board to production in 23 blazing months." *Goddamn,* I thought. *Ads!* I had been so focused on mining the articles that I didn't think to read *Time* for the ads.

There's a less philosophical and more prosaic reason to have multiple editors mark a source: there's a lot to read, and we do have editorial deadlines to keep. After all, lexicography is entirely a commercial enterprise. Editors have to meet deadlines because we need to publish a dictionary at a certain point in time to increase sales; we need to sell a certain number of dictionaries a year to pay all our expenses; if we can't meet our expenses, then we need to find ways to save money; saving money, as most modern American workers know today, usually involves getting rid of people or processes that you need to do your job. As much as I would like it, I can't spend the day with my feet on my desk, languorously reading instead of tackling a particularly nasty definition (let's say, "as").

The reading and marking list is an illusion: given enough time, you will end up reading things you didn't want to. When one of my colleagues left to go teach, I inherited part of her reading and marking—in particular, the political magazines. Though I don't mind discussing politics, I hate reading anything that smacks of a political screed or rant, yet now I had weekly periodicals full of them to sift through. Eventually, we all give up some of our early cherished sources simply because we don't have the time to read them. *Car and Driver* is no longer delivered to my desk, nor is *Popular Mechanics*. I am these days dutifully slogging through *The Cambridge Companion to Postmodern Theology*. There is no one on staff to foist that one on. Kyrie eleison.

And yet. Most lexicographers are compulsive readers, and reading and marking teaches you to be a *close* compulsive reader. You can't help it: once you start, you cannot—no matter what—stop. I have interrupted dinners to take blurry cellphone pictures of the menu for the citations files; I have shushed my children to transcribe that someone on public radio used the word "ho-bag";* I have swerved to the side of the road to take pictures of road signs when they feature interesting vocabulary; I have gotten in the habit of taking the complimentary soaps when I travel, not because I like complimentary soaps, but because sometimes they have really interesting copy on them. Here is a partial list of items that I've seen waiting to be sent to the typists for citations (and not all of them put there by me):

- frozen TV dinner boxes
- diaper boxes
- beer bottles

---

* We generally don't take citations of spoken English, because it's too easy to mishear a word you aren't familiar with or transcribe it with a spelling it doesn't have; think of all the people who type "beaucoup" as "boku." But, c'mon: ho-bag. On public radio.

- medication inserts
- matchboxes
- pictures taken from family albums (sorry, kids, you were standing under a sign that advertised a "dinor," and that is a very rare and specific regional spelling of "diner," and neither of you cares about that picture anyway—you didn't even know I had it until you saw me take it to work)
- the packaging from a set of Odor-Eaters
- cereal boxes
- take-out menus
- cat food bags (empty)
- concert announcements or programs
- mail-order catalogs of wide variety and scope
- labels torn off skeins of yarn
- the Yellow Pages. The *entire* Yellow Pages.

Even when you do your damnedest to shut it off, you can't stop reading and marking. You can still enjoy reading, of course, but you will always have a mental hangnail that catches on certain words and hurts until you attend to it. You may be reading the latest best seller, taking it in as smooth as silk on glass, and your eye jerks to a stop at the word "fuckwad." *Should I?* you think, and a small voice from within pleads with you *not to,* dear God, we probably have thousands of instances of "fuckwad" in the citations file, this is not linguistically interesting at all, please just let it go—and before your inner hedonist has finished, you have already grabbed a pencil and piece of scrap paper and are transcribing the quotation to bring into the office the next day. I imagine it's like being a podiatrist: after a while, the whole world is nothing but feet.

A job where you read all day can be a pleasure, to be sure, but it can also ruin you. Words cease to be casual, tossed off, and able to be left alone. You are that toddler on a walk, the one who wants to pick up every bit of detritus and gunk and dead insect and dog crap on the sidewalk, asking, "What's that, what's that, what's that?" while a parent with better things to do tries to haul your over-inquisitive butt away.

Out of the corner of my eye even now I can see an oatmeal canister crammed onto a shelf in my pantry, emblazoned with the words "Quick Cook Steel Cut Oats." "Quick cook." "Steel cut." Hmm. I wonder.

Pardon me: I have a package of oatmeal to vandalize.

Surfboard

On Defining

B ack in the stuffy editorial conference room, Gil leans back in his chair and sucks his teeth. He seems to do this whenever he's about to embark on a long explanation that he knows will whistle clear over our heads but will contain important information we will need if we get on with this lexicography shtick.

He sucked his teeth a lot that first year.

Today, he announces, we will start talking about definitions—specifically, the kinds of definitions we will be writing and the kind we won't be writing. "We'll begin," he says, "with real defining."

My fellow new hires and I give each other surreptitious side-eye. We were under the impression that writing definitions for the oldest dictionary maker in America would, you know, constitute real defining. As it turns out, there are several kinds of defining in the world, but the two big ones that lexicographers must wrestle with are real defining and lexical defining. Real defining is the stuff of philosophy and theology: it is the attempt to describe the essential nature of something. Real defining answers questions like "What is truth?" "What is love?" "Do sounds exist if no one is around to hear them?" and "Is a hot dog a sandwich?" This is the sort of defining that many budding lexicographers imagine doing: sitting at a leather-topped desk in an office made of warm wood, being erudite, and getting your philosophy on. You'd get to stare into the middle distance and palm books of wisdom and decide whether love is an action, a feeling, a myth. From somewhere outside—a passing car, perhaps—you'd hear the strains of music. Rhythms would thump while the KLF asked, "What time is love?" and you would smile, because you are a lexicographer, and only you can tell the KLF exactly what time love is.

This is a happy fiction (it was my happy fiction, in fact). Lexicographers don't do real defining. In fact, the hallmark of bad lexicography is the attempt to do real defining. Lexicographers only get to do lexical defining, which is the attempt to describe how a word is used and what it is used to mean in a particular setting. The questions we answer are, "What does 'beauty' mean in the sentence 'She's a real beauty'?" or "What does 'love' mean when someone says they love pizza, and is that the same use of 'love' as when they say they love their mom?"

But when people go to the dictionary and look up "love," they expect to see us explain what it *is*. You can tell by the comments that people leave at the entry online that they don't care about all this highfalutin faff ("strong affection for another arising out of kinship or personal ties," or "attraction based on sexual desire," or "affection based on admiration, benevolence, or common interests"):

- L ong O vercoming V alues E ffect ~ love ?
- What is Love?? God is Love! "For God so LOVED the world, that he gave his only begotten son!"
- Love is the desire for something to live to the fullest of its ability.
- Strong magic feeling, which is expressed each another people, and it's need to all
- I think love is a big con and like religion or so called metaphysics can be moulded into anything people want the word to mean.
- Love is so much more than that
- The meaning of love in your dictionary is wrong. The meaning of love is the Jonas Brothers.*

---

* It's not limited to "love," either. "I DO NOT THINK A COUCH HAS A BACK OR ARMS. IT IS SIMPLY A FLAT SURFACE TO LIE OR SIT

The distinction between real defining and lexical defining often sounds like some ass-covering hairsplitting. Lexicographers aren't saying that the essential nature of love is affection; we're saying that's how the word is used. But the speaking, writing public chooses to use the word "love" over "affection" because love signifies something more than affection, doesn't it? Love has to be different from mere affection.

Lexicographers wobble across this tightrope constantly. Yes, it's true, the *thing* love is different from the *thing* affection, but the *word* "love" has a bunch of different uses that overlap some of the uses of the *word* "affection." If you are a philosopher, that answer is unsatisfying, but it's the best one that a lexicographer can give.

Once budding lexicographers have surrendered their idea of what lexicography is, they must learn the jargon, and it is through mastery of the jargon that they begin to realize how complicated a dictionary entry can be. The word being defined is the "headword"—never do we call it "the word being defined." The definition is called "a definition" (phew) or "a sense," particularly when there's more than one of them. Different senses are marked by sense numbers (1, 2, 3, and so on). Closely related senses can be made into subsenses: those are marked by letters after a sense number (1 *a, b, c, d,* and so on). Sometimes, if you are very lucky, there are very closely related subsenses that you can link together and subdivide once more into subsubsenses, which are marked after the subsense letter with a number in parentheses: 1 *a* (1), (2), *b, c* (1), ad nauseam. Now, each sense can, within itself, have several equal defining statements, which we call "substitutes" just because there aren't enough "sub-" words to learn. Substitutes are separated by a boldfaced colon, unless your

UPON. A CHESTERFIELD IS A SOFA WITH TUFTING USUALLY LEATHER. I WOULDN'T USE DIVAN OR DAVENPORT WHICH I THINK IS ARCANE. LOUNGE IS A VERB. SETTEE IS A SMALL SOFA USUALLY WITH TIGHT UPHLOSTERY INSTEAD OF LOOSE CUSHIONS. SQUABS SHOULD BE EATEN."

substitute is a binding substitute (a sort of ur-substitute which is followed by subsenses that are examples or subsets of the binding substitute), in which case it is followed by a lightfaced, roman colon.
The whole megillah—headword, senses, subsenses—is an "entry."
And while you learn the lingo, you also know that you will have
to code-switch between lexicography jargon ("sense," "headword")
and words that normal people understand ("definition," "word"),
which is frustrating because you are learning about the precision
of language, and here you have to be wicked imprecise in order to
communicate with people. This is good practice for learning how
to write definitions.

One of the first things you need to do when writing a dictionary is decide if a word merits entry. This is a concept that rankles
many people for completely different reasons. As we've already
seen, many people feel that some words simply don't deserve to be
entered into the dictionary because that somehow legitimizes what
they consider to be a piss-poor, wrong usage.

On the other side of the argument are the inclusionists, people
who believe that every word in use, ever, should be entered in the
dictionary. It doesn't matter if it was common in 1400 but fell out of
use with Shakespeare; it doesn't matter if it was written down once;
it's a word and it deserves to be entered. Inclusionists have always
been around—Webster himself groused about the lack of Ameri-
canisms in other dictionaries—but it was easier to silence them
when you laid out the strictures of print publishing before them.
Few people buy reference books to begin with; the ones who do
rarely buy multivolume references; if multivolume references don't
sell, then we must focus on single-volume references; publishing a
single-volume dictionary that is twenty inches thick is impossible
and cheating.

Once dictionaries began to move online, inclusionists began
poking holes in that line of reasoning. Electronic dictionaries have
no space restrictions, so why shouldn't we enter all the words ever
used? But we still run into one major speed bump in the quest for an

exhaustive dictionary of English: lexicographers are a dying breed. Language, we've established, moves much faster than lexicography. There are not enough of us around to even *see* every word in the language, let alone *define* every word in the language.

There are a number of open-source dictionaries or online glossaries where people enter their own words and definitions, but the best ones all have one thing in common: they have some sort of editorial staff sweeping up behind the amateur definers. That sounds unbearably snobby, but it's borne out of long experience with user-submitted definitions. Merriam-Webster has run its own little experiment in the open-source dictionary, allowing people to add a word, its part of speech, a source, and a definition to an online database. It became immediately apparent that people did not natively know how to write a dictionary definition.

Nancy Friedman, a copy editor and commercial naming specialist, sent me a Twitter link to a T-shirt that featured the definition of "hella" (a California adverb that means "very"):

hella

hell•a \helə\

adverb
1. an excessive amount
2. large quantity
3. more than above what is necessary

synonyms:
1. surplus

antonyms:
1. lack, deficiency

No, I e-howled, this is terrible defining! The copywriter managed to get the part of speech and the pronunciation right (both terribly difficult jobs) but then defined an adverb with (1) a noun definition, (2) another noun definition that is missing an "a" and is essentially the same definition as the first one, and then (3) a completely unidiomatic, confusing, vaguely adjectival definition. What the hell does "more than above what is necessary" even mean? "Hella" is *so much more* that we have to unidiomatically slap synonymous prepositions all over this definition to get that point across? This definition makes as much sense as saying "over over what is necessary," which is to say, it doesn't. Try substituting those definitions into a perfectly idiomatic sentence using "hella":

That album is *hella* good.

That album is *an excessive amount* good.

That album is *large quantity* good.

That album is *more than above what is necessary* good.

Dude, do you even English? That defining job is hella bad. That's why lexicographers have to be trained in how to write definitions.[*]

The one cardinal rule of writing definitions that every lexicographer learns in their first days, but which is completely opaque to the average dictionary user, is that nouns need to be defined as nouns; verbs as verbs; adjectives as adjectives; and adverbs as something vaguely adverbial, if you can. Every part of the entry needs to match its function. If you include an example sentence, it needs to use that word with the same part of speech that you've defined it as.

A word has to meet three criteria for entry into most general dictionaries. It needs first to have widespread use in print, which is part of why lexicographers do all that reading. A word that appears only in *Wine Spectator*, for instance, is probably not well-known outside the magnum of oenophiles who read *Wine Spectator*. But if

---

[*] You'll find a better definition of "hella" on page 103. And confidential to copywriters: You can actually hire a lexicographer to write this for you! It won't cost you an arm and a leg, because we are accustomed to working for hella little compensation.

the word shows up in *Wine Spectator* and *Today's Chemist at Work* and *VICE* and the *A.V. Club,* then it's probably well-known enough to merit entry.

A word also has to have a long shelf life, though what constitutes a long shelf life depends on the dictionary that's being edited, the evidence you manage to find for that word, and the reality of what modern communication has done to language. It's not necessarily that the language is growing faster today than it did in 1600; no one really knows what sorts of words were being used in 1600 apart from what we have a written record of, so no one can reputably make that claim. It's more accurate to say that with increased general literacy, better access to printed materials, and the birth of the Internet, where anyone—even a T-shirt company—can publish something online and gain readers, we're more aware of how quickly language grows. And holy crap, does language grow quickly. A word that in 1950 might have taken twenty years to come to popular attention and use now may take less than a year. This means that you have to evaluate the types of sources very carefully, and you have to make judgment calls, at times, on whether a word has staying power.

These are dangerous, because no one really knows where a word is going to go, and your judgment call may end up being terrible. In the early 1980s, one of our editors decided that the word "snollygoster," meaning "an unprincipled or shrewd person," was not really in use anymore, and to free up some space for something new and exciting, they dumped the entry from the *Collegiate*. About ten years after that, a notable TV personality began using "snollygoster" because it was the perfect word to describe a politician. America is now on the cusp of a "snollygoster" revival, and, boy, do we feel stupid. We also have to gamble on the tech of the future, which is impossible. Twenty years ago, no one had any idea that the common verb that means generally "to search the Internet for something using a search engine" was going to be "google," and a tweet was something that came out of a bird's mouth.

Once you've determined that a word has widespread use and a

decent shelf life, the third requirement is that it has what we call "meaningful use"—that is, whether the word is used with a meaning. What a dumb criterion, you think: all words are used with a meaning!

Not necessarily. The one that every lexicographer offers as proof is "antidisestablishmentarianism." It's a word plenty of people are familiar with, but most of our citational evidence for it is in lists of long words, not in running prose, and when it does appear in running prose, it appears in sentences like "'Antidisestablishmentarianism' is a long word." When tasked with prying meaning out of a bunch of citations like that, you quickly discover that "antidisestablishmentarianism" is rarely ascribed a meaning in text. It's not the only one. "Pneumonoultramicroscopicsilicovolcanoconiosis" —a word that puzzlers and lexicographers call "P45"—sure looks like and sounds like the name of a great disease, and it is entered in our *Webster's New International Dictionary, Second Edition,* but it does not have any meaningful use. In fact, it appears to have been coined by the president of the National Puzzlers' League in 1935 just to see if dictionaries would fall for it. We did. We're a little more careful now.

We trot this rubric out all the time as lexicographers—widespread, sustained, and meaningful use—and then follow up with "If a word meets the criteria for entry, then it's time to draft a definition." But there is an intermediary step we don't talk about at all: you have to define before you can define.

All words are defined contextually, so before you can know that there's a new sense of a word to be entered, or a new word, you have to read the collected evidence for it and determine if that marked use is covered by the existing entry. It's not always an easy task: just as words can slide around between parts of speech, so can they slide around between meanings. For instance, what do we do with the "cynical" in this sentence: "It was concluded that students experiencing loneliness report a greater level of unhappiness, display signs of detachment during social interactions, and are more cynical and dissatisfied with their social network." This use of "cynical" doesn't seem to quite fit the existing "contemptuously distrustful of human nature" meaning, as in "Voters have grown *cynical* about politicians and their motives," nor does it fit the meaning that refers to human conduct being primarily motivated by self-interest, as in "It was just a *cynical* ploy to win votes." It seems rather to mean "pessimistic"—not that the students are contemptuously distrustful of human nature, but that they are certain that the terrible status quo will continue to be terrible. But if one is distrustful of human nature, and contemptuously so at that, then wouldn't it follow that the cynical person doesn't expect things to turn up sunshine and flowers? Back to the citation. Do you shrug and toss it onto the "contemptuously distrustful" pile? Is this a new, possibly emerging meaning? If it's not, do you need to revise the entry to cover this use?

The longer you define, the better you become at determining how close to a definition a citation falls and how far away it needs to be for it to be its own sense. Meaning is a spectrum; you are only describing the biggest data clusters on that spectrum. Madeline Novak puts it this way: "There's a meaning there, and it could be sliced up any of a variety of ways, none of which really capture the whole thing. You're going to be dissatisfied with it no matter what, so you're kidding yourself if you think you've pinpointed it. There's still stuff oozing around the edges."

All the editors at Merriam-Webster go through a few months of training to learn how to parse the grammar of a word, how to read and sort the citations, and then how to write a definition that fits any new uses of that word.

There are a handful of tricks we use to get us in line, the first being the formulaic definition. You know what these are: they're dictionaryese. "Of or relating to" blah-blah-blah; "the quality or state of" yadda yadda; "the act of" et cetera. They exist not because we're lazy but because they can be helpful ways of tagging a definition as a particular part of speech, and definers can use formulaic definitions to help orient themselves. They can also be helpful tools to link together linguistic cousins. If I define "devotion" as "the quality or state of being devoted to (someone or something)," I've subtly communicated to the reader that "devotion" is closely related to the word "devote."

While formulaic definitions are helpful at times, they can also be too restrictive. This is when lexicographers lean on their second tool: substitutability.

The idea behind substitutability is that a well-written definition should be able to slot into a sentence in place of the word being defined, and while the result may be verbose, it won't sound wrong (as the definitions given for that "hella" T-shirt above do). Substitutability can actually help you scale down a long definition. If I were defining "hella" without using substitutability, I would probably come up with something long-winded and full of dictionaryese, like "to an excessive degree." And it works: "That T-shirt is [to an excessive degree] awesome." But using substitutability, I'm more likely to define "hella" as "very" or "extremely": "That T-shirt is [very/extremely] awesome."

While you are getting the hang of writing nounal and verbal definitions, you must also master dictionary house style. Every publisher has a house style, or a house stylebook: that's where the publisher lists how a particular word, or compound, or bulleted list will appear in all of its books. This is for consistency, one of the Holy Grails of practical lexicography. None is pure enough for such a quest; at Merriam-Webster, this is where the Black Books come in.

Every editor at Merriam-Webster deals with the Black Books at many points during their tenure. The Black Books are the in-house set of rules for writing a dictionary (commonly called a style guide) as conceived and written in punctilious detail by the former editor in chief Philip Babcock Gove, for the creation of *Webster's Third*. They are named for the black clothbound binders in which the single-spaced memos find their eternal repose.

The Black Books are formidable. They are, for the most part, the brainchild of Gove, and so reflect his borderline pathological attention to detail. Gove wrote a memo for our editors called "PUNCTUATION and TYPOGRAPHY of VOCABULARY ENTRIES" that begins, "This memo is concerned primarily with *how* and does not, unless expressly stated, cover *when* or *why,*" and he means it. In that memo, Gove goes on to lay out, in excruciating detail, the basic pattern for all Merriam-Webster definitions. The memo is thirty-three pages long. It even lays out for you where in definitions you are allowed to put spaces.[*]

Don't think that Gove was a windbag: he was a New Englander and valued sparse efficiency in all things (including lexicography). So it says something that the memos are so long. To be thorough as a lexicographer is to pay attention to the smallest of details. This is not a haphazard, minor-leagues approach to defining. Go granular or go home.

The Black Books also reflect Gove's notoriously brusque manner, no doubt gained from an early career in the Navy. Memos begin, "Editorializing has no place in definitions," or "Godlove's psychophysical defs of color names and their references had better be regarded as sacrosanct." Sir, yes, sir!

There is an otherworldly quality to the books themselves. For such important documents, they are housed in odd nooks and crannies in the office—in a short bookshelf near the former editorial secretary's desk, on top of a deserted maze of cabinets that contain the paper galleys for earlier copies of the *Collegiate*. One set resides with the president of the company; another wanders the office and

---

[*] On either side of a boldfaced colon; after a semicolon that introduces a sense divider like "especially" or "specifically"; after (but not before) a lightfaced colon that is used to mark a series of subsenses; after each definition if followed by a subsequent sense or usage note (which is introduced with an em dash—no space after the em dash, though); between the major elements of the entry, like headword, pronunciation, etymology, date; and, obviously, between the words in a definition.

shows up in odd places without warning. One morning I left my cubicle and paused to see what grotesquerie the life sciences editors had been looking up in the medical encyclopedias near my desk* when I saw two of the Black Books lurking dustily on the corner of the encyclopedia table. I flipped the cover of the topmost volume open; it was a collection of defining technique memos. Just opening the cover, I could smell 1952 waft out: typewriter ribbon and mimeograph paper tinged with stale tobacco, laid over a base note of Gove's perpetual disappointment and irk.†

Individual books (and each of their subsequent editions) have their own style guides, because what worked for Gove in the 1950s doesn't always work for us today. That said, each of those style guides, no matter how many hundreds of pages it runs to, relies ultimately on the Black Books. If you have a question about anything having to do with the mechanics of defining, you'll find the answer there. Obviously, no one wants you to stutter up to their cubicle covered in flop sweat and asking how to write an adjective definition again; it's much easier to direct you (wordlessly, scowling) to the Black Books for your answer.

The only real way to master house style is to practice it, which is what all editors at Merriam-Webster get to do when they are plucked, fresh-faced and wet behind the ears, from the vast sea of editorial candidates and plopped, still wriggling, down at desks with editing homework. The best way, our senior editors felt, to learn how to define was to spend some time in quiet, reflective imitation.

---

* The medical encyclopedias are always open to gruesome pictures of injury or deformity, made gruesomer by the regulation black band over the patient's eyes. But it's not all life sciences' fault: one co-worker, about three glasses of wine deep, revealed that if he passed the table and saw that the daily medical offering was relatively tame, he'd flip through until he found something suitably gross.

† **irk** *n* -**s 1** : IRKSOMENESS, TEDIUM <the *irk* of a narrow existence> **2** : a cause or source of annoyance or disgust <the main *irk* is the wage level> *(MWU)*. What a lovely little précis on lexicography.

First we begin by going through the fifty-odd pages of defining theory that Gil and Steve have come up with over the years. This gets into the minutiae of the definitions and defining process itself, and it is based—you guessed it—on the Black Books. You are then handed a sheaf of paper and asked to edit the definitions found on it, all of them having been taken from earlier Merriam-Webster dictionaries. You get another such worksheet for where to enter phrases, another one that asks you to fix the capitalization of older entries, and another that asks you to fix the inflected forms of older entries. This is existentially unnerving, because these definitions are taken from published dictionaries, which means they were written by people who had more training and practice than you do. It is your *memento moron:* no matter how smart and excellent, remember that you, too, will fuck up.

Soon, you learn how to tell the difference between a boldfaced colon in four-point type and a lightfaced colon in four-point type. You learn to tell when something wasn't written using the right formula or when a definition accidentally editorializes. You learn when words get labeled "usu. cap" and when they get labeled "sometimes cap." You even go over the standard proofreader's marks so you can read galleys and old defining slips and know the difference between your bold and italic. And you feel as though you are scrambling up an avalanche, desperately looking for any foothold you can.

Once the worksheets are done, every new hire is given a batch of practice defining to go through; mine was a chunk of *B* and some sundries in other parts of the alphabet. You will define these words as if they were being entered: you must write your definitions on buffs, you must make sure you've got everything right, and you will date stamp them just so the practice becomes muscle memory. Then you will hand them over to Gil or Steve to be thoroughly smashed to bits.

Because I am a sentimental pack rat, I kept my practice defining slips and every once in a while pull them out and marvel at how bad a definer I was. I routinely forgot important style issues: half of my definitions don't start with the boldfaced colon, and I used sense numbers for definitions that only have one sense (a major no-no: "What's sense 2? You can't have a sense 1 if you don't have a sense 2," Gil would harrumph).

More frustrating were the things that I did wrong that weren't easily corrected:

> jugate n - s 1 : a collectible (as a button or coin) showing the heads of two political figures; esp : a collectible showing the heads of a presidential candidate and his running mate

I have committed a venial sin against the style guide (that damned sense number), but two mortal sins against the evidence. First, the subsense after "especially" is too broad as I've written it: the most common use of the word "jugate" doesn't refer to just any collectible, like a spoon or ceramic salt and pepper shakers, but to a campaign button. I've covered the broader use in the first sense, but the point of the "especially" is to zero in on the most common and specific use. The subsense after the "especially" should read "a campaign button showing the heads of a presidential candidate and his running mate."

But that's not the worst of it. I have also, as Gil pointed out, gendered the definition when I didn't need to. He struck the "his" from "his running mate." "It is conceivable," he said afterward, while going over my definitions with me, "that a woman will run for president at some point, and if she does, this definition will need to be revised. So why not write it in a way that the gender of the candidate doesn't matter." I was gobsmacked: here I was, a recent graduate of a women's college, getting schooled on gendered language by *an old guy.* And rightly so: I brought to the definition my own assumptions about the gender of people who have in the past run for president. But a good lexicographer weighs the untold future as well as the told past and present: Is it so inconceivable that a woman could run for president? By assuming that the gender-neutral "he" was going to be fine here, because presidents are all men, I had committed the sin of editorialization.

I also had problems—as most new definers do—figuring out just what information to include in a definition. My scratch definition of "naja" is "a crescent-shaped pendant made by the Navajo people." Is it just made by the Navajo, or do the Navajo wear them as well? Is it worn by other people? If a white tourist stops at one of the ubiquitous roadside gift shops you find throughout the Southwest and buys a necklace with a naja, then wears it, does it cease to be Navajo? Does it cease to be a naja? Would it be better to say it's characteristic of the Navajo? And what does *that* mean? Joan Narmontas, our senior life sciences editor, says of defining, "It's complex systems made simple," but my definition is its inverse: a simple system made needlessly complex. There's not quite enough information in this scratch definition; it ends up leaving the dictionary user with more questions than answers.

And I brought plenty of my own assumptions and biases about what makes a good dictionary definition with me, as we all do. I was tasked with defining "outershell" and gave the definition as "a protective covering." Gil revised the definition to read "an outer protective covering." At our next meeting, I protested—you're not supposed to use the word you're defining in the definition! It is a truth universally acknowledged (and enforced) by American language arts teachers everywhere!

"Well," he said, grinning, " 'outer' is not the word being defined here." I pressed anyway—does "outer" need to be there? It looked a little, well, lazy. It was important, he said: you need to convey where the covering is, that an outershell is, in this case, something you wear over your clothes or put over an item.

I was perturbed. "Covering," to me, already conveys outsideness, not insideness. It is *covering* something; there is something *inside* it; it is *outside* the thing it's covering. Q.E. Motherfucking D. Gil ignored my botheration and we moved onward, but I secretly thought he was needlessly nitpicking.

Pride goeth before a fall: that afternoon, while proofreading, I discovered that there is a covering around the heart called the peri-cardium, but it is not outside; it is inside the body. The pericardium is inside the body, and the heart is inside the pericardium. I threw my head back and indulged in a quiet bleat of frustration. I was never, ever going to get the hang of this.

Two days later, I was sitting in class with Gil while we began going through our *B* batches. I trained with two other editors, and it was common for Gil to have us read our definitions aloud so that we could benefit from hearing how dumb we all were. We went through a few entries, then got to "birdstrike." The other two editors went first, with Gil giving them some constructive critique about scope, usage, whether you need to split the word into two senses, and how we can probably just make do with one. Then he looked at me:

birdstrike n : a collision in which a bird or flock of birds hits the engine of an aircraft

Gil rolled my definition around in his mouth for a bit. "All right," he said. "That's a pretty good definition."

I'm sure he gave some constructive critique, but I didn't hear any of it. I was on cloud nine. After months of banging my way through training and feeling, at almost every turn, like I knew little about most things and definitely nothing about English, I had some glim-mer of hope: *I drafted a pretty good definition.* It wasn't all needless nitpicking; it was *needful* nitpicking. We finished the session, and I went back to my desk, pulled my standard-issue monthly planner toward me, and wrote in the square for September 1, 1998: "Gil/ birdstrike: PRETTY GOOD DEFINITION."

I still pull the calendar out at times, to remind myself that it can be done.

There are more oddities in lexicography. The first is the weirdest and appears to be consistent across all traditional dictionary pub-lishers: no one starts writing a dictionary in *A*. Ever.

When I asked Steve about this—dumbfounded, because where

else do you start but at the beginning?—he gave two answers. First, every dictionary—not dictionary publisher, but every book that publisher puts out—has its own style guide, and it takes definers a while to settle into that guide. Hell, sometimes it takes a few letters for the style guide to even be *finished*. Starting about a third of the way through the alphabet, in short letters like *H* or *K*, gives editors time to settle into the new style before getting to some of those bigger letters. Many dictionaries are revised from *H* (or thereabouts) onward to *Z*, and then *A* through *H* (or thereabouts), with the first middle bunch of letters (*H*, maybe *I*) getting another revision.

History bears out this process. Thomas Elyot, a sixteenth-century lexicographer, talks about this in the (incredibly long) dedication and preface to his dictionary. He started in *A*, farted around a bit until he got the hang of defining, and then, he says, "Wherfore incontinent I caused the printes to cesse, and beginninge at the letter M, where I lefte, I passed forth to the last letter with a more diligent study. And that done, I eftesones returned to the fyrst letter, and with a semblable diligence performed the temenant." If eftesones returning to the fyrst letter was good enough for Thomas Elyot, it's good enough for us.

The second reason we don't start in *A* is a little more mercenary: back in the days of yore when dictionaries were actually reviewed, reviewers would inevitably start looking at definitions in the first chunk of the book. It takes so long to write a dictionary, and the style file will inevitably change as you go along. You don't want reviewers catching a style change midway through *A*, do you? *A* through *D* would be, as the last letters worked on, as close to stylistic perfection as possible. No reviewer is going to look too closely at *K*.

You also discover that not every letter in the alphabet has the same number of entries, and therefore lexicographers look forward to (or dread) certain letters. Pick up any desk dictionary, disregard the front and back matter, and pinch letters *A* through *D* between your fingers: you'll find that *A, B, C,* and *D* make up about a quarter of your dictionary. *E, F,* and *G* are middling. *H* is long; we can chalk that up to the surprisingly large number of words that begin with "hand-" and "hyper-." *I, J,* and *K* are relatively tiny. Then you begin the long middle section of the alphabet: *L, M, N, O,* and *P,* which always seem longer than they should be, probably because they go by so quickly in the ABC song. *Q* is a barely registered dip in the road, and you're back into *R,* velocity maintained, corners rounded. *T* is a decent size, and *U* surprises you (all those "un-" words). *V* is a comparative breeze; *W* is about as long as it sounds—double *U. X, Y,* and *Z* are nothing, nada, the long stretch after the marathon.

You'll notice a letter missing from that litany, and that is because it merits special mention. *S* is, to put it in the modern vernacular, the worst. It is the longest letter in the book and an absolute heartbreaker, because you can see the end of the alphabet from it, and you know that once you clear *S,* you are moving on to *T–Z,* and half of those are barely even letters. But *S—S* goes on *for-fucking-ever.* Exactly 11 percent of your dictionary is made of words that begin with *S.* One-tenth of your dictionary is made up of one twenty-sixth of the alphabet. I bet the guy in the picture who supposedly went home and shot himself was in the middle of *S* when he did.

It's not just the length of the letter but the content as well that can get to you. Emily doesn't mind *S* as much as she does *D,* because *D* is long and filled with horrible words (like "despair," "dismal," "death," and "dejected"). "It's depressing," she said. "And even that starts with *d*!" I am not fond of *G* because it contains "get," "give," and "go," and those are horrible entries,* but I love *J* because it is short and has "jackass" and all its sibling entries in it (including not only "jackassery" and "jackassness" but "jackass bark," "jackass bat," "jackass brig," "jackass clover," "jackass deer," "jackass fish," "jackass hare," "jackass kingfisher," "jackass penguin," "jackass rabbit," and "jackass rig").

---

* For an elucidation on the horrors of defining short words, read the chapter "Take."

There are occasions, however, when even *S* holds a secret delight or two in the form of a pink, such as the one I found among the citations (or "cits" for short) for "sex kitten":

sex kitten
sex pot
There is no essential difference in these defs [definitions], but
they're not the same. Some differentiation shd be made.

The pink was written by one of our former physical science editors infamous for commenting as brusquely as possible on things beyond his remit. The files are littered with his pinks, most of them gruffly correcting a defect that he's perceived (correctly or otherwise) with an existing definition—any existing definition, not just one touching on the sciences. This is one of his more frustrating pinks. If he thought that the definitions could be differentiated, he clearly had some idea how while writing the note but decided to withhold that information.

Another one of our science editors who was reviewing the batch later was apparently irritated by this note, and decided to comment on what he no doubt saw as needless meddling. His typewritten response to the note about "sex kitten" reads, "I will no doubt regret saying this but I think you have misconstrued the meaning of 'physical' science somewhere along here."

But a pink's a pink. Steve acted on it for the *Tenth,* adding the word "young" to the definition for "sex kitten."

Lexical definitions come in a handful of philosophical-sounding flavors—ostensive, synonymous, analytical, truncated, periphrastic. These are fancy names that describe, in order of attempt, what each native English speaker does or attempts to do when called upon to explain what a word means. Everyone everywhere can do ostensive defining: it's the act of physically showing a person what the word means. When a beaming, sleep-deprived parent asks his infant, "Where's your nose?" and the baby blops a fist onto the middle of her face, that is ostensive defining.

Most dictionaries avoid ostensive defining because it's hard to do ostensive defining with anything remotely abstract: How do you point at "sad" or "concept" or "for"? Ostensive defining also limits you to one example of a type: cups come in a wide variety of shapes, sizes, colors, and materials, but you may only have a red plastic disposable cup handy when someone asks, "What's a cup?" We understand that there's wide variety in some things (cups) and not in others (okapis), but dictionaries are not set up to adapt to a user's mental pictorial database of things. That said, we do indulge in adding ostensive defining to our dictionaries from time to time in the form of pictures or illustrations. We trust our users to be able to read the definition of "gable"—"the vertical triangular end of a building from cornice or eaves to ridge"—and figure out what part of the building that definition refers to, but sometimes it's easier to provide an illustration of a roof with a line pointing to the gable. "Picture dictionaries" or "visual dictionaries," which are usually geared toward children who can't read yet or for English-language learners, make heavy use of ostensive defining.

As with ostensive defining, nearly everyone can come up with synonymous definitions: they are simply definitions that list other better-known synonyms of a word. Your great-auntie Rose calls someone a "schlemiel," and when you ask what "schlemiel" means, she tells you it means "idiot" or "fool" or "dupe" or "chump" ad infinitum.* You ask what "beautiful" means, and someone responds with "pretty." This sort of defining gets ingrained in us through a collective childhood of vocabulary quizzes and standardized tests. Dictionaries do quite a bit of synonymous defining because we claim it makes semantic relationships between different types of

---

* English has a lot of synonyms for "fool" or "idiot." Perhaps you take this to mean that English speakers are mean-spirited; I simply reply that necessity is the mother of invention.

words apparent. It also just so happens to be a lot easier to read a one-word synonym than to decipher a lengthy definition.

The jump from synonymous defining to analytical defining is a big one. Analytical definitions are the most common ones you'll find in dictionaries, the ones that read like they were written by a team of neurodiverse robots—the ones that take years of practice to write.

A definition begins with what we call the "genus," the overarching category that describes what, at heart, the "definiendum," or word being defined, means.* The genus term must be broad enough to encompass the wide variety of uses for that word, but not so broad that it provides inadequate direction. Definienda should be, our training documents say, placed in the smallest genus that can contain them, lest they rattle around in there and irritate you. Sometimes this is easy: "snickerdoodle" is clearly "a cookie" and not "a dessert" (which lumps it in with pudding, pie, and ice cream) or "a meal" (which makes it an appetizer or entrée). More often, it's not as simple. What genus term works best for "surfboard"? "A piece of sporting equipment," perhaps? No: the genus in that phrase would be "piece," which is so broad that it can refer to everything from an opinion (speak your *piece*) to a portion of food (a *piece* of pie) to a gun (a mobster's *piece*) to a partner in a sexual interlude (a mobster's *piece*). You begin a long meander through your mental thesaurus. "A plank used for surfing." Better, but remember that the genus term—in the sense that you mean it—must be entered in the dictionary you're working on. You look up "plank" to see that it generally describes a long piece of wood that is much narrower than the average surfboard. Back to the proverbial drawing board. "A panel used for surfing" is no good: "panel" in this sense usually refers to something used as a finished surface, like wood panel, or a small section of a door. "A platform used for surfing": nope, because the pertinent meaning of "platform" here begins, "a

---

* All terms are Latin because everything sounds smarter in Latin.

usually raised horizontal flat surface," which implies that there's something underneath the platform that is raising it. But—couldn't that be water? Perhaps, but horizontal? Are surfboards always in a horizontal orientation? What if I stick it upright into the sand—does it cease to be a platform? This line of thought smacks of overthinking; you move on. What about "a slab used for surfing"? You picture a longhair riding a tombstone.

You realize that the best genus term for "surfboard" is "board," and you instinctively shudder with memories of Gil and "outershell." But you aren't using the word "surfboard" in the definition of "surfboard," you reassure yourself; you are using the word "board." Still, it stings a bit: it will be read as lazy, even though it's the best genus term available. It is, after all, called a surf*board* and not a surfplank or a surfslab. The only thing left is to move on to explaining how this board is different from all others.

In a standard analytical definition, the genus term is the broad category that encompasses the headword, but the differentiae are the descriptors that differentiate each member of that category. ("Differentiae" is plural; there's usually more than one in a definition.) "Administration," "couch," and "surfboard" all feature the genus term "board," but only one of those things is used for surfing, and it's differentiae that do that work.

Considering that a definition is made up mostly of differentiae, there's not much in the Black Books or our training materials on the specifics of writing differentiae. There are a handful of very general suggestions and fewer hard-and-fast rules offered as guidelines, but differentiae across a dictionary can be so varied that it's difficult to make generalizations about them. The definer is left to their own devices, primarily a knowledge of how English moves that's based on an insatiable appetite for reading material.

The first problem you encounter is trying to decide what information to include in the differentiae: What's vital to knowing what this word refers to, and what's extraneous information that will at best distract and at worst confuse? In the case of a word like "surfboard," the differentiae seem pretty clear. How is this board different from all other boards? It is, obviously, used for surfing, and this is clearly a no-brainer in terms of including this bit in your definition.

This board is also what some people would call "long" and "narrow," though both these metrics are highly subjective (and lexicographers know that). Some people who ride what are called longboards—surfboards that are longer than the "long" you are thinking of here—consider the average surfboard stubby, and a water-skier would consider a surfboard comically wide. But you are not defining for the longboarder or the water-skier—you are defining for the mythic Everyperson, and it stands to reason that something that is as wide as an arm's length and as tall as a person would be considered, proportionally speaking, "long" and "narrow" by Everyperson.

This board is also—and this strikes you as an important detail—buoyant, because it has to carry the weight of a person and not drag them immediately to the bottom of the sea. Shamefully, this point did not occur to you. You only noticed it because one citation in your batch is from an article called "Surfing Physics," and it notes that surfboards are buoyant because they are less dense than the water underneath them.

You begin to scratch out a definition and place your differentiae: "a board that is long, narrow, and buoyant and which is used for surfing." A perfectly adequate, though inelegant, definition. "Long," "narrow," and "buoyant" can modify "board," and moving them before the genus gives you the tidier "a long, narrow, buoyant board used for surfing." Congratulations: you've just saved twenty-five characters and one turned line. The spirit of Gove compels you to check the definition of "surf," and you find that in our brave, new age "surf" doesn't just refer to getting on a long, narrow, buoyant board and riding waves; it also refers to sitting on your large, spreading, squishy butt and clicking through web pages. Maybe "used for surfing" needs a little modification. "The act of surfing" could apply to either Internet or oceanic surfing, but "the sport of surfing" makes it clear you're referring to the wave "surf" and not the web "surf." Maybe leave "the sport of" in and let your sprachgefühl pick at it, seeing if it survives the ravages of your Germanic affliction. You are slowly getting there.

Unfortunately, you cannot slowly get there: you need to quickly get there. Lexicography in America is a ruthlessly commercial enterprise, just like the rest of publishing. Your scholarship and care mean bupkes if no one buys or uses your dictionary.

This means that the production schedule rules us with an iron fist. The *Collegiate Dictionary,* to take a good example, takes about two or three years to revise for a new edition. For most people, that project timeline seems ridiculously long: Three years to add some words to a dictionary? Cry me the proverbial river, lexicographers.

But a new edition doesn't mean you're just adding new words. The bulk of a lexicographer's work is actually in reviewing existing entries and revising them. I didn't draft the entry for "surfboard," but I have reviewed it more times than I've actually seen a surfboard in the wild. We do the same thing in reviewing an entry as we do in writing one: we read all the citations for that word, weigh the evidence, and futz with the definition as necessary. The *Collegiate Dictionary* has, as of this writing, about 170,000 entries with about 230,000 definitions, give or take, to review. In reviewing, you'll find that in the last decade or so editors have found problems with various entries and so sent pinks to those entries; you will take care of those pinks as you review and revise. Every entry, whether revised or reviewed, goes through multiple editing passes. The definer starts the job, then it's passed to a copy editor who cleans up the definer's work, then to a bunch of specialty editors: cross-reference editors, who make sure the definer hasn't used any word in the entry that isn't entered in that dictionary; etymologists, to review or write the word history; dating editors, who research and add the dates of first written use; pronunciation editors, who handle all the pronunciations in the book. Then eventually it's back to a copy editor (usually a different one from the first round, just to be safe), who will make any additional changes to the entry that cross-reference turned up, then to the final reader, who is, as the name suggests, the last person who can make editorial changes to the entry, and then off to the proofreader (who ends up, again, being a different editor from the definer and the two previous copy editors). After the proofreaders are done slogging through two thousand pages of four-point type, the production editors send it off to the printer or the data preparation folks, and then we get *another* set of dictionary pages (called page proofs) to proofread.

This process happens continuously as we work through a dictionary, so a definer may be working on batches in *C*, cross-reference might be in *W*, etymology in *T*, dating and pronunciation in the second half of *S*, copy editors in *P* (first pass) and *Q* and *R* (second pass), while the final reader is closing out batches in *N* and *O*, proofreaders are working on *M*, and production has given the second set of page proofs to another set of proofreaders for the letter *L*. We all stagger our way through the alphabet until the last batch, which is inevitably somewhere near *G*, is closed. By the time a word is put in print either on the page or online, it's generally been seen by a minimum of ten editors. Now consider that when it came to writing the *Collegiate Dictionary, Eleventh Edition*, we had a staff of about twenty editors working on it: twenty editors to review about 220,000 existing definitions, write about 10,000 new definitions, and make over 100,000 editorial changes (typos, new dates, revisions) for the new edition. Now remember that the 110,000-odd changes made were each reviewed about a dozen times and by a minimum of ten editors. The time given to us to complete the revision of the *Tenth Edition* into the *Eleventh Edition* so production could begin on the new book? Eighteen months.

You can see, then, why these definition goofs happen. Is it any wonder that when faced with that pressure, one editor working his way through the *Third* and toward an early grave defined "fishstick" as "a stick of fish"? You can almost see the oily sheen of desperation on the page: there, this batch is done, I'm done, get me out of here.

A definition like the one at "fishstick" seems incongruous when compared with other definitions in the *Third*. Unabridged dictionaries don't just include more entries but longer definitions with more complex differentiae than are found in abridged dictionaries. An unabridged dictionary gives a lexicographer the space to stretch out a little bit, because users expect to see more of everything in an unabridged dictionary. But this leads to problems: When space isn't an issue, how do you know when to stop?

It was evidently very easy to lose sight of the forest for all that delicious xylem and phloem. This is one (now infamous) definition of "hotel" found in *Webster's Third:*

> a building of many rooms chiefly for overnight accommodation of transients and several floors served by elevators, usually with a large open street-level lobby containing easy chairs, with a variety of compartments for eating, drinking, dancing, exhibitions, and group meetings (as of salesmen or convention attendants), with shops having both inside and street-side entrances and offering for sale items (as clothes, gifts, candy, theater tickets, travel tickets) of particular interest to a traveler, or providing personal services (as hairdressing, shoe shining), and with telephone booths, writing tables and washrooms freely available

Dancing compartments! Travel tickets! Candy! Where are these hotels today?

Lexicographers tend to fall into one of two categories when it comes to writing definitions: lumpers and splitters. Lumpers are definers who tend to write broad definitions that can cover several more minor variations on that meaning; splitters are people who tend to write discrete definitions for each of those minor variations. This seems to be a natural inclination: lumpers have a very hard time teasing out the micro-meanings covered by their broad definitions, and splitters have a very hard time collapsing their incredibly concise definitions into one. Emily and I are splitters; Neil is a lumper; Steve can do both, though the more he defines, the more he tends toward lumping. That definition of "fishstick" was written by a lumper; that definition of "hotel" was definitely written by a splitter.

The definition of "hotel" highlights one of the biggest problems in writing definitions: things change, and you are a lexicographer, not a clairvoyant. Back in the 1950s, when this definition for "hotel" was written, places that called themselves hotels did have some (or all) of these amenities. The lexicographer who wrote this definition evidently wanted to distinguish a hotel from other accommodations (like motels or inns) and thought—reasonably—that mentioning what sorts of services were available at a hotel compared with, say, a motel would help orient the reader. But these details of swank hotel life from 1950 are very different from the modern reality; some things you think are a given about how a word is used and what it means will inevitably change. You must consider every detail, every word you place in a differentia: Is this specific enough while being general enough to allow for change?

You will find, as you read the citations for "surfboard," that there are plenty of citations about new space-age materials (circa 1980) being used for boards. Is it worth mentioning that surfboards aren't always wood? You search the definition of your genus term, "board," to see whether non-wood materials are covered in that definition. They are, but as you scrunch up your face and consider the citations, you get that familiar, crinkling feeling at the back of your brain. When you think of surfboards, you think of wood, and you'd wager that most people who see the word "board" in reference to a big flat thing probably think of wood as well. There's an awful lot of chatter in your evidence about how amazing these new space-age materials are and—yes, there it is—even mention of them in an NPR interview transcript about the inventor of the surfboard. It seems like mentioning that surfboards aren't always wood might be a good idea.

Fortunately, for Merriam-Webster editors, there is a good detail hedge we can use: the parenthetical adjunct. It's a device wherein we can give in-definition examples of a range without committing to the elements in that range. "A long, narrow, buoyant board made of wood, fiberglass, or foam and used in the sport of surfing" is a fabulous definition for right this very second, but what if some bright surfing engineer starts making boards out of a special kind of plastic? Or carbon fiber? Or what if they invent an entirely new polymer that your tiny word-bound brain can't even conceive of in this moment, and that becomes the industry standard for surfboards in a few years? You can give yourself an out by using the parenthetical adjunct instead: "a long, narrow, buoyant board (as of wood, fiberglass, or foam) used in the sport of surfing." The "as" signals that the list that follows isn't exhaustive; the parentheses give a visual clue that this is secondary information; and the words themselves tell you some of the more common members of that range. This parenthetical adjunct tells you that surfboards are generally made of wood, fiberglass, or foam, but it also doesn't rule out surfboards made of a sentient plastic that molds to the surfer's foot and biometrically adapts to the rider's surfing style, communicating with each molecule of water in the ocean underneath to produce the optimal wave for maximum gnarliness.

There are other hedges that show up in definitions across all publishing houses: words like "especially" or "specifically" that are used within a definition actually join two separate but very closely linked senses of a word, or "broadly" which does the same thing in reverse.[*] When do you use "broadly" and when do you use "specifically" or "especially"? It is, like much of lexicography, a matter of feel.

With all these devices, it can be easy for the dictionary user and the lexicographer to become lost in the labyrinthine complexity of a word's differentiae. Differentiae must be restrictive clauses; after all, you are restricting the genus to a specific type. And they are

---

[*] **sex·ism** *n* **1** : prejudice or discrimination based on sex; *especially* : discrimination against women *(MWC11)*; **man** *n* . . . **1c** : a bipedal primate mammal (*Homo sapiens*) that is anatomically related to the great apes but distinguished especially by notable development of the brain with a resultant capacity for articulate speech and abstract reasoning, is usually considered to form a variable number of freely interbreeding races, and is the sole living representative of the hominid family; *broadly* : any living or extinct hominid *(MWC11)*

often subordinate clauses—that is, clauses that modify something that came in front of them. You can be as careful as possible and still end up with one of those subordinate clauses hanging there between two clear antecedents:

> **dog** \\'dȯg *sometimes* 'däg\ *noun* -s **1 a** : a small- to medium-sized carnivorous mammal (*Canis familiaris* synonym *Canis lupus familiaris*) of the family Canidae that has been domesticated since prehistoric times, is closely related to the gray wolf, occurs in a variety of sizes, colors, and coat types as a pure or mixed breed, is typically kept as a pet, and includes some used in hunting and herding or as guard animals

Here, which word does the clause "that has been domesticated since prehistoric times" modify? It could be "mammal," or it could be "Canidae." But isn't this sort of microscopic focus on antecedents just arrant nitpicking? Probably not to the person who reads this definition and thinks that all members of the family Canidae have been domesticated since prehistoric times, so it's totally fine to bring the dingo inside the house.

We all use tricks to organize our differentiae. Sometimes I pull out a pad of paper and chart them to make sure they all refer to the right thing:

genus	1st order	2nd order
board		
	long	
	narrow	
	buoyant	
	(made of wood, fiberglass, foam)	
	used in the sport of surfing	

That gets more difficult as the definition gets bigger:

genus	1st order	2nd order	3rd order

a building
    of many rooms
        for overnight accommodation
            of transients
    and several floors
        served by elevators,
  usually with a large open street-level lobby
        containing easy chairs,
  with a variety of compartments
        for eating,
        drinking,
        dancing,
        exhibitions,
        and group meetings
            (as of salesmen or
            convention attendants),
  with shops
        having both inside and
        street-side entrances
        and offering for sale items
            (as clothes,
            gifts,
            candy,
            theater tickets,
            travel tickets)
            of particular interest to a
            traveler,
        or providing personal services
            (as hairdressing,
            shoe shining),
  and with telephone booths, writing tables, and washrooms
  freely available

I'm sorry, what word were we describing? I got caught up in the dancing compartments again.

"In an odd way," Steve Perrault says, "I tend to feel that the definition is an imperfect thing any way you look at it. A definition is an attempt to explain a word's meaning using these certain conventions, and you have to distinguish between the definition of a word and the meaning of a word. The meaning is something that resides in the word, and the definition is a description of that. But a definition is an artificial thing."

It's true. Emily worked on the top ten most looked-up words on our main website, and those ten words took her twelve months to finish. There is only so much you can do in capturing meaning in a definition. "While I definitely get the itch to just quit and move on," Neil explains, "ultimately there's a problem to solve with defining, and I ask myself if I've come any closer to solving it. It's like the asymptote on the Cartesian plane: you might get closer and closer to the solution but never reach it."

He offered a better paraphrase one day when I was complaining about an entry: "Words are stubborn little fuckers."

Pragmatic

On Examples

Writing a definition is only half of your entry-related job at Merriam-Webster. The other thing you must do is either write or find example sentences for that definition.

Example sentences are given at an entry in order to illustrate the most common uses of that word. It's a sly way to give the user a little more information about what sorts of words the headword appears with. For example, "galore" is defined as "abundant, plentiful," and ends with a usage note: "used postpositively." Rather than making our dictionary users sigh with frustration and start flipping toward *P,* we just give an example that explains what "used postpositively" actually means in the real world: <bargains *galore*>. And so on: skim through the examples at "aesthetic," and you will see that it's one of those adjectives that can be used prepositively to modify nouns (<her *aesthetic* sensibility>), but it can't be used after a verb without making you sound like an art student trying too hard (<her sensibility was very *aesthetic*>). "Coffee," it turns out, can be used as a mass noun (<I love *coffee*>) as well as a count noun (<give me two *coffees* and no one gets hurt>). The verbal illustrations at "liberal" show you which senses are the political ones (<he voted a straight *liberal* ticket>) and which have to do with generosity (<she was a *liberal* donor to the charity>) or liberal arts (<a *liberal* education>, though these days that's often read as political even when it's not).

You may notice as you flip through the dictionary that some of the example sentences aren't even sentences; they're fragments. That's a holdover from the print days, when including the subject of a sentence (and the punctuation) might turn a line, which turns the page, which requires a new folio, which swallowed the spider that caught the fly, and so on. This is a reasonable explanation from a production standpoint, and a complete slap in the face to English and literacy from most dictionary users' standpoints. Teachers will write in and angrily ask how they can possibly teach their students proper grammar and punctuation if *the dictionary* can't be bothered to use it?* Even that is changing, however: there's room online to put in both a subject *and* terminal punctuation, thereby (we hope) saving students of English from utter inevitable idiocy.

You'll also notice that some example sentences have an attribution and some don't. These are different types of examples: the unattributed type are what we in the biz call "verbal illustrations," and the ones with attributions are called "authorial quotations." The authorial quotations are examples taken directly from our citation files as we've collected them. You'd think this is an easy task—after all, we've already read through all the citations for this word, and you should just be able to grab one—but like many other things in lexicography, this is not the case.

Finding a suitable quotation for a dictionary entry is near impossible, because quotations used in dictionaries need to meet three main criteria: they need to illustrate the most common usage of the word; they need to use only words that are entered in that particular dictionary; and they need to be as boring as humanly possible. Writers generally want to catch and hold your attention, and so they write things that are full of narrative interest, clever constructions, and tons of proper names. These things are a delight to read, and because of that they make for the worst example sentences possible.

The goal of a dictionary is to tell people what words mean and

---

* I have no good answer for that, which is perhaps why I am a lexicographer and not an English teacher.

show them how they are used in the most objective, dispassionate, and robotic way possible. People do not come to the dictionary for excitement and romance; that's what encyclopedias are for. They just want to glance at an entry, get a sense of what the word they're looking at means, and then get back to finishing their homework, love letter, or all-caps, keyboard-mashing screed.

In order to make sure that there's no lexical cowlick sticking up out of an entry, lexicographers carefully weigh each part of an entry to make sure that the whole thing is balanced, and we pay particular attention to the example sentences and the definitions they are paired with. Which grabs you first? If the definition: good, because that's what people want. If the example sentence: try again. The example sentence should be less interesting than the definition.

The problem, of course, is that the definitions are generally pretty boring; that is after all the lexicographer's wheelhouse. "Concerned with or relating to matters of fact or practical affairs : practical rather than idealistic or theoretical," reads the first definition of "pragmatic." Yes, very sexy if you are into words with more than three syllables. But for the rest of us, this is Typical Dictionary: no sparks or sizzles here, just matte, bland, and, well, *pragmatic.* One hopes for a great quotation as just deserts* for making it through two polysyllabic definitions, maybe something snarky and biting by Mencken, Ambrose Bierce, W. C. Fields even.

With some words, like "pragmatic," you soon discover that many writers use the word without quite knowing what it means:

> Aren't politicians supposed to pander? Aren't they supposed to be pragmatic to a fault—focusing on short-term relief and eschewing serious, long-term problems like reforming the health care system and attacking structural deficits?

---

* **de·sert** \di-ˈzərt\ *n, pl* **-s** . . . **2 :** deserved reward or punishment—usually used in plural <got their just *deserts*> *(MWCII).* I leave it to you to determine whether example sentences are reward or punishment.

You're a bit confused: Aren't these politicians "concerned with or relating to matters of fact or practical affairs"? Are shortsighted responses actually "pragmatic to a fault"? Gil didn't cover American politics in your Style and Defining class. This is just one of 463 citations for "pragmatic." You feel the day stretch out before you, taffy-wise.

Considering all this, it's no surprise that looking for a really good quotation to use at the entry takes longer than writing the definition. When I ask Emily about quotations, she confirms that for her it is the "hugely, hugely time-consuming part" of working on an entry. I ask Neil about quotations, and he exhales and crumples a bit, as if I've sucker punched him. "I feel like I'm living in the abyss of Google News," Neil says, noting that most of the resources that we work with at Merriam-Webster aren't written for lexicography, and so their search capabilities (particularly for lexicographers, who would love nothing more than to be able to search for, say, the transitive use of a common verb) aren't adequate to the task. They return too many hits to easily and quickly sift through; the metadata of publication name and date might be wrong; they're full of false positives for the word you're looking for. "It's tricky; it can feel tedious." Later, he says, "I just accept that I'll be underwater." I know the feeling.

In lieu of suitable examples from real writers, lexicographers at Merriam-Webster sometimes write example sentences themselves. This is vastly more difficult than it sounds. Lexicographers are people who are, despite the low pay and the mockery, deeply in love with English—they love to play and muck around in it—and it is very hard not to want to make other people fall in love with English too. So in spite of the interdiction against narrative interest, it occasionally seeps in. The definition of "portly" that means "dignified" includes the sentence fragment <walked with the *portly* grace of the grande dame that she was>, and you can picture the tableau perfectly: a crinolined and corseted matriarch, all bustle, with a fascinator of feathers and an exquisite wooden cane, processing down the avenue with practiced, straight-backed elegance. A lovely image; Gove would have struck everything after "grace" for being too long and unnecessary.

The other big problem with writing your own examples is that you sometimes write out of your own experiences, which are often not the experiences of the people who will be reading this dictionary. You may get "obscure" in your batch of defining and decide to add a verbal illustration to the "not well-known" sense of the word, so you go with <an *obscure* Roman poet>—a perfectly idiomatic and blessedly short example. But consider your audience: How many Roman poets are they reading on the regular? Aren't *all* Roman poets fairly obscure these days? It's not as though the youth are quoting Catullus or Sextus Propertius left and right, or folks at the diner talk about what a raw deal Bibaculus got. It's easy for lexicographers to forget that they are not the gold standard for "normal."

You also end up with verbal fatigue—a condition whereupon your sprachgefühl deserts you as soon as you need it the most. When called upon, you not only can't think of any use that suits the definition, but you completely forget English altogether. Little words, like prepositions and adverbs, slip effortlessly through the sieve that your mind has become, so you write <a *pragmatic* man absorbed by practical details> and aren't sure whether "absorbed by" is actually idiomatic English. Should it be "absorbed with"? You weigh the two mentally, and you even do a corpus search to see which is more common, but you still can't tell anymore. The word "pragmatic" has ceased to be anything but elaborate chicken scratch. Where your sprachgefühl was, there is only an empty ache where it used to dig its fingers into you.

This is the point at which you slink out of your chair and scuff aimlessly over to someone else's desk. When they look up at you, you will bleat, "Help, is it 'absorbed with' or 'absorbed by'?" I have sent many an e-mail to Emily and Neil that began, "Help, I can't English [*sic*]." This is the mercy of being part of an editorial team: it's likely that not all of you will lose your minds at exactly the same time.

There are some fairly strict rules in place for writing verbal illustrations. First and foremost, no jokes or anything that could possibly be construed as a joke. Do not write <she's just a harmless *drudge*> at "drudge," because there are only about fifty people in the English-speaking world who will get that reference, and they are all sitting within a twenty-five-foot radius of you, worrying about their own entries. You are writing for the dictionary, not *Puns Monthly*.

You must also excise all potential double entendres from the book; they say that the best editors have a sharp, sharp eye and a filthy, filthy mind, and they are right. Editors are, at heart, twelve: if we can construe something as a fart or sex (or a fart *and* sex) joke, we will. This is a double-edged sword as you write verbal illustrations: the elevation of your adult duty is constantly pulling against the gravity of your native gutter thinking. Duty must prevail because duty ostensibly pays the bills, and so <I think we should *do* it> gets changed to <I don't want to *do* that>; <That's a *big* one!> becomes <That's a *big* fish!>; <He *screwed* in the lightbulb> becomes nothing at all. After a while, you see double entendres everywhere: you remove every single verbal illustration at "member" and "organ" for obvious reasons, you scrutinize the verbal illustrations at "wind" extra hard just to make sure there's no secret fart joke in there, and you wonder if you should science-up the verbal illustrations at "organism" because it's just a few letters off from "orgasm," and no doubt someone will read sex into <complex *organisms*>.

(And yet here I must confess that I am aware of two good double entendres that have made it into our dictionaries and have stayed there. The first is in a paperback dictionary at the entry for "tract" and references a boob joke from *Monty Python and the Holy Grail:* <huge *tracts* of land>. The second is in our middle-school dictionary, at the entry for "cut." It reads <cheese *cuts* easily>, and I hope that it has given much joy to countless fart-obsessed middle schoolers and perhaps even convinced them that dictionaries are, if not cool, at least not boring and stupid.)

Once you have removed all vestiges of fun from your verbal illustration, you must go through another pass and remove names. You may think it'd be a great way to win friends and get people to buy dictionaries—hey, anyone named Larry, you're in the dictionary at the entry for "awesome"!—but it's fraught with peril. Who will think of Trisha, the woman who just broke up with a Larry, who then picks up the dictionary and sees <Larry is the *paradigm* of class>? Trisha might be tempted to get nine hundred of her social media friends to write to us and tell us that we need to change the verbal illustration to read <Larry is the *paradigm* of a lying sack of shit, and Trisha is glad she dumped his ass>. There is no comfort to be had in using the names of famous people, either. <Bill Clinton was the *president* of the United States> will earn you long political rants from both ends of the spectrum that inevitably culminate in chest-beating pant-hoots of disdain or admiration that make you feel like an extra in a Leni Riefenstahl film. There is no name under the sun that will not earn you some sort of abuse: write <Mother Teresa was a *holy* woman> and you'll get people complaining that they don't want to have Catholicism crammed down their throats by the dictionary.

In addition to names, be very careful about pronouns and how you use them. English pronouns, gendered as they are, tend to inspire a lot of teeth grinding in general use, because they end up communicating something about the user's views of men and women whether the user wants them to or not. It's a pronounal catch-22. Don't even think about writing <he enjoys *working* on his car>, you misogynist, unless you also include the sentence <she enjoys *working* on her car>, though this is an inclusion that the copy editor won't let you make because it is ridiculous and redundant to have both in the entry. Don't try to smooth over your idiocy by changing that to <he enjoys *working* on her car>—what, you think that women need a man to work on their cars for them?—or <she enjoys *working* on his car>: How dare you emasculate men by assuming that they can't work on their own cars! Further, what about people outside the gender binary? Can't they work on their cars, too? But write <they enjoy *working* on their car> and the peeververein will descend to bewail your use of the singular "they," though it's not exactly transparently singular here.

This goes well beyond pronouns, of course. You must avoid any hint of perceived bias anywhere in the verbal illustration. Your illustration for "conservative" that reads <the *conservative* party blocked the measure> will be read as saying that people who identify as conservative are obstructionist; change that to <he votes a straight *conservative* ticket>, and you'll hear from people who think that the dictionary is trying to tell them how to vote. Even something you consider to be as innocuous as possible—<I love pizza a *lot*>—could end up garnering unwarranted criticism. Never mind that this illustrates "lot": someone will write in to ask, "How can you *love* pizza; are you a pervert?"*

Further, be aware that writing a verbal illustration like <tomorrow is *supposed* to be sunny> may be problematic, because there are supposedly people out there who will assume that if they look up "suppose" in the dictionary and read <tomorrow is *supposed* to be sunny>, that means tomorrow will, in fact, be sunny, and they will write in and complain when tomorrow is not sunny. According to one senior editor who worked on the *Third*, Gove himself prohibited these types of verbal illustrations on the grounds that the reader wouldn't be able to distinguish between a dictionary and a Magic 8 Ball (my paraphrase) and would take us at our word. What if tomorrow *isn't* sunny?

It is best, in fact, to assume that every verbal illustration you write will offend someone, somewhere, at some point.

---

* We hear an awful lot about the entry for "love." I have received some form of this complaint for years, though not specific to pizza.

All this can send an editor skittering over the edge in their own quietly unhinged way. Here is a list of verbal illustrations, compiled by a proofreader, that used to appear in two of our children's dictionaries:

<a man overboard>
<discovered arsenic in the victim's coffee>
<the baby was abandoned on the steps of the church>
<it was as if you had lost your last friend>
<when you have no family, you are really on your own>
<blow up the bridge>
<carried a knife about him>
<felt as I was dead>

Perhaps they are a little depressive, you counter, but how else are you going to illustrate words like "overboard" and "arsenic" and "knife"? Well reasoned. If only those were the words those examples were illustrating:

<*a* man overboard>
<*discovered* arsenic in the victim's coffee>
<the baby was *abandoned* on the steps of the church>
<it was *as if* you had lost your last friend>
<*when* you have no family, you are really on your own>
<blow *up* the bridge>
<carried a knife *about* him>
<felt *as* I was dead>

Just as the verbal illustrations are not the place to try to hone your skills as a novelist, they are also not the place to work out your feelings about your latest breakup or other assorted existential crises. If I am copyediting your batch and see a string of verbal illustrations like <I wonder *why* I do this job>, <*thinking* dark thoughts>, and <*all* hope is lost>, I will stop to wonder if you are okay, and then I will have to leave my desk and speak to you in person, which will terrify us both.

If example sentences are such a pain in the ass to find and to write, then why not leave them out? Who will miss them? Surprisingly, lots of people will. One of the most common requests we have gotten over the years is for more example sentences in our dictionaries. From a linguistic point of view, this makes sense. People don't learn language in individual words but in chunks of language. Think about any foreign language you've learned (or attempted to). What's the first thing you learn? Usually how to say "Hello, my name is [Kory]. How are you?" You don't learn the word for "name," and then learn the conjugation of "be" (and good thing, too, because it is stubbornly irregular in most languages). You don't learn the interrogative "how" and the various declensions of the second-person pronoun. All that comes later when you have a little something to hang that information on. You learn two complete, if rudimentary, sentences, and that gives you the confidence to keep moving forward—until you reach the subjunctive, anyway.

The point of example sentences in dictionaries isn't just to fill out space and drive lexicographers to a nervous breakdown but to help orient the user in terms of a word's broader context, its connotative meanings, its range, its tones. In all the things that people look for in writing—narrative, color, dialogue—it must be bland, yet it must be lexically illuminating, showing formality of tone and collocative use, sounding completely and utterly natural even if it is the most highly constructed sentence you've ever written. It's a difficult balance to get right.

Six years into my tenure at Merriam-Webster, I was working on a reference book that was heavy on verbal illustrations. The senior editor who was managing the book and overseeing my work was an excellent editor, but not one who was free with compliments or encouragement. More than once during the project, I opened e-mails from him that asked me what, exactly, I was thinking while working on thus-and-such batch. I often left the office during that era wondering if maybe I should pack it in and go work at a Renaissance Faire instead.

One difficult afternoon, I sent him an e-mail about a batch I was copyediting, asking him for thoughts on another editor's verbal illustration. He answered at length, crabbed and cantankerous, then ended his miserere with an unlooked-for compliment. "'Gobs'—of all things—perhaps is an example of your commendable creativity. You took a difficult word, and created a sentence in which that particular word looks at home."

The verbal illustration I came up with was <has *gobs* of money>. Perfectly idiomatic, short, and utterly boring: I felt like I had finally arrived.

Take

On Small Words

We were working on revising the *Collegiate* for its eleventh edition, and we had just finished the letter *S*. For the *Collegiate,* it was broken up into two batches, so by the time that last batch in *S* had been signed back in, the editors were not just pleased; we were giddy. You'd go to the sign-out sheet, see that we're into *T,* and make some little ritual obeisance to the moment: a fist pump, a sigh of relief and a heavenward glance, a little "oh yeah" and a tiny dance that is restricted to your shoulders (you *are* at work, after all). Sadly, lexicographers are not suited to survive extended periods of giddiness. In the face of such woozy delight, the chances are good that you will do something rash and brainless.

Unfortunately, my rash brainlessness was obscured from me. I signed out the next batch in *T* and grabbed the galleys for that batch along with the boxes—*two boxes!*—of citations for the batch.[*] While flipping through the galley pages, I realized that my batch—the entire thing—was just one word: "take." *Hmm,* I thought, *that's curious.* Lexicography, like most professions, offers its devotees some benchmarks by which you can measure your sad little existence, and one is the size of the words you are allowed to handle.

---

[*] The *Eleventh* was an odd duck production-wise: the citations we needed to review for the new edition straddled the divide between paper and database. So though we had a database in place when the *Eleventh* was being written in the late 1990s, we reviewed citations in print. I do miss those boxes of citations, if I'm being perfectly, stupidly honest.

Most people assume that long words or rare words are the hardest to define because they are often the hardest to spell, say, and remember. The truth is, those are usually a snap. "Schadenfreude" may be difficult to spell, but it's a cinch to define, because all the uses of it are very, very semantically and syntactically clear. It's always a noun, and it's often glossed because even though it's now an English word, it's one of those delectable German compounds we love to slurp into English.

Generally speaking, and as mentioned earlier, the smaller and more commonly used the word is, the more difficult it is to define. Words like "but," "as," and "for" have plenty of uses that are syntactically similar but not identical.* Verbs like "go" and "do" and "make" (and, yes, "take") don't just have semantically oozy uses that require careful definition, but semantically drippy uses as well. "Let's do dinner" and "let's do laundry" are identical syntactically but feature very different semantic meanings of "do." And how do you describe what the word "how" is doing in this sentence?

It's not just semantic fiddliness that causes lexicographical pain. Some words, like "the" and "a," are so small that we barely think of them as words. Most of the publicly available databases that we use for citational spackling don't even index some of these words, let alone let you search for them—for entirely practical reasons. A search for "the" in our in-house citation database returns over one million hits, which sends the lexicographer into fits of audible swearing, then weeping.

To keep the lexicographers from crying and disturbing the people around them, sometimes these small words are pulled from the regular batches and are given to more senior editors for handling. They require the balance of concision, grammatical prowess, speed, and fortitude usually found in wiser and more experienced editors.

I didn't know any of that at the time, of course, because I was

---

* See the grammatical rabbit hole of one use of "but" in the chapter appropriately titled "But."

not a wise or more experienced editor. I was hapless and dumb, but dutifully so: grabbing a fistful of index cards from one of the two boxes, I began sorting the cards into piles by part of speech. This is the first job you must do as a lexicographer dealing with paper, because those citations aren't sorted for you. I figured that "take" wasn't going to be too terrible in this respect: there's just a verb and a noun to contend with. When those piles were two and a half inches high and began cascading onto my desk, I decided to dump the rest of the citations into my pencil drawer and stack my citations in the now-empty boxes.

Sorting citations by their part of speech is usually simple. Most words entered in the dictionary only have one part of speech, and if they have more than one, the parts of speech are usually easy to distinguish between—the noun "blemish" and the verb "blemish," for example, or the noun "courtesy" and the adjective "courtesy." By the time you've hit *T* on a major dictionary overhaul like a new edition of the *Collegiate,* you can sort citations by part of speech in your sleep. For a normal-sized word like "blemish," it's a matter of minutes.

Five hours in, I had finished sorting the first box of citations for "take."

It is unfortunate that the entries that take up most of the lexicographer's time are often the entries that no one looks at. We used to be able to kid ourselves while tromping through "get" that someone, somewhere, at some point in time, was going to look up the word, read sense 11c ("hear"), and say to themselves, "Yes, *finally,* now I understand what 'Did you get that?' means. Thanks, Merriam-Webster!" Sometimes, in the delirium that sets in at the end of a project when you are proofreading pronunciations in six-point type for eight hours a day, a little corner of your mind wanders off to daydream about how perhaps your careful revision of "get" will somehow end with your winning the lottery, bringing about world peace, and finally becoming the best dancer in the room.

But nowadays, thanks to the marvels of the Internet, we know exactly what sorts of words people look up regularly. They generally don't look up long, hard-to-spell words—no "rhadamanthine" or "vecturist" unless the National Spelling Bee is on TV.* They tend to look up words in the middle of the road. Some of the all-time top lookups at Merriam-Webster are "paradigm," "disposition," "ubiquitous," and "esoteric," words that are used fairly regularly but also in contexts that don't tell the reader much about what they mean.

This also means that the smallest words, like "but" and "as" and "make," are not looked up either. Most native English speakers know how to navigate the collocative waters of "make" or don't need to figure out what exactly "as" means in the sentence "You are as dull as a mud turtle." They recognize that it marks comparison, somehow, and that's it. But that's not good enough for lexicography.

It is also a perverse irony that the entries that end up taking the most lexicographical time are usually fairly fixed. Steve Kleinedler notes that one of the *American Heritage Dictionary* editors overhauled fifty or sixty of the most basic English verbs back in the first decade of the twenty-first century. "Because he did that, they don't really need to be done again anytime soon. That was probably the first time they'd been done in forty years." This isn't dereliction on *The American Heritage Dictionary*'s part: these words don't make quick semantic shifts. "Adding new idioms to these entries: easy-peasy," Steve says. "But in terms of overhauling 'take' or 'bring' or 'go,' if you do it once every fifty years, you're probably set."

That's not to say that these tiny words don't have semantic shift at all. Emily Brewster had the indefinite article "a" in one of her defining batches for the *Eleventh,* and she "found" a new sense of the word. I put "found" in quotations for a reason: the semantic shift that Emily outlined in her overhaul of "a" isn't new. Her care-

---

*   **rhad·a·man·thine** \ ˌra-də-ˈman(t)-thən, -ˈman-ˌthīn\ *adj* : rigorously strict or just *(MWU)*
vec·tu·rist \ˈvekchərəst\ *n, pl* -s : a collector of transportation tokens *(MWU)*

ful reading of the citations for "a" and her splitter nature led her to tease out a finer meaning of "a" than had been previously recorded. The new sense: "—used as a function word before a proper noun to distinguish the condition of the referent from a usual, former, or hypothetical condition," as in "With the Angels dispatched in short order, *a* rested Schilling, a career 6-1 pitcher in the postseason, could start three times if seven games were necessary against the Yankees."

"It was one of my most exciting days as a lexicographer for sure," Emily says. "The process was simpler than it sometimes is because I didn't have to go back and forth in my head about whether the meaning was already covered or not; it was immediately apparent to me that it wasn't. From there it was just a matter of formulating the definition itself. I felt very proud of myself when it was all done."

It seems ludicrous—all that futzing for *"a"*? No one pays attention to little words like this. Everyone knows what they mean, and all this foofaraw has exactly zero impact on the way we live our lives. Then again, debate over the meaning of "is"—one of the simplest words in the English language—helped set in motion the impeachment of a sitting U.S. president.

Q: [Mr. Wisenberg] . . . Whether or not Mr. Bennett knew of your relationship with Ms. Lewinsky, the statement that there was "no sex of any kind in any manner, shape or form, with President Clinton," was an utterly false statement. Is that correct?

PRESIDENT CLINTON: It depends on what the meaning of the word "is" is. If "is" means is, and never has been, that is one thing. If it means there is none, that was a completely true statement.

So perhaps not precisely *zero* impact.

The citations sorted, I decided to tackle the verb first. The entry for the verb is far longer than the entry for the noun: 107 distinct senses, subsenses, and defined phrases. And, perhaps hidden in all those cards, a few senses or idioms to add.

You will recall that when one works with paper citations, the unit of work measurement is the pile. Every citation gets sorted into a pile that represents the current definitions for the word, and new piles for potential new definitions. I looked at the galleys, then my desk, and began methodically moving everything on my desk that I could—box of pinks, date stamp, desk calendar, coffee—to the bookshelf behind me.

My first citation read, "She was taken aback." I exhaled in relief: this is simple. I scanned the galley and found the appropriate definition—"to catch or come upon in a particular situation or action" (sense 3b)—and began my pile. The next handful of citations were similarly dispatched—a pile for sense 2, a pile for sense 1a, a pile for sense 7d—and I began to relax. In spite of its size, this is no different from any other batch, I reasoned. I am going to whip through this, and then I am going to take a two-week vacation, visit my local library, and *go outside.*

Fate, now duly tempted, intervened. My next cit read, "Reason has taken a back seat to sentiment." I confidently flipped it onto the pile with "taken aback" and then reconsidered. This use of "take" didn't really mean "to catch or come upon in a particular situation or action," did it? I tried substitution: reason did not catch or come upon a backseat.* No: reason was made secondary to sentiment. I scanned the galleys and saw nothing that matched, then put the citation in a "new sense" pile. But before I could grab the next citation, I thought, "Unless . . ."

When a lexicographer says "unless . . ." in the middle of defining, you should turn out the lights and go home, first making sure you've left them a supply of water and enough nonperishable food

---

* This is not an error. For whatever reason, people tend to use the open compound "back seat" in the phrase "take a back seat" but the closed "backseat" when referring to the seats behind the driver. English!

to last several days. "Unless . . ." almost always marks the beginning of a wild lexical goose chase.

There is a reality to what words mean that is amplified when you're dealing with the little words. The meaning of a word depends on its context, but if the context changes, so does the meaning of the word. The meaning of "take" in "take a back seat" changes depending on the whole context: "There's no room up front, so you have to take a back seat" has a different meaning from "reason takes a back seat to sentiment." This second use is an idiom, which means it gets defined as a phrase at the end of the entry. I started a new pile.

My rhythm had been thrown off, but upon reading the next citation, I was confident I'd regain momentum: ". . . take a shit." Profanity and a clear, fixed idiom that will need its own definition at the end of the entry—yes, I can do this.

Only "take a shit" is not a fixed idiom like "take a back seat" is. You can also take a crap. Or a walk, or a breather, or a nap, or a break. I scanned the galleys, flipping from page to page. "To undertake and make, do, or perform," sense 17a. I considered. I tried substitution with hysterical results: "to undertake and make a shit," "to undertake a shit," "to undertake and do a shit," "to undertake and perform a shit." This got me thinking, which is always dangerous. Can one "perform" or "do" a nap? Does one "undertake and make" a breather? Maybe that's 17b, "to participate in." But my sprachgefühl screeched: "participate" implies that the thing being participated in has an originating point outside the speaker. So you take (participate in) a meeting, or you take (participate in) a class on French philosophy. I tentatively placed the citation in the pile for 17a, then spent the next five minutes writing each sense number and definition down on a sticky note and affixing it to the top citation of each pile. My note for sense 17a included the parenthetical "(Refine/revise def? Make/do/perform?)."

I sat back and berated myself a bit. I have redefined "Monophysite" and "Nestorianism"; I can swear in a dozen languages; I am not a moron. This should be easy. My next citation read, ". . . arrived 20 minutes late, give or take."

What? This isn't a verbal use! How did this get in here? I took a pinched-lip look around my cubicle for the guilty party—someone has been in here futzing with my citations!—then realized I was the guilty party. Clearly, I needed to refile this. But where? After five minutes of staring at the citation, I took the well-trod path of least resistance and decided that maybe it's adverbial ("eh, close enough"). Yes, I'll just put this citation . . . in the nonexistent spot for adverbial uses of "take," because there are no adverbial uses of "take." My teeth began to hurt.

I placed the citation in a far corner of my desk, which I mentally labeled "Which Will Be Dealt with in Two or Three Days."

Next: ". . . this will only take about a week." My brain saw "take about" and spat out "phrasal verb." Phrasal verbs are two- or three-word phrases that are made up of a verb and a preposition or adverb (or both), that function like a verb, and whose meaning cannot be figured out from the meanings of each individual constituent. "Look down on" in "He looked down on lexicography as a career" is a phrasal verb. The whole phrase functions as a verb, and "look down on" here does not mean that the anonymous He was physically towering over lexicography as a career and staring down at it, but rather that he thought lexicography as a career was unimportant or not worth his respect. Phrasal verbs tend to be completely invisible to a native speaker of English, which is why I was so very proud of spotting one at first glance. I created a new pile for the phrasal verb "take about," and then my sprachgefühl found its voice: "That's not a phrasal verb."

I squeezed my eyes shut and silently asked the cosmos to send the office up in a fireball right now. After a moment, I realized that my sprachgefühl had picked loose a bit of information that fell neatly to the bottom of my brainpan: the "about" is entirely optional. Try it: "this will only take a week" and "this will only take about a week" mean almost the same thing. The pivot point for meaning is not "take" but "about," which means that this use of "take" is a straightforward transitive use. I flipped the card onto the pile for sense 10e(2), "to use up (as space or time)."

It had been an hour, and I had gotten through perhaps twenty citations. I sifted all my "Done" piles into one and grabbed a ruler. The pile of handled citations was a quarter inch thick. Then I measured the cit boxes. Each was full. Each was sixteen inches long.

Over the next two weeks, the tensile strength of my last nerve was tested by "take." My working definition of "desk" expanded as I ran out of flat spaces to stack citations. Piles appeared on the top of my monitor, in my pencil drawer, filed between rows on my keyboard, teetering on the top of the cubicle wall, shuffled onto the top of the CPU under my desk. Still I didn't have enough space: I began to carefully, carefully put piles of citations on the floor. My cubicle looked as if it had hosted the world's neatest ticker-tape parade.

When dealing with entries of this size, you will inevitably hit the Wall. If you run, or have tried to run, then you are familiar with the Wall. It's the point in a run when you are pushed (or pushing) beyond your physical endurance. Your focus pulls inward on your searing lungs, your aching calves, that hitch in your right hip that is probably because you didn't stretch but might just be a precursor to your lower body literally[*] exploding from the effort you are putting forth. The ground has tilted upward; your feet are made of concrete and are fifty times bigger than you thought; your neck begins to bow because even the effort of holding your fat melon upright is too much. You are not euphoric, or Zen, or any of the other things that *Runner's World* magazine makes running look like. You are at the Wall, where you are nothing but a loose collection of human limits.

I hit my human limits about three-quarters of the way through the verb "take." As I looked at a citation for "took first things first," I felt myself slowly unspooling into idiocy. I knew the glyphs before me had to be words, because my job was all about words, and I

---

[*] Sense 2.

knew they had to be English, because my job was all about English. But knowing something doesn't make it true. This was all garbage, I thought, and as I felt my brain slip sideways, and the yawing ache open up in my gut, one thought flitted across my mind before I slammed headlong into the lexicographer's equivalent of the Wall: "Oh my God, I'm going to die at my desk like in that urban legend, and they will find my body under an avalanche of 'take.'"

That night over dinner, my husband asked if I was okay. I looked up at him, utterly lost. "I don't think I speak English anymore." He looked mildly alarmed; he only speaks English. "You're probably just stressed," he said. "But what does that even mean?" I whined. "Just thinking about what it means makes my brain itch!" He went back to looking mildly alarmed.

It took me three more days to finish sorting the citations for the verb "take." I was ecstatic—yes, I had done it!—and then immediately depressed: shit, I still had to actually do defining work on "take," and I still had the noun to go! Lucky for me, I had decided to use the sticky notes to make changes to existing entries. "Make, do, or undertake" didn't end up getting a revision in the end, but a rough handful of senses needed expanding or fixing; one definition meant to cover uses like "she took the sea air for her health" had been unfortunately phrased "to expose oneself to (as sun or air) for pleasure or physical benefit," which I hurriedly changed to "to put oneself into (as sun, air, or water) for pleasure or physical benefit" so as not to encourage medicinal flashing.

On the floor were my piles for citations that I needed to mentally squint at a bit more and piles of citations for new senses of "take." It was late in the afternoon, the sun slicing gold along the wall. Before I took care of those, I decided to reward myself by answering the e-mail correspondence I had let accumulate while I had been ears-deep in "take." I'd start afresh in the morning.

The next morning, I came into work and discovered that the overnight cleaning crew had decided to move all the piles I had left on the floor, dumping them into a cascade of paper on my chair. It was a cinematic moment: I dropped my bag and stared openmouthed at the blank spaces where twenty or so piles of citations used to sit. As my sinuses prickled, I realized, almost too late, that I was about to cry, and if I cried, I would most certainly make noise. I left my bag in the middle of the floor and went to the ladies', where I leaned against the paper towel dispenser and wondered if it was too late to go back to the bakery and have people throw cakes at my head.

Lexicography is a steady plod in one direction: onward. I was doing no good standing there with my head on the cool plastic. Besides, a few of my colleagues were waiting for me to move so they could dry their hands. I re-sorted the tidy stack the cleaning crew left and papered every flat surface within five feet of my cubicle with "DO NOT MOVE MY PAPERS!!! KLS!!!!" I sat grimly in my chair and decided that a little fun was in order: it was time to stamp the covered citations and file them away.

When you're done working on an entry, the paper citations get put in one of three places: the "Used" group, which are the citations used as evidence for every existing definition in the entry; the "New" group, which holds the citations for each new sense you draft; and the "Rejected" group, which holds the citations for any use whose meaning isn't covered by the existing entry or by a newly proposed definition. Used and new citations are stamped by the editor who worked on the entry to mark that they were used for a particular book. When the whole floor was consumed with a defining project, you'd occasionally hear a sudden rhythmic thumping, like someone tapping their toe in miniature. It was an editor stamping citations.

I took out my customized date stamp and began marking the covered cits, pile by pile, as used. After the first handful, I stamped a little more exuberantly, and my cube mate hemmed in irritation. No matter. I had no punching bag to pummel; I had no nuclear device to detonate. But I had a date stamp, and by the power vested in me by Samuel Johnson and Noah Webster, I was going to put this goddamned verb to bed.

•

That small act of brutality against index cards marked the other side of "take." After I reshuffled the citations from the floor back into new piles, the verb went smoothly. I wrote and rewrote and rewrote some more. I got up from my desk to run proposed revisions and new entries past a few colleagues, and after climbing out of their hiding places, they were very helpful. I teased a new sense out of sense 6f, "to assume as if rightfully one's own or as if granted," which covered uses like "she took all the credit for it," and created sense 6g: "to accept the burden or consequences of" to cover "she took all the blame for it"—a little splitty by lexicographical standards, but a distinction that Steve thought was good enough to leave in. I came up with verbal illustrations for the more opaque senses of "take." Momentum begets momentum: I was suddenly able to see that "take the plunge" was a fixed idiom, "give or take" should be covered at "give," that these three piles of citations for uses that are kinda-sorta close to the meaning of 12b(3) ("to accept with the mind in a specified way") can be covered by 12b(3) if I change the definition by two words, that this phrasal verb I had a pile for had its own entry in the dictionary and so I can happily foist it on some other unsuspecting editor. It only took two days of scribbling and shuffling to finish the verb. When it was done, I took no break for e-mail but went straight on into the noun—a blissfully manageable twenty piles. And when that was done, in mere days, I was so pleased with myself that I pushed back from my desk, looked left and right to make sure that no one was within glancing range, and then emphatically punched the air and mouthed "YES."*

I marched my finished batch back to the galley table, flipped the sign-out sheet back several pages—we were already in *U*—and signed "take" back in. It had taken a month of nonstop editorial work.

A month, I have come to discover, is not that long in lexicographical terms. In 2013, the University of Georgia hosted the biennial

---

* I saved the hooting and hollering for when I was outside.

meeting of the Dictionary Society of North America, an academic society for lexicographers, linguists, and logophiles interested in dictionaries. One of the attendees was Peter Gilliver, a lexicographer from the *Oxford English Dictionary,* who joined a crew of us for dinner.

We had the restaurant mostly to ourselves, and talk turned shopwise. We discussed the differences between defining for the *OED,* which is a historical dictionary with over 600,000 senses, and defining for the *Collegiate Dictionary,* a relative lightweight at about 230,000 senses. While discussing this, I announced to the table that I had done "take" for the *Eleventh Collegiate,* and it had taken me about a month. One of the academics at the table shook his head. "Wow."

Peter piped up. "I revised 'run,'" he said quietly, then smiled. "It took me nine months."

The table burst forth in a chorus of "Jesuses!" *Nine months!* But of course it did. In the *OED,* "run" has over six hundred separate senses, making the *Collegiate*'s "take" look like kid stuff.

I lifted my glass of wine from the other end of the table. "Here's to 'run,'" I said. "May it never come up for revision again in our lifetimes."

Bitch

On Bad Words

When you spend all day looking carefully at words, you develop a very detached and unnatural relationship with them. It's much like being a doctor, I imagine: a beautiful person walks into your office and takes off all their clothes, and you spend all your time staring raptly at the sphygmomanometer.

Once you get them in your office and have their clothes off, all words are the same for a lexicographer. Words that are crude, vulgar, embarrassing, obscene, or otherwise distasteful get treated just as clinically as science terms and other general vocabulary. It takes some getting used to. A new editor was recently sitting quietly at her desk, when two other editors walked by, engrossed in a conversation. "Should we have cock at all?" asked one editor as they sailed down the cubicle aisle. "It's got shithead in it, it's got turd in it . . ." That was all she heard before they were out of earshot.

Such a conversation is completely normal when you're trying to figure out what words should go into which dictionary. I have spent years trying to convince horrified correspondents that the appearance of a profanity in a dictionary is merely a record of the word's written uses, and no tender young child is learning profanity from the dictionary anyway. Taboo language of all sorts has been recorded since the earliest days of English dictionaries: John Florio's 1598 dictionary uses the verb "fuck" in his translations of Italian. And though Johnson and Webster refused to enter such

low language—Johnson for the aesthetics of it and Webster for the
moral impropriety—there's no denying that it was very much in
use. So my unrufflable attitude to all manner of taboo words is not
callousness on my part, nor the sly coolness of using taboo words
to seem much hipper than I actually am, but simply part of my job.
Very few entries faze me. Until the day I looked up the *Collegiate
Dictionary* entry for "bitch":

bitch *noun* \ˈbich\
1 : the female of the dog or some other carnivorous mammals
2 a : a lewd or immoral woman
b : a malicious, spiteful, or overbearing woman—sometimes used as
a generalized term of abuse
3 : something that is extremely difficult, objectionable, or unpleasant
4 : COMPLAINT[*]

It wasn't an entry I had consulted before, but I was considering
adding a new sense of the word and so needed to review it. As I
reread it, I tilted my head, as if listening for a sound that wasn't
there. Then I heard it: this wasn't marked in our dictionary as taboo.

Dictionaries mark taboo language in a variety of ways. Most
common are labels at the beginning of the definition to warn you:
"offensive," "vulgar," "obscene," "disparaging," and the like.
Unfortunately, these labels can be opaque at best. What's the difference, for instance, between "vulgar" and "obscene," or "offensive"
and "disparaging"? Don't offensive words disparage? If something's obscene, isn't it also vulgar, and vice versa?

The documentation in-house is shockingly thin on how to determine whether a word should be labeled "vulgar" or "obscene."

---

[*] Those definitions in small caps are what we call synonymous cross-references.
They are synonyms of the meaning in question, and so fuller analytical definitions can be found at the cross-referenced entry. Unsurprisingly, they are a
space-saving hedge that allows us to use single words as definitions (verboten
per the Black Books).

Nothing in the Black Books, nothing in our more recent style guides, no e-mails from Gil or Steve about litmus tests we can put a word through to determine what to call it. If there's nothing in the style files, then we have to assume that the giants who went before us thought this was so commonsensical that it didn't merit mentioning. We must turn to the dictionary for answers to these questions. What does "vulgar" mean when used of words? The appropriate definition teased out from the *Unabridged* is "lewd, obscene, or profane in expression or behavior : INDECENT, INDELICATE" with the orienting quotation <names too *vulgar* to put into print> by the serendipitously named H. A. Chippendale. Not promising: after all, "obscene" is right there in the definition. "Obscene" in turn is defined in the *Unabridged* as "marked by violation of accepted language inhibitions and by the use of words regarded as taboo in polite usage." Alas, "taboo" provides no more direction: "banned on grounds of morality or taste or as constituting a risk : outlawed by common consent : DISAPPROVED, PROSCRIBED." There are very few words that are, as the *Unabridged* puts it, "outlawed by common consent." And what constitutes "common consent"? What my granny thinks is taboo language is different from what I think is taboo language; what is indecent to one person is perfectly fine to another. Even more frustrating: what is indecent to one person *in one context* is perfectly fine to that same person *in another context*. If I am walking down the street and a strange man calls me a "man-hating bitch," I will react differently than I would if one of my friends commented on my gumption by calling me a "tough old bitch." These three definitions are an ouroboros of subjective vagueness, gagging on its own tail.

Of course, I can't label this "vulgar to some, obscene to others, sometimes vulgar to still others, sometimes offensive, mostly disparaging," because our style rules don't allow for it. Our style rules don't allow for this because that's a ridiculous statement. I find I'm bothered by the lack of a label in the *Collegiate*. But when the force of a profane word or slur is felt and perceived differently person to person, how can lexicographers possibly concisely communicate, with one label, its full range of use?

"Bitch" as a word goes back to the turn of the first millennium, when it was used as the name for a female dog, appearing quite a bit in hunting and husbandry texts where the keeping, breeding, running, and whelping of bitches was discussed. In the "dog" use, it was unremarkable: a handy little word. It's likely that the single-mindedness of a dog in heat is what gave "bitch" its extended meaning: "a lewd woman." Around 1400, this sense began showing up in texts; one early citation gives us a line that sounds like it's been pulled straight from the liner notes of a heavy metal album: "þou bycche blak as kole [thou bitch black as coal]." By the time Shakespeare used the dog sense of "bitch" in *Merry Wives of Windsor,* the "lewd woman" sense had seeped into the language. Tellingly, most of our early evidence for this use of the word comes from plays, satires, and other tawdry tales—the pulp fiction of early English. The "lewd woman" sense of "bitch" was, in 1600, therefore considered at the very least informal.

The dictionary makers of the sixteenth century knew about "bitch," of course, because they were cultured men who read about hunting. It's also likely that they knew about and read the plays, satires, and morality tales that used the other meanings of "bitch"— the "lewd woman" sense and another rarely used sense referring to contemptible men. But early dictionaries included entries only for the dog-related sense of "bitch," even though the written record, such as it is, shows that the "lewd woman" sense starts to pick up more use in the mid-sixteenth century, when most of these men were writing their dictionaries. (The general term of abuse for a man doesn't have much of a rise in use at all.) They might have thought the meanings were too vulgar to consider entering. It's also worth considering that early dictionaries were essentially résumés and mash notes rolled into one, so it behooved a lexicographer to consider the station and tastes of a potential patron. If including vulgar words meant that the lexicographer lost a high-powered connection at court, then the obvious answer was to omit the vulgarity in the work.*

Leave it to Samuel Johnson to break the mold; his 1755 *Dictionary* is the first to include a definition for the woman-centric sense of "bitch." It's a striking entry for a number of reasons, not least of which was that Johnson had made it clear that he wasn't about to keep track of slang and nonstandard words for his *Dictionary*. It just so happened that some well-respected Restoration writers (and a handful of nobles, for that matter†) used this sense of "bitch" often enough in their poems and satires that Johnson considered it an established part of English.

That's not to say that he thought the word could be used freely. Instead of defining this woman-centric use as "a lewd woman," which is surely what the most common uses of the word meant, he defined it as "a name of reproach for a woman." It's not a straight-up analytical definition of "bitch"; it's a usage warning and a definition rolled into one.

While some early lexicographers pandered to the delicate sensibilities of the properest of the aristocracy, some went in the other direction toward sensationalism and instead focused on producing the previously mentioned canting dictionaries. "Cant" refers to a type of slang used by various groups on the seedy outskirts of society: thieves, Gypsies, criminals, scoundrels, loose women, and

---

* Florio translates the Italian *fóttere* and its derivatives with register-appropriate slang: "to jape, to sard, to fucke, to swive, to occupy." One must consider the possibility that Florio's patrons were so overwhelmed by his praise in the five dedications that prefaced *A Worlde of Wordes* that they perhaps never made it to *F.* Or maybe they just expected such profanity from Italian.

† Charles II's court was notoriously ribald as a reaction against the Puritan reign that came before. John Wilmot, the Earl of Rochester and an infamous libertine—and given the era, that's saying something—was one of the foremost poets of the age. His poetry mentions masturbation, dildos, homosexuality, incest, and uses the word "fuck" liberally. Take that, Puritans.

loud drunkards. Whatever base, whatever low, whatever dangerous: these dictionaries attempted to catalog it.

The sordid wordbooks weren't all created for love of money; there was actual scholarly interest in "low" language. By the eighteenth century, serious lexicographers were interested in cant. John Ash, for instance, included a number of vulgar and cant words in his 1775 dictionary. He was an English Baptist minister, but his religious calling didn't stop him from both snagging most of Johnson's entry for "bitch" and being the first lexicographer to enter both "cunt" and "fuck" into a general-language, monolingual English dictionary and, unlike Bailey, define them in English.

In 1785, Francis Grose, an educated gentleman with a knack for a good story, published *A Classical Dictionary of the Vulgar Tongue,* which entered both cant and what Grose called "those Burlesque Phrases, Quaint Allusions, and Nick-names for persons, things and places, which from long uninterrupted usage are made classical by prescription." It was the first general dictionary devoted to the bottom end of the vernacular, not just canting slang. Grose and his assistant, the aptly and delightfully named Tom Cocking, didn't just sit over a good dinner and concoct vocabulary: they went on midnight strolls through London, collecting slang words from the docks, the streets, the taverns of ill repute, and the slums, then publishing them in Grose's work. It would be fair to say that Grose and Cocking therefore probably had a very good grasp of how vulgar terms were being used in that moment by ordinary people.

Grose includes this entry for "bitch":

> BITCH, a she dog, or dogess; the most offensive apellation [*sic*] that can be given to an English woman, even more provoking than that of whore, as may be gathered from the regular Billin[g]sgate or St. Giles's answers, "I may be a whore, but can't be a bitch."

A Classical Dictionary of the Vulgar Tongue includes a good number of impolite and rough words; it is worth noting, then, that he calls "bitch" "the most offensive" name a woman can be called. The big lexicographers stuck with Johnson's shorter treatment. Webster steals Johnson's treatment for his 1828 *American Dictionary* and also eschews a label: the definition itself was warning enough. Joseph Worcester, another American lexicographer,* included it in his 1828 abridgment of Johnson's *Dictionary,* also stealing Johnson's treatment, though he makes the choice to omit it from his own 1830 *Comprehensive Pronouncing and Explanatory Dictionary of the English Language.* He notes in the preface that he will not "corrupt the language," and indeed no profanity of any sort is found in Worcester's 1830 *Dictionary* or in any of his following dictionaries.†

But the lure of Johnson was too strong. By 1860, Worcester had caved to "bitch" and added Johnson's second definition to his dictionary. This was the status quo until the end of the nineteenth century. The "name of reproach" definition remained unchanged in dictionaries for well over a hundred years, from 1755 onward.

The actual uses of the word, however, were not so stable. You can get a lovely sense of the rich verdure of "bitch" by reading through the archived proceedings at the Old Bailey, London's chief criminal court from 1674 through 1913. The testimonies, which read like British police procedurals, are rife with "bitches," and few of those for the dog. Most uses of "bitch" found there are the term of abuse directed at women, but as early as 1726 we also find evidence of the word "bitch" used of a gay man:

> There were 8 or 9 of them in a large Room, one was playing upon a
> Fiddle, and others were one while dancing in obscene Postures, and

---

* For more on the soap-opera-worthy relationship between Joseph Worcester and Noah Webster, skip over to the chapter "Marriage."

† "Damn," "hell," and "ass" (referring to the donkey) aren't considered profanity by Worcester. They're in the Bible and so perfectly holy words. The "stupid person" sense of "ass" isn't in the Bible, but it is in Shakespeare, which is a close second.

other while Singing baudy Songs, and talking leudly, and Acting a great many Indecencies. —But they look'd a skew upon Mark Partridge, and call'd him a treacherous, blowing-up Mollying Bitch, and threatned that they'd Massacre any body that betray'd them.

The use of "bitch" as a derogatory term pointed at men predates the Old Bailey: it goes back to 1475 ("Be God, he ys a schrewd byche"). It certainly didn't have the use that the woman-centric "bitch" did, but it shows up with some regularity, especially in the eighteenth and nineteenth centuries. Henry Fielding uses it in *Tom Jones,* and Robert Burns uses it in his Scottish dialect poems of the late eighteenth century. This derogatory use even snuck into college slang of the early nineteenth century: at Cambridge, the student who always served during tea (taking the maid's or mother's place) was called "a bitch." The thrust of each of these uses was clear: men who were called "bitches" were feminized, or less than men.

The eighteenth century thus saw "bitch" bifurcated into two main meaning trunks: one trunk that referred to all things female and feminine, and a new trunk that instead tapped into the difficulty of controlling a bitch in heat. From this, we get the sense of "bitch" applied to difficult or uncontrollable things; from the mid-eighteenth century onward, "bitch" is applied to fortune, poverty, necessity, a boat that stubbornly resists repair, the star that ruled over Lord Byron's love life, and so on.

All these uses of the noun "bitch,"* attested to in a wide variety of sources and not a one of them entered into a dictionary for hundreds of years.

"It doesn't have a label?" Emily asked, frowning. "Really. None?"

We were standing in her kitchen, scuffing around in our socks,

---

* This isn't even taking the verb "bitch" into account—a verb that began life in the sixteenth century and, by 1900, meant everything from "to go whoring" to "to spoil something" to "to complain" to "to drink tea."

having a glass of wine and talking about the day. It's an occupa-
tional hazard that work follows the lexicographer home. You spend
all day elbows-deep in the language, so it's inevitable that you can't
scrub it all off when you leave the building.

We began running through the scenarios together. Could it be,
we wondered, that somehow the label got dropped accidentally? It
did happen: revision slips occasionally went missing, having been
clipped to the wrong galley or having fallen off entirely. Maybe the
data I was looking at just wasn't up to date. Emily leaned on the
counter. Maybe, she offered, the usage note about the word being a
generalized term of abuse was meant to cover both the non-"whore"
sense of "bitch" when used as a slur against women *and* the "weak,
ineffectual" sense of "bitch" when used as a slur against men. She
moved her wineglass from one hand to the other. "A usage note
could take care of both."

"Only if it's its own sense," I said. "This usage note is attached to
the 'malicious, spiteful, or overbearing woman' sense."

"So it can't be in reference to men."

"No."

"Or just . . . women in general. Like women who don't respond
to assholes who catcall them on the street."

"Or women who don't play into hyper-feminized stereotypes."

"Right."

"You know, 'bitches get shit done,' that sort of use. Though,"
I said, "I suppose that's really a reclamation of the slur. Which
means—"

"Oy," she groaned, and took a very large gulp of wine.

Jo Freeman's pamphlet *The BITCH Manifesto* was written in 1968
and published in 1970, right as second-wave feminism crested. The
year of the manifesto's creation, "sexism" was first used in print,
and the first public protest against restrictive abortion laws happened in New York City; the year of its publication, the feminist
activist Bella Abzug was elected to Congress, and two branches of

the Lutheran Church in the United States began ordaining women. What Americans thought about women—and how they talked about them—was in flux. Jo Freeman decided it was time to control the narrative on one particular word that had been applied to women. "A woman should be proud to declare she is a Bitch," Freeman writes, "because Bitch is Beautiful. It should be an act of affirmation by self and not negation by others."

One part of many identity movements is linguistic reclamation. This is a process by which a maligned group—women, gay men, people of color, the disabled, and so on—take an inflammatory slur that's been directed at them as a group and begin using it themselves as an identity marker of pride. It's done to remove power from the oppressor, the linguistic version of catching an arrow shot at you in flight.

But reclamation isn't always so straightforward. First, it assumes that the community which is maligned is just that—a single community, rather than a diverse group of people who happen to share a particular ethnicity, sex, gender, sexual orientation, or state of life. Take the case most often held up as a reclamation success story: "queer," which was reclaimed by the AIDS activist group Queer Nation in the 1990s. Through the 1990s and the first decade of the twenty-first century, "queer" came to be used as a tongue-in-cheek synonym for "gay," even appearing in the titles of TV shows like *Queer as Folk* and *Queer Eye for the Straight Guy.* It was adopted as a label within the gay community first to describe gayness in all its manifestations, then to describe those who didn't want to identify within the traditional binaries: gay/straight, man/woman, male/female. It is just one identity available to those who find their home in the LGBTQIA movement.[*]

And yet, its reclamation was not as universally successful as portrayed. John Kichi, a gay man in his sixties, was horrified in 2013 to

---

[*] Lesbian, gay, bisexual, trans (here referring to either transsexual or transgender), queer, intersex, and asexual. The initialism is still expanding and in flux.

find "queer" listed as a gender on a job application. "I think queer harkens back to a time when being gay was a documented medical abnormality," he told a local news station. "Every one of my gay friends is appalled by this."

The same uneven pattern of reclamation is happening with "bitch." Feminists (mostly white) began to reclaim it in the 1960s and 1970s, while plenty of other women rejected—and continue to reject—the attempt. No matter how commonplace the word became in culture, the naysayers claimed, it was still used negatively. The authors of a 2009 paper in *Sociological Analysis* summarize the anti-reclamation argument: "As feminism taught us long ago, the personal is political; women who normalize 'bitch' also normalize sexism."

The point of linguistic reclamation is to kill the potency of a slur. If I turn "bitch" on its head and use it to refer to a strong-willed, strong-minded woman, isn't that use just as valid—if not more so—as the original slur, or are the authors of that *Sociological Analysis* paper right that "putting 'bitches' into the atmosphere, over and again, sends the message that it is acceptable for men to use the term"?

What if the women reclaiming the word are black women wresting it from male rappers? Does that give the reclamation more—or less—legitimacy? And who gets to say how legitimate black use of "bitch" is? And isn't it pretty racially untranscendent to talk about "black women" reclaiming "bitch" as if all black women were part of the same community? What about other women of color?

What happens if men try to call women "bitch" as a compliment? What happens if straight men do it? How about gay men, or men who identify as feminists? Are men even allowed to be a part of the reclamation process? While we're at it: use of the female dog sense of "bitch" has declined over the last thirty or so years, and now you're just as likely to see "she-dog" or "female dog" or even "girl dog" in print as you are to encounter this sense of "bitch." Can I still call a bitch "a bitch"?

And at the heart, a personal conundrum: How does a lexicographer, who sits within a particular cultural moment, with their own thoughts, feelings, experiences, prejudices (known and unknown), and assumptions—who is tasked with describing, to the best of their ability, the main denotative and connotative meanings of a word—adequately capture and communicate this mucky, hot mess?

Lexicography is linguistic surgery. There's a ritual preparation, a laying out of instruments (pencils, notepads, computer mouse, database). Sometimes there's music in the operating room; sometimes just the whir of machines and the thin-ice silence of concentration robing you like a blanket. There is the first slice into the patient, which could be the beginning of a very long morning full of unexpected complications or the start of a procedure so routine a seasoned surgeon could do it in their sleep.

Surgeons and lexicographers exist within a strange lived duality: your patient—human or verbal—is at once an anonymous sum of parts that you can label, work on, know. Yet at the same time, those parts work in concert with other parts to form a person with a name, a family, a community, a dog, bills, a history, a mystery scar on the chin that you, in your expertise, cannot account for. You are an expert of the part and cannot hope to describe the whole.

It comes down to what's there and how it got there: the meaning of "bitch" as it is applied to women. There are currently two senses to wrangle:

2 a: a lewd or immoral woman
b : a malicious, spiteful, or overbearing woman—sometimes used as a generalized term of abuse

I knew the history of each use, but I was curious about the history of the definitions themselves. The more I thought about the definitions, the more they itched and prickled. Yes, "bitch" has been used of a woman who is *held to be* lewd or immoral; it has been used of a woman who is *held to be* malicious, spiteful, or overbearing. But is that the same as "bitch" being used of a woman who *is* lewd or immoral or who *is* malicious, spiteful, or overbearing? I scooted back from my desk as quietly as possible—my desk chair, a metal and cork contraption from the mid-1960s, squonks like a goose being sat upon, regardless of what high-tech oil I squirt into its decrepit bearings—and padded over to the consolidated files, where all the historical evidence for "bitch" was held. The drawer was jam-packed; the evidence for "bitch" was nine linear inches of paper.

The evolution of the definition is split between two different dictionaries: the unabridged dictionaries, which go back to the 1860s and have changed names a few times, and the *Collegiate* dictionaries, which were originally abridgments of the unabridged dictionaries. The paper trail begins with the entries from the first *Webster's New International Dictionary* of 1909, an unabridged dictionary. There is just one card in the stack, a drafted entry for what was then sense 2 of "bitch," complete with editing marks:

> 2. ~~An~~ opprobriously, ~~name for~~ a woman, esp. a lewd woman; also :
> ~~in~~ less offensively, ~~applied to~~ a man. "Landlord is a vast comical
> bitch." <u>Fielding</u>.

This definition doesn't appear in *Webster's New International Dictionary,* however. What appears in the 1909 is the unedited first half of that definition: "an opprobrious name for a woman, esp. a lewd woman." There are no notes explaining why the "also" was deleted.

For *Webster's New International Dictionary, Second Edition,* released in 1934 (and so referred to in-house as W34), the definition was overhauled again. It was given as "Opprobriously, a woman, esp. a lewd woman; also, formerly, less offensively, a man. *Vulgar.*" This is where the revision proposed decades earlier had ended up, with one notable addition. The assistant editor who wrote this defi-nition, Percy Long, appended a note to his definition: "The citation from the Sat. Review shows that temper as well as morals may be stigmatized by the word. Colloquially it is used to indicate ill will or meanness quite as often as lewdness." The note is undated, but we can assume it was written prior to 1931, when John Bethel, an assistant editor, left this riposte: " 'also, formerly, . . . a man.' This is of course all wet in its use of 'formerly.' It's extremely common in 1931." Bethel's note was rejected.

There's significant chatter in the editorial files about the revisions needed to the *Second*'s definition. John Bethel left a mammoth note in May 1947, breaking down just how wrong the definition found in the *Second* is. He calls for a separation of the one broad sense into separate subsenses for applications to women, men, and things; notes that the use of "bitch" of men is still in use, regardless of what W34 says; and notes that "bitch" as it was used in the mid-1940s wasn't merely "colorless"—that is, merely another word for "woman"—but did imply that there was something wrong with the woman who was being called a "bitch." He closes his note with "In the specific applications the term often, of course, implies 'loose morals,' but in other contexts it (? almost equally often) implies spitefulness or some other extreme flaw of disposition."

Bethel retired in 1952 and moved to the Bahamas but was kept on as a consultant. He tried again to press for a separation of senses in 1954, and another assistant editor, Daniel Cook, took up the charge a year later.

The real changes to the definition came with the 1961 *Webster's Third New International, Unabridged.* The revision of "bitch" for the *Third* fell to Mairé Weir Kay, an associate editor for the *Third*. She was a formidable, no-nonsense woman who demanded excellence and could be brusque or intimidating if she found your work lacking. For most of the post-*Third* years, she was functionally (though not titularly) the editor in chief and was known for the almost forty years she was on staff only as "Miss Kay." She was, in short, the embodiment of the reclaimed "bitch."

The files show her crisp date stamp on a host of citations and

notes dating back to the 1920s. There are two drafted definitions
of hers for "bitch" in our files, from 1956, when primary defining
on the *Third* was under way. Taken together, her revisions are as
follows:

> 2 a : a lewd or immoral woman : trollop, slut—a generalized term
> of abuse b : woman; esp : a malicious, spiteful, and domineering
> woman : virago—usu. used disparagingly
> 3 archaic : man—sometimes used disparagingly

The synonymous cross-references make us wince today. "Trol-
lop," "slut," "virago"? What about Bethel's comment that the word
as used nowadays often refers to the male view of the woman and
not the actual character of the woman? Miss Kay hedged on that by
adding the two usage notes: "a generalized term of abuse" and "usu.
used disparagingly." This is the lexicographer's loophole: when this
word is used to disparage, this is the meaning that speakers and
writers of the word give it.

The third sense was struck by Cook, though there is enough evidence in the files to support it. Sense 2a made it in without edits.
Sense 2b was edited down by Cook to "a malicious, spiteful, and
domineering woman." The general meaning of "woman"—the one
that gets used when men lean out their car windows and scream
"Hey, bitch!" at a woman whose character they cannot comment on
because they do not know her; the one that was used in testimony at
the Old Bailey in the seventeenth century, as in "I'll see you hang'd,
you Bitch!"—was gone. The usage label that Miss Kay added, "usu.
used disparagingly," was also gone. In its place is a definition with
no usage warning, no qualifying label, nothing. Lexicographically,
this use of "bitch" is no different from the use of the noun "baseball" or "milk" or "sweetheart."

Also of note: the "and" in 2b. By this definition, the word "bitch"
is only applicable if the woman in question is malicious, spiteful,
and domineering. If she's benignly domineering or meek yet mali-

cious, then this sense of "bitch" doesn't apply. But looking through the citations marked as "used" for this entry, it's clear that the "and" is a misstep: it really should be "or." Small words have big consequences.

The evolution of "bitch" in the *Collegiate* is more varied. The first edition of the *Collegiate* (published in 1898) used the same definition for "bitch" that the unabridged 1864 *American Dictionary of the English Language* had used: "an opprobrious name for a woman," which was a gussied-up version of Webster's 1828 definition. For the *Seventh Edition* in 1963, the definitions were revised along the lines of the definitions in the *Third:* "a lewd or immoral woman" and "a malicious, spiteful, and domineering woman." The *Collegiate* now had two meanings of "bitch" that were clearly disparaging yet did not carry any stigmatizing label.

It wasn't until the *Tenth Edition* of the *Collegiate* that a usage note showed up in the entry again—this time, at the "malicious, spiteful, domineering" sense. The usage warning was introduced thanks to Susan Brady, one of our associate editors, who left a pink for the copy editor noting that a label was warranted at the entry. Steve, acting as copy editor, inserted the suggest note: "—sometimes used as a generalized term of abuse." Gil, acting as final reader, stamped the note as closed. Closed or not, the note was annotated one more time: our editor in chief, Fred Mish, didn't dispute Gil's decision, but did make his feelings clear with a comment on the pink. "But most often," he wrote, "it means just what the definition says and is not generalized." This exchange happened in the final stages of defining for the *Tenth;* it was 1992.

"Uuuuuugh," my fellow lexicographer Jane Solomon groaned. We had been talking about editing and the difficulty of not bringing your own views and biases to an entry, and I mentioned "bitch." What was wrong with it, she asked, and I held up my index finger— *wait for it.* It didn't even have a "disparaging" label, I told her. She answered, "*Ohhhh,* oh God."

We had started the conversation talking about the word "micro-aggression." It's a relatively new term that refers to the small slights or comments directed particularly at a member of a minority group that could be perceived as inconsequential but are in fact some sort of attack. Mansplaining is often seen as a type of microaggression: a woman can never have the last word, even on something that she's the expert on. Jane had been tasked with defining "microaggression" for one of the online dictionaries she worked on, and we had been talking about the difficulty of getting rid of unconscious editorial bias in definitions that touched on sensitive issues, like "microaggression." She went back and forth with the editor reviewing her entry; Jane had run the definition by a friend who was a civil rights activist to make sure that she had gotten a good grasp on the word's denotative and connotative meaning. But the edits made to her definition were from what she considered to be "a rich, white perspective, unfortunately." Her editor had changed the force of the definition so that the word "microaggression" referred to comments that were merely *perceived* to be offensive. "But, *no,*" she said, "they're just offensive—but offensive in a way that's not always obvious to the person who is perpetrating the offense."

The problem that lexicographers face with a reclaimed word like "bitch" is the same problem that Jane's struggle with the definition of "microaggression" is, just writ large. The force of the word's full meaning is contained in something that lexicographers can't measure: the interplay between intention and reception. What's more important: the intention of the speaker or the reception by the hearer? If I walk down the street and hear a man I do not know, hanging out of his car window, yell, "Nice, bitch!" at me, I will probably not respond as if he had yelled "Nice day!" I will feel disparaged; therefore, I will assume that he meant to disparage, even if he meant to compliment.

Would I feel differently if a woman yelled it at me? Maybe—that depends on my previous experiences with women calling me and each other "bitch," the use of "nice," the tone of voice the caller delivers the statement in, what mood I'm in at that exact moment, how old I am (for I find, as I get older, that I can be bothered less and less with randos on the street hollering dumb shit at me and am more apt to return the insult in kind, thereby proving their initial claim that I am, in fact, a bitch), and whether I think the holler refers to me or, let's say, my teenage daughter who might be walking with me. Is this my own bias against men using "bitch"? Absolutely, one informed by a lifetime of having men sneer "bitch" at me for any reason, all reasons, and no reasons. Can I, in that two-second interlude as the car passes by, even pretend to divine the speaker's intention? And further, I need to consider the possibility that, what with people being such complex animals with palimpsested feelings, the man or woman in question doesn't quite know what exactly *they* mean when they yell "Nice, bitch!" at me.

There's always another person in this equation, not just the speaker and the hearer: the bystander. Because this is what the lexicographer is, in the end—a linguistic bystander. We are not involved in the initial back-and-forth; we only hear about it later, and then in flat prose. What are we to make of citations like these?

- an actress recently described as the reigning *bitch* of the movies.
- It contains his two most memorable characters: Leila Bucknell, the irresistible siren and invincibly successful *bitch,* who manages to be financed by a succession of lovers without losing her position in smart society.
- . . . was a hard *bitch.*
- "So someone calls you a *bitch*?" says Tanisha of BWP. "That's what they call any woman who's tough and good at business. We say, wear the title as a badge of honor and keep getting yours."

Are these uses of "bitch" generalized abuse? Disparaging? It's hard to tell. Some of the citations are so short that you can't even tell if the referent is a woman or a man. The last citation is clearly a remark on the reclamation of "bitch," but it doesn't give you enough information to tell what, exactly, Tanisha of BWP thinks the unreclaimed "bitch" means.

Some dictionaries take on reclamation not with standard definitions but with short essays. Dictionary.com has a short essay on "bitch" that explains that the force of the word depends on who says it and what the intention behind it is. It goes on to talk a bit about the reclamation of "bitch" in the broadest of strokes. It's imperfect, of course—whole books could be written about the word "bitch"—but it's a start, and as dictionaries move online, it's something that more publishers could indulge in.

But this doesn't do away with the two major difficulties of defining reclaimed slurs. The first is that lexicographers have to try to give a general overview of the most common uses of a word, which means that lexicographers need to place themselves squarely in the middle of the most painful lexical interactions and pick them apart to describe them. The reason why lexicographers are loath to wade into this mess leads to the second difficulty: lexicography has historically been (and, frankly, continues to be) the province of well-off, educated, old white dudes. There are today likely more women who are lexicographers than men, but the landscape of lexicography is still overwhelmingly beige. Our own biases are difficult to see, and lexicographers don't always do a good job of setting them aside, because we are only human and eternally under deadline. Daniel Cook couldn't see in 1956 that the second sense of "bitch" really was disparaging; Fred Mish struggled with the same statement in 1992. The people who pointed out that "bitch" was disparaging when used of women were both women, editors who had lived the experience of "bitch."

Modern lexicographers are trained to be objective and leave their own linguistic baggage at the door; modern lexicography is set up to make the definer anonymous and incorporeal. But language is deeply personal, even for the lexicographer: it's the way that we describe who we are, what the world around us is, delineate what we think is good from what we think is bad. The nursery rhyme "sticks and stones may break my bones, but names will never hurt me" is a lie that every five-year-old knows in their deep waters. Words hurt, because they are one of the only socially accepted ways we can attack each other, and suddenly the retiring lexicographer is right in the middle of the melee. When a white lexicographer has to edit the entry for "nigger," they are aware of the centuries of attack the word represents. They are also aware of the attempts to reclaim the word, to wrest from the oppressor that power to unmake a person, and to use the worst slur imaginable as a point of pride. They know they are outside this reclamation. They know that they are, by dint of their whiteness, their education, their position in society, implicated in part of the problem that "nigger" represents. How can that white lexicographer possibly do right by the word "nigger" and all the various opinions on it?

Words are not just personal but corporeal. Lexicographers can grow inured to slurs while defining them—how many times can you read the word "bitch" before it stops even looking like an English word?—but we all have our own lived experiences in the world that prove words have substance. We write them with our hands, we speak them with our mouths, we bear the scars they inflict in our bodies: the fish-line twist of my mother's mouth, sucking on "bitch" like a canker sore as she talks about what it was like to be a woman manager in manufacturing; the three droplets of spittle that hitched a ride with the affricate and flew from the mouth of my dad's friend, in profile against the western sun, as he called his ex-wife a bitch; the heat rash of anger and embarrassment (why embarrassment?) that flares up my cheeks as the cacophony of the city splits like a curtain and allows "bitch" to hang in the spotlight for an airless moment; the fist that clenches in my chest as the car rounds the corner, trailing male laughter and a whiff of gasoline.

Posh

On Etymology and Linguistic Originalism

A person's cubicle is, in some ways, like a storefront church. It's clearly got its purpose—come worship at the altar of the Almighty Nine-to-Five. But because it's not hidden away and anyone can walk past and peer in to see what we're about, we trick it out with little cultural markers that tell the passersby something about the religious inside. The main place of devotion, the desk, is occupied primarily with the tools of our worship: computer, books, files. Around the periphery are the things we carry with us to remind us and our fellow clerics that work is not all that we are: totems and fetishes that we arrange (intentionally, ritually) to advertise the essence of what's inside us. Steve and Madeline both have an abundance of plants in their cubicles; one of our cross-reference editors has set up pictures of her cats (and other people's cats) along the long banked bookshelf each of us has to keep multiple dictionaries open at once. Dan has a few desk toys and some *Far Side* cartoons; Emily has a few artistic photographs and postcards within her view to balance out the feng shui of the giant, inflatable *Collegiate Dictionary* with arms and legs that she won at a company luncheon and that sits on her bookshelf, overseeing her duties like Pharaoh watching the children of Israel.

And then there's Jim Rader's cubicle. Jim's cubicle is not an altar to language but a terrarium of language, a place where language slowly, slowly grows, breathes, takes shape. It's also a marvel of space-time. There is no way that much paper can fit inside a six-by-six-foot work space and allow a human to comfortably work in there, yet all you need to do is walk by and peer over the piles of dictionaries to confirm that, no, Jim's in there, leaning back in his chair, even. One wall of his work space is a high bookshelf, stuffed to overflowing with titles like *Alt-mitteldeutsch Etymologisches Wörterbuch* and *Old Frisian Etymological Dictionary;* his standard-issue desk is literally (sense I) buried underneath a static wave of loose papers, a good number of them covered in a fine scrawl of Proto-Indo-European roots. There are stacks of books on, near, and under his desk that are micro-feats of engineering, the sorts of constructions you hold your breath around for fear of toppling them, but Jim swivels in his chair without regard for them. He will lean back and plop his feet on his desk in a clear spot that wasn't there when he began to unfold, or reach out for a book buried under a sheaf of papers and find it comes neatly into his hand. The rest of us gawp, as if Jim were an alchemist or magician, a Level-Ten Word Mage. He is, in a sense: he's an etymologist.

If logophiles want to be lexicographers when they grow up, then lexicographers want to be etymologists. Etymology is the study of the history and origins of words, lexical genealogy, and etymologists are the practitioners of it. Lexicographers love the nerdy intricacies of a language, trading esoteric factoids like baseball cards, but etymologists master the nerdy intricacies of language, not just a language—language morphology, phonology, and history as a whole. The amount of information they know is almost superhuman. A while ago, after a trip to Finland, I brought in Finnish candy to share with the office. Jim stopped by my desk. "Finland," he said. "Puhutko suomea?" *Do you speak Finnish?*

I blinked. It's rare to meet a Finnish speaker outside Finland, and especially one in your own office. "En puhu paljon suomea. Puhun vähän," I answered. *I don't speak much Finnish. Just a little.* "Entä sinä?" *And you?*

"Ei," he said, shaking his head. "En puhu suomea." *No,* he said in Finnish. *I don't speak Finnish.*

\

This isn't peculiar to Jim. Steve Kleinedler recounted listening to Eric Hamp, one of the more famous etymologists of the modern era (insofar as there are any famous etymologists of any era), explain what a Pan-Scandinavian pronunciation of "Häagen-Dazs" would be, respecting the umlauts and everything, though the ice-cream brand's name is definitely not Scandinavian and so can't really be pronounced in any of the Scandinavian languages. Then Eric talked for half an hour about the Albanian word for "milk." Patrick Taylor, one of the etymologists for *The American Heritage Dictionary,* is in some remote part of central Asia learning Kurmanji—for no other reason than learning an obscure language. "Some of his etymologies take things back to Middle Chinese or Akkadian," notes Steve. "He's crazy. I love it."

Part of why people love etymology is because it tells a story about English and a word's place in it, and sometimes that story tells you something about the culture or time period in which that word blossomed. It makes words literally relatable: "virulent" is just a dumb SAT word that means "malignant" or "intolerably harsh or strong" until you find out that its root word is the Latin *virus,* "poison," the same word that gave us "virus" (no surprises there) and that is akin to the root words for "bison," "weasel," and "ooze."* From that point forward, "virulent" is no longer the province of pundits and English teachers eager to get you into the best colleges; it becomes the hoity-toity East Coast cousin at the weird Virus family reunion, keeping its distance from its muskier relatives.

English is full of these delights, and we eat them up like penny candy. They're not only fun but informative: Why do we call them "sideburns"? It's a play on the name of the Civil War officer who made them popular, General Burnside. Why do we call practical

---

* The Latin *virus* is a wonderfully evocative yet tidy word: it can mean "poison," "stench," "venom," or "slimy liquid." It got its distant tie to "ooze" because of the "slimy liquid" sense, and to "weasel" and "bison" for the "stench" sense.

and unflappable people "phlegmatic"? Because we used to believe that they were unexcitable because they had an overabundance of phlegm in them. Why do we say that someone's "worth their salt"? Because in the ancient world salt was such a valuable commodity that we used to pay people in it (and this is why you also get a *sal*ary). Ah! we cry, and e-mail this factoid to all our friends: see, there's *a reason*!

This is also what makes etymology dangerous. It's easy to assume that no matter how convoluted and ridiculous English seems to be today, it can be straightforward and logical if we trace it back to its beginnings. It's a beguiling idea: that there's a golden plumb line of logic that English follows, and we just need to snag it to unravel the mysteries of this language. Noah Webster himself succumbed. The etymologies given in his 1828 dictionary are based on a complex etymological system he devised himself that assumes all words in all languages stem from one common source language—a language he calls Chaldee.

Webster's push to relate all words was not a linguistic one but an existential one. The section of his *American Dictionary*'s introduction that is titled "Origin of Language" gets right down to brass tacks: "We read, in the Scriptures, that God, when he had created man, 'Blessed them and said to them, Be fruitful and multiply and replenish the earth and subdue it, and have dominion over the fish of the sea, &c.'" Webster goes on to explain that as the Bible says, we all must have spoken one language from creation onward until our innate dickishness (my paraphrase) played out at the Tower of Babel, when God punished our hubris by making us speak different languages—all of which are equally ancient even if they have undergone some changes over the years. Everything, for Webster, should be able to be traced back to an ancient Semitic language, Chaldee. And trace things back he did:

BECK, *n.* A small brook. *Gray.* This word, Sax. *becc,* Ger. *bach,* D. *beek,* Dan. *bæk,* Sw. *back,* Pers͟ bak, a brook or rivulet, is found in the Ir. Ar. Ch. Syr. Sam. Heb. and Eth., in the sense of *flowing,* as tears, weeping. Gen. xxxii. 22 It is obsolete in English, but is found in the names of towns situated near streams, as in *Walbeck;* but is more frequent in names on the continent, as in *Griesbach,* &c.

According to modern scholarship, just about every part of that etymology is wrong. "Beck" comes from Old Norse, which is not listed here, and "beck" is *not* found in Irish, Arabic, Chaldee, Syriac, Samaritan, Hebrew, and Ethiopic in the sense of "flowing, as tears." There *are* words in German, Dutch, Danish, and Swedish that look a lot like "beck" and refer to a small brook, but that's likely because all those words are probably from Old Norse as well. Even his claim that the word is obsolete in English is wrong: it's used in Britain.

This problem with Webster's etymologies underscores an important point about etymology. As Anatoly Liberman, one of the etymologists for the *OED,* has said, "Everything in etymology is conjecture and reconstruction." Webster's etymologies were hit or miss, but they were based on a mostly coherent system that, if you look at it through Webster's lens, is completely logical. "He had the notion that derivations can be elaborated from one's own consciousness," said James Murray, the first editor of the *OED,* and this is the tack that many language lovers and armchair etymologists today take. If the forms match and they seem logical, then how can it be disputed? I had one correspondent tell me that we were incorrect in saying that "sushi" is Japanese: The correspondent's family was Polish, and their grandmother used to eat raw fish and call it *szukajcie,* and this was long before sushi became popular. "Sushi" is close in sound to the Polish *szukajcie,* so the origin of "sushi" must be Polish.

I tell Jim about this theory, and he actually laughs out loud. Ridiculous, he says, and here is where rubber hits the proverbial road, where the difference between the amateur and the professional is laid bare. The earliest uses of the English word "sushi," he tells me, come from travelogues written by Westerners traveling to Japan in the late nineteenth century, which makes sense because there was rising interest in Japan, which had been closed to Western contact for hundreds of years but reopened during the Meiji dynasty, after Matthew Perry's 1853 voyage to the nation. English speakers had consistent contact with Polish speakers as far back as the sixteenth century through trade, and though there was an influx of Poles seeking asylum in England in the mid-nineteenth century, Polish just didn't lend as many words to English as Japanese did. Besides, he finishes, *szukajcie* is the second-person plural imperative form of *szukać,* which actually means "to seek," not "raw fish." He's nonplussed. "This is settled," he says. "Why would this person think otherwise?"

I shake my head, not so much in answer to his question as in wonder at his answer.

The process of finding a word's etymology is about as abstruse as lexicography gets, which is pretty damned abstruse. Etymologists begin their process by working backward. They start pawing through the written record until they've found the earliest Modern English use of the word in question. Then they use a combination of education, research, and (frankly) hunches to move even further back. If the word goes back to Early Modern English, around 1500 or 1600, then the etymologist looks at the context, the spelling, where and who and how the word was used. "Specter," for instance, goes back as far as 1605 in English—nothing earlier. But the etymologist also knows from their training that because of its orthography "specter" is likely not a native English creation. That initial *sp* followed by that *ct*—those are the morphological marks of an Italic language, not a Germanic language (of which English is one). It's very well-known that the Italic language that English speakers have historically had the most contact with is French; the etymologist doesn't have to poke too far to find the sixteenth-century French *spectre,* which means "specter," and the Latin *spectrum,* which means "appearance" or "specter."

Like the language itself, etymology isn't fixed. New scholarship, new sources, new ideas, come to light. People assume that etymologies are either so self-evident that they don't need study or so opaque that the etymologist is literally creating the history out of nothing. Some incantations, a little hand waving, some adverbs, and hey, presto: out of nowhere appears the etymology of "ghost." The books in Jim's cubicle are not for show: he actually refers to the *Old Frisian Etymological Dictionary* to try to find cognates of words that might be coming into the language. And he's always scouring the Internet and other sources for new information. Can you prove that the hairstyle-specific word "mullet" predates the Beastie Boys' 1994 song "Mullet Head"? That sort of information could have etymological implications.

Etymologists give all words their due, and sometimes even more than their due, no matter what the subject matter. In one of the early batches for the *Unabridged Dictionary,* Jim wrote some extensive etymology notes for words like "blephar-" (a scientific prefix meaning "eyelid") that began like this:

Eric Hamp (in *Glotta,* vol. 72 [1994], p. 15) suggests *g^wlep-H-ro- from the base *g^wlep- (whence *blépein*). The variants in initial *gl-* found in Doric—*glépharon* for *blépharon*—are explained by Hamp as outcomes of word-initial *g^wl- with syllabification of the *-l-,* yielding *gul-,* reduced by analogy to *gl- (see his earlier article "Notes on Early Greek Phonology," *Glotta,* vol. 38 [1960], p. 202).

He also left equally scholarly notes at entries like "twerking" ("The hypothesis suggested therein that *twerk* is altered from *work* does not seem convincing. Expressive deformation of a neutral word is not a customary method of English word formation and hence is a rather ad hoc explanation in this case"), the MDMA meaning of "molly" ("In the United Kingdom a parallel name for a powder or capsule form of the drug is *mandy,* which bears somewhat greater resemblance to the initialism *MDMA.* There appears to be no compelling reason to take *molly* as a clipping of *molecular*"), and "asshat," which drily mentions the movies *Raising Arizona* and *City Slickers* before offering a final etymological analysis: "The current meaning of *asshat* may be a reanalysis, perhaps in part based on the expression 'have one's head up one's ass' (meaning 'to be obtuse, be insufficiently conscious of one's surroundings'), perhaps in part due to simple phonetic similarity to *asshole.* A more precise history will depend on the location of further attestations."

It's not all "molly" and "asshat." The etymologies of some words are, for the lexicographer and average joe alike, boring. ("Father" comes from the Old English word *fæder,* which means "father"—big whoop.) But the words that excite etymologists rarely excite anyone else. While working on the *Unabridged Dictionary,* Jim reviewed the etymology for the word "chaus," a word that refers to an Old World cat and that gets very, very little use. Jim dug into the files, and then dug some more, and some more. It turned out that "chaus" stemmed ultimately from a misreading in one manuscript tradition of a word in Pliny's *Historia naturalis* of the word *chaum.* The correct reading is probably *chama.* "Chaum—the *-ma* was read as *-um.* I actually found some manuscripts of Pliny." He pauses. "Yeah, I really got into this."

Prior to the *Unabridged,* the etymology of "chaus" was listed as "origin unknown," which is the wide-open field where armchair etymologists frolic. There are many assumptions about what "origin unknown" means, and none of them are right. To the etymologist, "origin unknown" means that while there may be theories regarding a word's origin, there's no direct evidence that those theories are true. But to most people, "origin unknown" seems to mean "Please send us your best guess as to where this word came from, because we are idiots."

Nowhere is this more evident than in the correspondence we get on the word "posh." The adjective is first attested to in English in the beginning of the twentieth century, meaning "elegant" or "fashionable," and its earliest use appears in a book called *The British Army from Within:* "The cavalryman, far more than the infantryman, makes a point of wearing 'posh' clothing on every possible occasion—'posh' being a term used to designate superior clothing, or articles of attire other than those issued by and strictly conforming to regulations." This suggests military slang, perhaps, but scholars can find no use of an adjective "posh" prior to this. The record seems to drop off a cliff.

That hasn't stopped people from telling us where the word comes from. In the days of steamer travel between England and India, wealthy patrons traveling with the Peninsular and Oriental Company reserved the choicest cabins on the ship, which were the ones that got the morning sun but were shaded in the afternoon—no air-conditioning in the nineteenth century. These cabins were on the left side of the ship on the way out, and the right side on the way home, and so were stamped "P.O.S.H." to indicate that the ticket holder had a cabin that was *p*ort side out, *s*tarboard side *h*ome. The "posh" ticket, then, was for the moneyed, elegant folk, and it was this association with wealth that gave us the "elegant" and "fashionable" sense of "posh" we know today.

This is a fabulous story: it conjures images of women in bustles swooning on deck, canapés, servants in white linen shuffling deck chairs about for the quality. It's also one of those great historical tidbits that sinks into the language and presents a finely sculpted detail to the modern reader. It's beautiful—and total bullshit.

Etymology requires evidence, and in spite of all of the e-mails and letters we've gotten over the years (all the way back to the 1930s, in fact), there is bugger-all written evidence for this origin story for "posh." It's not that there's no one writing about these trips: there's lots of nineteenth-century literature out there about the British interactions with and trips to India. In fact, more and more of that writing is being made public, and we've turned up nary a contemporaneous hint that the "port out, starboard home" theory is true.

The first evidence we have for this theory goes back to a 1935 letter to *The Times Literary Supplement* of London:

> Sir,—In the Oxford New English Dictionary, the supplementary volume, the word "posh" is said to be of "obscure origin." There is reason to believe that it is made up of the initial letters of "Port Out, Starboard Home," an American shipping term describing the best cabins.

Right away, alarm bells sound. The current hagiography of "posh" is that it is British in origin, and yet here's a Brit claiming that it's an American shipping term. Further, the story *always* includes the tidbit about cabins and sun—it's an integral part of the story—and yet it's missing here. Again, this is the earliest citation we have for this theory, and already the details of the story have been confused.

There's another red flag: the acronymic etymology. In spite of the foot stomping over newer acronyms like "OMG" and "LOL,"* we really do love acronyms, and especially acronymic explanations for words. "*C*onstable *o*n *p*atrol," "*t*o *i*nsure *p*romptness," "*g*entlemen *o*nly, *l*adies *f*orbidden," "*w*ithout *p*assport," "*f*ornication *u*nder consent of the *k*ing" (or "*f*or *u*nlawful *c*arnal *k*nowledge," or "*f*orbidden *u*nder *c*harter of the *k*ing," or "*f*ile *u*nder *c*arnal *k*nowledge")†: all of them are the punch line for excellent stories about the supposed origins of those words, and they are all complete "*s*hip *h*igh *i*n *t*ransit." As a word group, acronyms are not very productive in

---

* For more information on the history of "OMG" that will make you pause, foot wavering in midair, sail over to the chapter "American Dream."

† We just cannot accept the fact that such a colorful word doesn't have an amazing story behind it, but *c'est la langue.*

English: they don't give us a lot of new words that stick around. The words that do stick around tend to be technical—"radar" from "*ra*dio *d*etecting *a*nd *r*anging," "laser" from "*l*ight *a*mplification by *s*timulated *e*mission of *r*adiation," "scuba" from "*s*elf-*c*ontained *u*nderwater *b*reathing *a*pparatus," "CAT scan" from "*c*omputerized *a*xial *t*omography." But these are transparent, and so uninteresting. We like our false acronymic etymologies to be sexier, like "*g*ood *o*ld *r*aisins and *p*eanuts" or "*n*orth, *e*ast, *w*est, *s*outh," and it's saying something about the field when "gorp" and "news" are considered sexy.

Acronyms also weren't terribly common until World War II, where they were deployed with aplomb. Unsurprisingly, most of the general words we have in English today that have true acronymic etymologies had their origins in the military: the aforementioned "radar," "GI" (originally "*g*alvanized *i*ron," if you can believe it, but misconstrued by soldiers and others as "*g*overnment *i*ssue"), "snafu" and "fubar" ("*s*ituation *n*ormal: *a*ll *f*ucked *u*p" and "*f*ucked *u*p *b*eyond *a*ll *r*ecognition," brought to you by government bureaucracy). It's true that a few of them snuck into English before the early twentieth century, but very few: "RSVP" (*r*épondez *s*'il *v*ous *p*laît) and "AWOL" (*a*bsent *w*ithout *l*eave) are the only two that could be considered general vocabulary, and some people will complain that one of those is not a proper acronym but an initialism and so doesn't count.[*]

The more elaborate, the more detailed a story about a word's origin is, the more skeptical the etymologist becomes. Look at the general vocabulary words that *have* come into English through interesting stories: look at "sandwich." The name was taken from

---

[*] Properly, an acronym is a word that is created from the initial letters or major parts of a compound term whose pronunciation is a word ("NAY-toe," "SNAF-oo"), and an initialism is an abbreviation created from the initial letters of a compound term, like "FBI," whose pronunciation is a collection of letters ("EFF BEE EYE"). "Acronym" gets used of both of these, however, and such use burns the biscuits of some.

the title of John Montagu, the fourth Earl of Sandwich and quite the gambler. He loved gambling so much that he once sat at the gaming tables for a twenty-four-hour stretch, so absorbed that he didn't stop to take a proper meal but ate cold beef between toast while playing. This bread-and-filling concoction became very much in vogue and came to be called a sandwich.

This is as good a verifiable story as you get in etymology: It's about wayward aristocracy and gambling and snacks. And it has some evidence to back it up—this story was taken from an account of the earl that was written and published during his lifetime, so if the earl wanted to refute it, he could. The account also mentions that the word "sandwich" for the bread-and-filling snack was in popular use in London during the late 1760s, which was contemporaneous with Montagu. The only thing etymologists are missing is a signed affidavit from Montagu himself and a sketch of the sandwich in question.

But you'll notice that the story's details are painted in broad strokes. There's no iconic cry from Lord Montagu asking for beef between bread; no triumphant win and subsequent mythology about the sandwich that made it a lucky charm of players; no shock from the onlookers that he refused to leave the gaming tables. The story we have is a good one, but it lacks a compelling narrative arc. Humans are inveterate storytellers. If history is lacking, we are happy to embellish it. And so, if a story behind the creation of a word has *too* many good details, etymologists grow suspicious.

And with "posh," the details change with remarkable frequency. The tickets were issued for journeys between England and Europe, for the shady side of the ship; or for any unspecified journey leaving Portsmouth, England, to ensure a sunny trip; or for journeys leaving Southampton, England, with the "posh" cabins getting the nice, scenic view and not the crappy one; or for journeys between England and America, so the afternoon sun would warm the passengers (or the morning sun—people are not clear on the position of the sun with regard to the assumed path of the voyage); or for

journeys between America and India, direction of travel unspecified, though it would have mattered, because those "posh" tickets
would have gotten the heat of the South Pacific sun traveling west
from San Francisco. There are so many variations on the story that
you need a map and a sextant to navigate them.

It's not as though lexicographers are actively working against
this theory for the origin of "posh." We have begged and pleaded
for evidence—stamped tickets, earlier uses that tie this somehow
to ship travel, journal entries, pamphlets. Anything that is contemporaneous for the era and written down would be the clincher
that substantiates this. The answer to our cries: crickets. One of
our etymologists wrote, on the back of a citation propounding the
stamped-ticket theory, "Attractive but undocumented. We should
live to see a ticket so marked."

The "port out, starboard home" theory isn't the only one that's
been proposed. Some people hold that the word is Urdu, an adaptation of *safed-pōś,* meaning "white clothed" and then "affluent" or
"well dressed." Others have told us tales of a screen in some courts
in the British Raj that was called a "posh" and that screened the
unwashed masses from the toffs. Some insist that "posh" comes
from "pasha," a word of Turkish origin that referred to a high-
ranking individual in the Ottoman Empire. Great theories all, and
completely unsubstantiated. Because there was a lot of published
material about the British Raj, you'd expect the Urdu word *pōś* to
show up somewhere in the writing of the early to mid-nineteenth
century and be explained as the Urdu word for "affluent" if this was
the origin, but the record is silent. Ditto on the screens, and the luxury
association with the P&O. "Pasha" came into English about three
hundred years before "posh" did, which means that if "posh" were
an adaptation of "pasha," we'd likely have some written evidence
linking the two together.

Linguists have a couple of theories that are slightly more probable than the ones proposed by our correspondents—that the adjective comes from the earlier noun that means "a dandy" or the earlier

slang noun for "money," or that it's somehow related to a one-off use of "push" in a P. G. Wodehouse story that means "fashionable," but even the best guesses of etymologists aren't good enough. We truck in hard facts.

This upsets people, because it bucks against their assumptions of what etymology is: the logical, fairy-tale story of English. But it would be sloppy scholarship to elevate an unsubstantiated theory to the level of researched etymology simply because that theory is au courant. Further, the way that English grows doesn't make sense. The history of English is full of messiness and illogic because the English language is a true democracy, built entirely by the people who use and have used it, and people, generally speaking, are messy and illogical. What genius, for instance, looked at the ragged edge of their sweater, laddering and unknitting itself with energy, and thought, "This is so bad that it's not just raveling; it's super-raveling. No: über-raveling. No, no, I got it: it's frickin' *un*ravel-ing! Like, unreal amounts of raveling. Yeah, I'm going to call this 'unraveling' from now on." Who thought that "pumpernickel" was a good name for a dark rye bread? Because when you trace the word back to its German origins, you find it means "fart goblin,"* and now you cannot help but blench *and* giggle whenever you see pumpernickel.

Some people can't deal with this wending and wandering. If English will not bend to their logic, then their logic will bend to English.

Devotees of what linguists call "etymological fallacy" ardently believe that the best uses of words—by which they mean the purest and most correct uses of words—are the meanings of that word's grandparent, or etymon. "Decimate" is the soldier most often called up for duty by fallacists. How dare, they trumpet, you use "deci-mate" to mean "to cause great harm to"? Its real meaning is "to

---

* Memorize this fact and become the life of your next party.

destroy one-tenth of," as is clear from its etymology (from the Latin *decimare,* "to select by lot and kill every tenth man"). So if you care about language, then you shouldn't use the hyperbolic extended meaning of "decimate." You should only use it to refer to destroying a tenth of something.

It is true that the earliest English use of "decimate" meant "to select and destroy one-tenth of." That's because when "decimate" was first used in English, it was primarily in contexts that described the harsh military discipline of the Romans. "Decimate" in the "one-tenth" meaning came into English in the late sixteenth century, and by the mid-seventeenth century its use had been expanded to refer to causing great harm. For about two hundred years, these two senses lived side by side without any peevery touching them.

In the late nineteenth century, however, Richard Grant White took it into his head that the extended sense of "decimate" was wrong because of its etymology—"to use decimation as a general phrase for a great slaughter is simply ridiculous"—and though it took a while for White's objection to be established, once it was, a long peeving tradition began. A handful of usage commentators in the twentieth century took up White's charge: the "greatly harm" sense of "decimate" was ignorant nonsense. Starting around this time, we have evidence of people's talking about "literally decimating" something—meaning they have selected and killed or destroyed exactly one-tenth of whatever the unlucky target is.

But even usage commentators can't ignore that "decimate" rarely means "to destroy one-tenth of" in English; it's most often used with that extended "greatly harm" sense that's been in frequent use since the late seventeenth century. This is truly logical: as Ammon Shea put it in his book *Bad English,* "How often does one really have the need to say, in a single word or so, that something has had exactly one-tenth taken from it?" Evidently, not very often. So the fallacists changed tack: "decimate" really means "to destroy one-tenth of," and by extension, then, it *can* mean "to greatly harm," but any uses of "decimate" that imply total annihilation are beyond the pale. This view shows up from the mid-1960s onward, and it is the objection raised in the usage literature nowadays.

Etymological fallacy is the worst sort of pedantry: a meaningless personal opinion trying to dress itself up as concern for preserving historical principles. It misses that language change itself is a historical principle: a language that doesn't change is a dead language, and as much as etymological fallacists seem to love the purity of Latin,[*] you'll notice that none of them have abandoned that whore English for it.

For people who love logic and straight lines, fallacists get squiggly if you press them on where, exactly, we draw the cutoff line for etymologically supported use and arrant anything-goes semantic nonsense. For instance, no fallacist suggests that we need to reorder the months of the year because the names for a bunch of them— September through December—don't match up etymologically with their placement in the calendar. *Septem*ber (seven) is the ninth month of the year; *Octo*ber (eight), the tenth; *Novem*ber (nine), the eleventh; and *Decem*ber (ten), the twelfth. No one complains that "redact" is now used to excise writing from text when its Latin root means "to put in writing." No fallacist objects now to words that came about through mistakes or misreadings, like "apron" (which was a fifteenth-century misapprehension of "a napron" as "an apron") or "cherry" (taken to be the singular of the Old French *cherise,* which Middle English speakers wrongly assumed was plural because of the final -*s*), because these mistakes are so very old and well established. If we were, however, to excise these from the language, how would we do it? Would we pick a watershed date for "right" use, and if so, which date? The death of Shakespeare? Dryden? Pope? The zenith of etymological fallacy would be to refuse to admit any words after the Norman Conquest or perhaps the Danelaw. You don't see any agitation for that, however; falla-

---

[*] Itself an impure language that underwent substantial change during the millennia it was in use. Sorry, fallacists.

cists know, in their hearts, that the language is going to keep changing, and no amount of tantrums or threats on their part will stop that.

I speak of etymological fallacy as if it were a new thing, but it's
truly not. People have been fomenting for an English academy, a
ruling body that shapes the language and decides what's official
and what's not, since the early eighteenth century. Daniel Defoe and
Jonathan Swift were the key movers: both felt that English needed
to be cleansed of impurities, polished, and subsequently policed.
Nothing new would get in unless the academy gave the new coinage its imprimatur. Defoe wrote, in his 1697 proposal, that "twou'd
be as Criminal then to *Coin Words,* as *Money.*" Swift, writing later,
noted snarkily that English was in such a terrible state that it has
"not arrived to such a Degree of Perfection, as to make us appre-
hend any Thoughts of its Decay."

French and Continental Spanish both have academies, founded
in the seventeenth and eighteenth centuries, respectively, and it is
true that they issue edicts on which constructions and words are
"allowed," and they have lexicographical arms that issue dictionaries with the "correct" words in them. Be that as it may, that
doesn't stop the French and Spanish from using whatever words
they damned well want.

The call for an academy of English fizzled, though there are still
stragglers to the game, either crying out for its creation or volun-
teering to be that academy. In its absence, though, people who yearn
for definitive guidance have created something similar: *The American Heritage Dictionary*'s Usage Panel.

When *Webster's Third* was released in 1961, it represented a
marked departure from previous Merriam-Webster dictionaries in
many ways, but the thing that gained the most notoriety was a new
Websterian adherence to describing as much of the language in use
as possible, including contested uses (like the extended sense of
"decimate"). There was a swift backlash from the literati of the day
who deplored what they perceived as laxity in Webster's defense of
the language. There was extensive bewailing of the death of English,

sped along by the "passel of double-domes at the G. & C. Merriam Company joint," as one *New York Times* editorial put it, and along with the pearl clutching came several high-profile requests to pulp the entire run of the *Third* and go back to the good old days of *Webster's Second,* which didn't shy away from using labels like "illiterate" and "uneducated." But Merriam sailed onward, heedless of the calls for reform (no doubt because the idea of junking the *Third,* a dictionary that took more than a hundred editors twenty-seven years to complete, sent the then president of the company into apoplexy). The *Third* was one of its flagship products, and the G. & C. Merriam Company would abandon it when hell froze over.

One James Parton, the publisher of *American Heritage* magazine, decided to do all he could to make it snow. In 1962, a few months after the release of the *Third,* he began buying up shares of Merriam stock with the view of buying out the company. His reason: the company "badly needs new guidance," and the *Third* was "an affront." His plans were to "take the Third out of print! We go back to the Second and speed ahead on the Fourth." When the hostile takeover failed, he did the next best thing: he created his own dictionary to right Webster's wrongs and give America the authority it clamored for.

The authority upon which *The American Heritage Dictionary* rested was its Usage Panel, a group originally of 105 writers, editors, and professors who were convened as a cabal of English experts, people who would decide which particular words and phrases were acceptable and which were not. Once a year, the lexicographers at the *AHD* send ballots to the panelists asking if they would find certain things acceptable in speech or writing. The first panel was reactionary in its founding—among the experts were a number of very vocal critics of *Webster's Third*—but some of their opinions are surprisingly moderate. The December 1964 ballot for "ain't," a word that was singled out in criticisms of *Webster's Third,* gives a slightly more nuanced approach than you would expect for a group of people who had it in for the *Third.* When asked about the accept-

ability of "I'm right about that, ain't I?" 16 percent of the panel
allowed it in speech, and 23 percent regarded it as more acceptable
in speech than "It ain't likely" (which was roundly dissed; only
1 percent of the panel found that acceptable in speech or writing).
Malcolm Cowley, author and literary critic, finished off his 1966
ballot for the first edition of *The American Heritage Dictionary*
with a cautionary epitaph, "There is always the danger that we, the
so-called authorities, should become too damned pedantic," and
Isaac Asimov pleaded, "My opinions are strong, but not necessarily
authoritative. Please realize that."*

Nonetheless, the panel has historically trended toward being linguistically conservative, particularly in eschewing both new meanings of old words and functional shift (that is, a word's moving from
one function to another, like the verbing of nouns). If there was
ever a haven for fallacists, the panel was it. And while they hold to
bits of etymological fallacy—in the early years of the twenty-first
century, 58 percent of the panel reported that in their own writing
they restricted the use of "dilemma" to refer to one of two options
rather than using it as a general synonym of a problem, because
its root "di-" means "two"—enough of the panel finds the positive
"awfully" and the great "fantastic" so unremarkable that usage discussions for these two words don't even appear in the latest edition
of *The American Heritage Dictionary*.

People who supposedly care about correct English love the
Usage Panel, but for reasons that are all smoke and mirrors. The
panel didn't have, and still doesn't have, authority to decide which
words are actually entered into the *AHD*. Steve Kleinedler says, "I
think everyone on the Panel recognizes the role of a dictionary. No
one has ever said, 'Ain't shouldn't be in,' or 'Irregardless shouldn't
be in.'" Good thing, too, because "irregardless" and "ain't" both

---

* Not everyone was as circumspect. The historian Barbara Tuchman, another
panelist, roundly rejected the use of "author" as a verb with "Good God, No!
Never!"

appeared in the first, most conservative edition of the book, and they continue in it today, stubborn barnacles of nonstandard English that can't be completely scraped off the hull of the language. (Interestingly enough, only 90 percent of the panel disapprove of "irregardless," which makes me wonder: Who are the turd stirrers infiltrating the panel?) Today, the panel comprises 205 people; they are, as a whole, much less linguistically conservative than their forebearers. Eighty-one percent of them, as of the 2005 balloting, have no problem with the extended sense of "decimate" that refers to widespread death, not just death restricted to one-tenth of a group, and 36 percent of them are fine with the sense of "decimate" that refers to extensive damage (as in "The crops were decimated by drought").

"These things can have a complex history," says Jim Rader, but few of us want to live with that complexity. We think that we have the right to go through the photo album of English's life and throw away the pictures that don't make sense—blurred pictures, or snaps from that unfortunate stage when it was surly and uncooperative. But those deviations from the plumb line contain surprises and delights not just about English but about the world we live in. "OK," which might just be one of the most widely understood English words in the world, came into being as an initialism from "oll korrect," which was a facetious misspelling of "all correct" that came about because of a short-lived fad in the early nineteenth century for intentional misspellings and the abbreviation thereof. And now you, too, know that there was a short-lived fad in the early nineteenth century for intentional misspellings.

English has survived through conquest and adaptation, and many of those adaptations are blunt mistakes and misreadings. A living language made by fallible people will not be perfect, but it will occasionally make for remarkable reading.

American Dream

On Dates

Lexicographers don't expect their readers—normal people who have a healthy relationship to reference works, which is to say, a casual one—to scrutinize every part of a dictionary entry. But there is one small part that ends up getting a lot of attention: four numbers hugged by parentheses. A date.

Dates haven't always been a part of dictionary entries. They are an innovation brought to market by historical dictionaries like the *OED,* and they're a feature primarily of historical dictionaries. By most general dictionary publishers, dates at entries were deemed impractical and uninteresting to the layperson. But those publishers were wrong: dates are popular.

Our dating project, as we call it in-house, has an odd history. Dates at entries were proposed by Merriam-Webster's then president, Bill Llewellyn, back in the 1980s. The reaction from the editorial department was extremely negative; the amount of work it would require to track down the dates of first written use seemed prohibitive. The company would need an army of editors scurrying around the country's libraries looking for dates for new and existing entries. Llewellyn wanted something that would make Merriam-Webster dictionaries more distinctive, and he told the editorial department that if it didn't want to add dates, that was fine, but then it needed to come up with something else. The senior editorial staff settled on adding usage paragraphs to a handful of entries in place of the dates. "Of course, what happened," says Steve Perrault, "is that when that was done and we presented them to Bill Llewellyn, he said, 'Okay, good, we'll put those *and* the dates in.'"

"That was an enormous project," says Joanne Despres, our senior dating editor, "because everything had to be dated from scratch." The daters, as we call them in-house, began by checking the *OED,* the granddaddy historical dictionary of them all, and then moved to more specialty dictionaries, like the *Middle English Dictionary* and the *Dictionary of American Slang.* From there, we moved into our own library and citation files. It was a massive undertaking but was finished in time for the *Ninth Collegiate* in 1983.

It turned out Llewellyn was right: everybody loves the dates in the *Collegiate.* So much so that we've begun adding them to entries in the *Unabridged Dictionary* as well.

At Merriam-Webster, the dates represent the first time that an English word was used in print (in English) with the earliest meaning given in that dictionary. You may be able to tell from the awkward and deliberate wording of that statement that there is plenty of misunderstanding about the nature of the dates.* The biggest misunderstanding is that a date of first written use is the date of that word's creation. At one conference I attended, a speaker noted that according to the *OED* Jane Austen was the first author to use the words "shoe-rose" and "shaving glass" in her novels—which says some interesting stuff about the sort of world that Jane Austen inhabited and depicted—but then went on to claim that Jane Austen invented these words because she was the first to use them in print. I maintained an outward detached, scholarly air as I listened, but inside I had slapped a figurative hand to my forehead, à la Homer Simpson. A little thought reveals that the idea is complete nonsense. Why would Jane Austen have created new words for very common items of the toilet—items that were in use and already had common

---

* Even though we explain what those dates represent in the front matter of the dictionary, which we evidently write and proofread entirely for our own amusement.

names—and use these new words, unglossed and unexplained, in her books? It's likely she wouldn't have. She would likely have explained, in running text, what a shoe-rose or a shaving glass is if she felt that her audience was going to be unfamiliar with it. She did not, because those words were already circulating in society by the time Jane Austen wrote her books.* Jane Austen is not the person to have coined those words.

Most words come into being first in speech, then in private writing, and then in public, published writing, which means that if the date given at the entry marks the birth of a word, the moment when it went from nothing to something, then Merriam-Webster must have an underground vault full of clandestine recordings of each word's first uttering, like something out of the Harry Potter books, only less magical. But the fact remains: because of how words are born, we will probably never know who coined a particular word and when they first used it, because language begins as something private and then moves into the public sphere.

Jane Austen will eventually lose her claim to "shoe-rose" and "shaving glass." Dates of first written use change frequently because new material comes to light, either by being published for the first time or by being digitized and easily searchable. "The number of full-text databases has multiplied, and now we're using them almost exclusively," says Joanne.

Dates can also change depending on the dictionary. Because we date to the first written use of the earliest entered sense of that word, we may have a different date for the word in the *Unabridged Dictionary* if there is an early obsolete sense in the *Unabridged* that isn't in the *Collegiate Dictionary*. "Actress" in

---

* "Shoe-rose" is used in *Pride and Prejudice* (1813), but a quick search turns up evidence of it in print back to 1801; "shaving glass" appears in *Persuasion* (1817, give or take), but I can trace it back to 1751. The *OED* entries for "shoe-rose" and "shaving glass" haven't been updated since 1914, but I'm sure that when the editors at Oxford get to *S,* they'll find my quick-and-dirty antedatings—and then some.

the *Unabridged Dictionary* is dated to 1586, and to 1680 in the *Collegiate*, because the *Unabridged* enters the earlier and obsolete sense "a woman that takes part in any affair," whereas the *Collegiate* only enters the common "a woman who is an actor" sense.

Because the dates are so precise in a way that seems measurable compared with the precision of a good definition—it's just a number!—they are the one part of a dictionary entry that many correspondents like to pick at, like scabs. Many people think that the dates don't describe the word but the thing represented by the word. "Boston marriage" (defined in the *Unabridged Dictionary* as "a long-term loving relationship between two women") is a good example. As best we can tell, the term wasn't used to describe this relationship until 1980, which some people decry as startlingly late. We have received long e-mails on the subject of hidden lesbianism throughout the ages, which are always educational but don't shed any light whatsoever on the term "Boston marriage." Some point out that Henry James described one such relationship in his 1886 novel *The Bostonians*; well and good, but he never used the phrase "Boston marriage" to describe that relationship, so we can't cite the book as the origin of the phrase.

Sometimes, a correspondent will forget what language we're dating in. "I noticed that some of the word origin dates are really off," one correspondent wrote recently. "For example, it says that 'brothel' was first used circa 1566, when in reality Tacitus used the term in his account of Rome burning as far back as A.D. 64." Tacitus did mention brothels in his *Annales,* but he used the Latin word *lupanaria* for them, and *lupanaria* has been translated into English as "brothel." That makes a good deal of sense, because Tacitus was a Roman (and therefore Latin-speaking) historian who flourished at the end of the first century A.D., a few centuries before English was even around as a language. Even when a word is borrowed directly from another language, we only look for evidence of that word that marks it as a fully English word. "Safari" was snatched into English from Swahili, but we are only concerned with the earliest point at

AMERICAN DREAM   •   193

which the word was clearly, undeniably English: "These Safari are neither starved like the trading parties of Wanyamwezi nor pampered like those directed by the Arabs."

We have a cadre of scholars and language lovers who are looking to antedate our date—that is, find an earlier use than the one we draw our date from. It's a natural impulse: everyone likes to one-up the experts, and the dates seem like a relatively easy place to do your one-upping.

On Twitter not too long ago, I was discussing the term "dope slap," which I had traced back (using what was available to me at the time) to Tom Magliozzi, one of the hosts of NPR's show *Car Talk*. A dope slap is, as Ray Magliozzi, Tom's brother, says, "kind of a quick slap to the back of the head when the recipient is unaware that it's coming," and when Tom Magliozzi first used it in a *Car Talk* blog post, it was clear that the dope slap got its name from the dopey target of the smack: "Well, the first thing I'd do is give that kid a dope slap for driving home after the oil light came on. When the oil light comes on, you should always stop the engine immediately." "I scoured all my sources and found nothing earlier than that," I said. "Which means that someone will antedate it immediately."

It only took fourteen minutes before someone chimed in to tell me that there was a Dope Slap Records putting out music in 1990. It's true that there was, but because this appearance of "dope slap" shows up in a name and not in running text, it's very difficult to tell what, exactly, it means. I said as much—good googling, but probably not an earlier date.

Six minutes later, my Twitterer found another instance from 1990, this time in running text: "the first annual Dope Slap Awards," used in reference to the video *Hockey: "A Brutal Game."* He was not going to give up; he was going to get his antedate, goddamn it. But all the same, there's nothing in that citation he linked to from *The Ottawa Citizen* to tell me that this "dope slap" refers to the upside-the-head smack that I was highlighting, and that's the particular sense that we're dating here.

Though my Twitter friend was wrong in this instance, well-researched efforts like his can turn up antedatings that we've missed. Joanne sighs when we talk about this. In one dating spreadsheet we use to keep track of where an antedating was found, there are sixty-five listed sources to check—everything from a rough couple dozen dictionaries of varying vintage, to newspaper databases and archives, to repositories of scholarly works (like JSTOR and PubMed), to our own editorial library, scattered throughout the building and definitely not digitized. There is no ur-script we can run on those databases to query all of them efficiently; there is no easy way to sift through the results; there is no program we can run to dump all the false positives we get (scanning errors, database errors, query errors, errors that appear like gremlins in the machine just to fuck with you). Each result has to be looked at by a dater and evaluated—and all that for hundreds of thousands of entries and under deadline. "We have to cover so much material. I don't have more than an average of fifteen minutes to research any given entry," says Joanne. "Some of these guys are spending days doing deep research into every obscure newspaper archive they can find." She shrugs. "They help us, you know, by digging this stuff up."

Because dating relies so much on meaning, it's just as squishy an enterprise as defining is. "It involves the same kind of semantic analysis that defining does, I suppose, although you don't have to be productive. You don't have to write the definitions, you just have to understand what's being said," says Joanne. But unlike defining, you have to hunt around for your source material, and this can lead the dater down a rabbit hole. Most uses that Joanne found of "day hike," which we enter in the *Unabridged Dictionary* defined as "a hike that's short enough to be completed in a single day," were nearly indistinguishable from the meaning of "a hike taken during the day," which is not entered in the *Unabridged Dictionary* and so is not the meaning that a dater is looking for. Searching through databases for uses of "day hike" turned up so many results for the "hike during the day" sense that Joanne eventually abandoned the method of searching in batches and went through everything she could from 1950 backward, year by year, looking for evidence of the "short hike" sense (as opposed to the "hike during daylight" sense) until she didn't find any uses of "day hike" referring to a short hike for several years running. This was her indication that she had probably found the earliest written use of "day hike" meaning "a short hike" that we were going to find. The date we give this sense of "day hike" in the *Unabridged* is 1918. There are earlier uses: they are for a sense that we don't enter, and so are invalid.

This is the bit that frustrates antedaters: earlier evidence may be rejected if it doesn't seem to clearly and completely fit the earliest given sense. "I'm very proud of 'American dream,'" says Joanne. There were several variations on the sense that's familiar to us now—"an American social ideal that stresses egalitarianism and especially material prosperity; *also* : the prosperity or life that is the realization of this ideal"—and she found a number of early citations that didn't quite fit:

The arrangements for shopping, like everything else, are divine. Public bands are playing seraphic music through the whole twenty-four hours, and you turn on the piece you like by telephone. Public buildings are palaces, and their equipment is a paragon of luxury. We only wonder how the unspeakable privileges of the city can be extended to the country, and who will be contented to stay in the country if they are not. The American dream is of city life.

This 1893 citation is excellent, but "it suggests material prosperity without the crucial element of egalitarianism," Joanne explains. It's not enough that the citation almost covers the current meaning: it must unequivocally do so. Could you read egalitarianism into that citation? Maybe, but it would be reading something into the citation, not basing your judgment on what's actually there.

The citation Joanne found as the first written use of this particular sense of "American dream" ironically tolls the bell for the
American dream itself:

> Every republic runs its greatest risk not so much from discon-
> tented soldiers as from discontented multi-millionaires. They are
> very rarely, if ever, content with a position of equality, and the
> larger the population which is said to be equal with them, the less
> content they are. Their natural desire is to be a class apart, and if
> they cannot have titles at home, they wish to be received as equals
> by titled people abroad. That is exactly our present position, and
> would be the end of the American dream. All past republics have
> been overthrown by rich men, or nobles, and we have plenty of
> Sons of the Revolution ready for the job, and plenty of successful
> soldiers deriding the Constitution, unrebuked by the Executive or
> by public opinion.

This citation sounds as if it were written last year. It's from 1900.
This is one of the joys of dating: everything is older than you
think it is. The linguist Arnold Zwicky has coined the term "the
recency illusion" to refer to the misbegotten assumption that anything that strikes you as new in language is a recent innovation,
when, in fact, it's not. Those dates in the dictionary prove that many
modern linguistic bêtes noires go back quite a ways. Clipped words
like "wevs" for "whatever" and "obvi" for "obviously" often show
up in the mouths (and in the texts) of youth and are therefore derided
as lazy. The articles bewailing the death of English at the hands of
young people with cellphones are too numerous to cite, but few
authors of these jeremiads against technology realize that clipping
slang predates the cellphone by centuries: John Gower used "hap,"
a clipping of "happening," in his *Confessio Amantis* ("A wonder
hap which me befell"), and that was written in the late fourteenth
century. Ah, but those horrid initialisms, naysayers cry—"LOL"
and "OMG"—surely a mark of modern laziness, moral decline, and

the end of Good English as we know it! Never mind that these nay-sayers use plenty of initialisms themselves—please RSVP ASAP and BYOB. Or that "OMG" goes back to 1917, when it was first used in a letter to Winston Churchill. What now? Shall we blame the decline of English on typewriters?

People rarely think of English as a cumulative thing: they might be aware of new coinages that they don't like, but they view those as recent incursions into the fixed territory they think of as "English," which was, is, and shall be evermore. The dates put the lie to that assumption. "The point at which [a word] entered the language is something that never occurs to people unless they see that date, and it just gets them to thinking a little bit about the history of the word," says Joanne. She's right: you realize that much of our vocabulary sits in a current of English that you don't see on the surface of your patch of river. The rise of Indian cuisine in America over the last thirty years means that more of us are familiar with the word "korma," but it first appeared in English in 1832. "Child support" sounds like a coinage born of the late-twentieth-century rise in divorce; in fact, the word dates back to 1901.

People also want to have some deeper connection with the word, to take responsibility for it, or to know some secret part of it. It's not enough to know how to spell a word or what a word means; you have to *know* it.

The most heartfelt people who write in are the ones who have come across an entry in our dictionary and write to tell us that they have a surefire antedating for us: they coined the word. This is almost always untrue, but the phenomenon is endlessly interesting. They always come with a personal story attached, with brilliant clarity of detail: I coined the term "wuss" in my dorm room at Princeton University in 1969, long before the date you give; you say that "noogie" appeared in 1968, but I grew up with kids getting and giving noogies in grade school, and I was already in graduate school by the time you say the word was created; I was born in

Staten Island in 1926, and by 1932 I was ordering ice-cream cones with jimmies, and by 1942 I was adding jimmies to ice-cream cones and sundaes as a soda jerk, which proves that your date of 1947 for the word "jimmies" is wrong. People are unswayed, even when we turn up hard evidence of the word in print that antedates their own date: "When I come back and give them earlier evidence, they continue, some of them, to assert that, no, no," says Joanne. They are claiming their stake in this language: the word "cyberstalk" or "vlog" or "ginormous" belongs to *them* first and foremost, regardless of the evidence to the contrary.

Though hunting down dates for words can sometimes feel like gearing up for a lexicographical pissing contest—can we beat the *OED*?—there is something inspiring and educational about tracing a word back to a particular point in time. You learn things about little lexical whims that ended up sticking: the fad for contractions in the seventeenth century that never went away, the mania for Latin hypercorrection through the nineteenth century. You realize that it's not just coincidence that we ended up with a bunch of food words from Yiddish and Chinese and Polish in the mid- to late nineteenth century: they're there as a direct result of the waves of immigrants who came to English-speaking countries in the nineteenth century. Chasing dates is a journey through history; sometimes you get to your destination quickly, and other times you get a long scenic drive past Winston Churchill's private correspondence.

Nuclear

On Pronunciation

It was Emily Vezina's first week of work, and she was still getting used to the atmosphere of the editorial floor. She had gleaned one office rule very quickly: no talking. So imagine her surprise when her mandatory reading of the *Third*'s front matter was interrupted by a voice, speaking at a normal volume and in a calm, measured tone: "Pedophile."

She shook it off—*ooookay*—and tried to return to reading front matter when she heard another voice chime in, equally dispassionate: "Pedophile."

Now it was getting creepy. The whole office was taking part, like some horrible incantation: person after person, down the row of cubicles. "Pedophile." "Pedophile." "Pedophile."

Suddenly at her arm was Josh Guenter, our pronunciation editor. He held a blue index card out to her, upon which was written the word "pedophile." "How do you say this?" he asked, and she obliged. "Pedophile," she said. He scratched something out on a pad of paper, nodded, and moved to the next cubicle, where another editor looked up, blinked, and announced "pedophile."

It was not some bizarre hazing ritual. He was polling the office to figure out how to order the pronunciations for the *Collegiate Dictionary*.

Anyone who visits the office can feel the busy quiet settle on them like a blanket. On a warm afternoon, it can be very hard to stay awake in the cosseted hum of computers and people breathing. So it was very odd, about a year into my tenure, to be standing in one of the more remote hallways on the floor looking for a German dictionary and hear what sounded unequivocally like conversation coming from a nearby office. Then I heard a laugh track. A pause, and then the interlude repeated: same murmured conversation, same laugh track. A light went on: I was standing outside the pronunciation editor's office. He was taking citations.

All lexicographers are collectors and collators of information, but the pronunciation editor is the only lexicographer who doesn't pay any attention to the Reading and Marking list or worry about finding space in their office for all the source materials they're sifting through. They collect pronunciations from instances of speech. That means, in short, that the pronunciation editor gets to spend all day watching TV. (Josh hesitates. "I spend more time on YouTube," he says.) There is a small television in his office, along with a radio, a tape recorder, and the requisite books spilling from shelves.

It may shock you to hear that the pronunciation editor doesn't just make up the pronunciations you find in your dictionary. "I'm flattered that you think I have a vocabulary of 100,000 words," says Josh, "but this is not me." The pronunciations found in dictionaries end up there through a process of collection, arranging, and analysis that is similar to the process used for definitions.

Taking citations for pronunciations (or prons, as the lingo goes) is a different critter, however. Context doesn't matter at all for pronunciations; what does matter is a clear articulation of the word in question. Pron citations come from three main sources: broadcast media (which includes radio, TV, movies, and cable), audio or video on the Internet (YouTube and podcasts being the big generators), and human contact (phone calls, the aforementioned office polls, and face-to-face conversations). Steve Kleinedler, who handles the pronunciations for *The American Heritage Dictionary,* has occasionally sent me links to promotional videos pharmaceutical companies have put together for various products. Both Josh and

Steve regularly call up companies, town halls, and famous people (mostly Nobel Prize winners and presidents) to ask them how they say the name of their product, their hometown, or themselves. If there's more than one pronunciation and Josh isn't sure which one to list first, he might go around with a clipboard and an index card for an office poll to see if he can get a better sense of which pronunciation is more common after making us all say something in our raspy, unused voices. When watching or listening to a source, Josh will transcribe what that source says onto a white citation slip, give the bibliographic evidence, and then file it away.

How Josh writes it down is the real trick. English is not a phonetic language—that is, there's not a one-to-one correspondence between a letter and a sound that it represents. So when it appears at the beginning of a word, the *g* in English has two sounds—the sound at the beginning of "girl" and the sound at the beginning of "giraffe"; *c* has three-ish sounds, depending on where it is in the word and what's around it—the sound at the beginning of "cat," the sound at the beginning of "citrus," and the sound in the middle of "politician"; and so on. That means that when writing down a pronunciation, you can't rely on the twenty-six letters in our alphabet to give an accurate representation of what was said. "SPRAHCH-geh-FYOOL"—huh? Is that \CH\ as in "chat" or as in the first raspy sound in "Chanukah"? Is that \AH\ as in "ax," or the first *a* of "again"? All that uncertainty means you might end up pronouncing "sprachgefühl" like "SPRATCH-gay-FULL" or "SPRUTCH-geh-FOOL," and you would be very wrong.[*]

That's why dictionaries use a proprietary alphabet[†] full of odd letters like $\bar{a}$ and ∂ and η. They help us accurately portray the pro-

---

[*]   Why do some pronunciations get set off in double quotation marks and others with backslashes? This is another esoteric lexicographical convention: phonetic renderings of a pronunciation get the quotation marks and normal letters, while actual pronunciations in the weird alphabet get set off by forward slashes.

[†]   And each company has its own proprietary alphabet, just to be difficult.

nunciation of "sprachgefühl" as \ˈshpräḵ-gə-ˌfᴕel\,* even if they do
drive people crazy because you need a key to decipher them. These
alphabets are phonemic, not phonetic. The letters in a phonetic system represent one sound per letter; the letters in a phonemic system
represent a group of sounds per letter, because an individual pho-
neme (the smallest unit of sound in an utterance, and the thing that
our pronunciation alphabets represent) can vary depending on your
accent and dialect. Take the symbol that we use to represent the *i* in
"pin": \i\. In a phonemic system, we tell you that \i\ is pronounced
like the *i* in "pin" regardless of how that vowel actually *sounds*
when it leaves your face. If, in your native dialect of English, you
say "pin" or "pen" or "payin" or "pehhn" when you read the word
"pin," that symbol represents all the *sounds* represented by that
vowel. This means that we can cover a variety of accents and dialects and not have to privilege one over the other. This means that if
you say \PIN\ for "pin" and "pen" (a phonological feature in some
parts of the country called pin-pen merger), but I say \PIN\ for "pin"
and \PEN\ for "pen," the dictionary doesn't, through its pronunciations, say that one of us is right and the other wrong. Those weird
alphabets allow for different phonological quirks.†

Pronunciation editors need training not just in phonemic and
phonetic alphabets but in listening. They need to know about the
phonological characteristics of most of the dialects in at least the
country they're writing in, if not a good sketch of the phonological
traits of English around the world. Josh asked where I was from at
one point, and when I told him, he said, "Oh, General Western. So
you have 'cot-caught' merger, and 'Mary-merry-marry' merger?"

---

*   KEY:
    \ā\ as in *a*ce; \a\ as in *a*sh; \ä\ as in m*o*p; \ē\ as in *ea*s*y;* \e\ as in b*e*d; \ə\ as in
    *a*b*u*t; \ī\ as in *i*ce; \i\ as in h*i*t; \ō\ as in g*o;* \ü\ as in l*oo*t; \ᴕe\ as in German
    füllen; \ˈ\ primary stress; \ˌ\ secondary stress.

†   Some folks ask why we don't make everything simpler by using the Inter-
    national Phonetic Alphabet instead of whatever weird system we're using,
    but the answer is in the name: "International Phonetic Alphabet." IPA, as it's
    called, isn't accent agnostic.

I evidently did, though I didn't know what those were until he explained that some dialects use different vowels for "cot" and "caught" and for each of the "Marys." I do not; when I talk phonology with people, I talk of the "cot-cot" and "Mary-Mary-Mary" mergers.

Because pron editors can hear these fine distinctions, they can also articulate these distinctions, so they're also often called upon to be the ones to record the audio pronunciations in the electronic dictionaries. When Josh was in grad school, before he worked for Merriam-Webster, he had been hired by *The American Heritage Dictionary* to record some pronunciations for its website; now he records the new pronunciations for ours. It's a relatively manageable job now, only a few thousand new words to research and say at most, but back in the mid-1990s we had the entire *Collegiate Dictionary*'s prons to record for the new website—close to 150,000 pronunciations. It was too many for one person. Four actors—two men and two women—were hired to record the vast majority of the pronunciations. Only two groups of words were held back and done in-house by our pron editor: words that had pronunciations with sounds that were difficult for native English speakers to make (like "sprachgefühl") and profanity. Peter Sokolowski remembers being in the hallway outside the pronunciation editor's office one day and hearing from within the office a very measured voice say, as blandly as possible, "Motherfucker. Motherfucker. Motherfucker." It was one of our old pronunciation editors, trying to get the intonation right for the audio file. He left a few years later to become a priest.

Audio prons are one of the great advantages of an online dictionary. You no longer need to figure out that ridiculous key; now you just click on the little speaker icon, and you can hear the word pronounced for you. Pronunciations in dictionaries have not always been so accessible.

Many early dictionaries, written as they were for those learning English as a foreign language, provide some basic guidance in pronunciation, though it's not where we moderns expect it to be. Often, the pronunciation help was given in a long section of prose at the beginning of the dictionary, sometimes disguised as grammar or orthography or prosody. Mulcaster's 1582 *Elementarie* (*"Vvhich Entreateth Chefelie of the Right Writing of Our English Tung"*) is a good early example. It gives lengthy explanations of the writing and sound of most of the letters in the alphabet before getting to his dictionary, though he is not exhaustive: he goes on about the sounds of *e* for several pages, but has two sentences devoted to the sound of *a* ("A Besides this generall note for the time and tune, hath no particular thing worth the obseruation in this place, as a letter, but it hath afterward in proportion, as a syllab. All the other vowells haue manie pretie notes").

Johnson handled pronunciation in the grammar that he appended to his 1755 *Dictionary,* and he set up his aim with a short excerpt from one Dr. Wilson, written in 1553. "Pronunciation," it begins, "is an apte orderinge bothe of the voyce, countenaunce, and all the whole bodye, accordynge to the worthines of such woordes and mater as by speache are declared. The vse hereof is such for any one that liketh to haue prayse for tellynge his tale in open assemblie, that hauing a good tongue, and a compelye countenaunce, he shal be thought to passe all other that haue the like vtteraunce: thoughe they hauve much better learning." In short, good words require good pronunciation, and good pronunciation will make you look smarter than everyone else in the room. Johnson claims that English has two pronunciation conventions: one that's cursory and colloquial, and one that's regular and solemn. Given Johnson's irascibility and use of the word "vitiate"* throughout the preface to his dictionary, you can guess which convention he feels has won out: the writers of English grammars have "established the jargon of the lowest of people as the model of speech."

---

* **vi·ti·ate** \ˈvi-shē-ˌāt\ *vb* **-ed/-s/-ing** *vt* **1** : to make faulty or defective : IMPAIR <the comic impact is *vitiated* by obvious haste—William Styron> **2** : to debase in moral or aesthetic status <a mind *vitiated* by prejudice> **3** : to make ineffective <fraud *vitiates* a contract> *(MWC11)*

Dictionaries, as Emily Brewster says, are aspirational texts, but the way we talk has always been a problem for the person aspiring to just the right social level. One must steer a steady path through a narrow strait: vulgarity, low, and classless speech on one side; prissy, overreaching affectation on the other. Is it low-class to pronounce "cadre" as \'ka-ˌdrā\ (KA-dray), or is it preening and pretentious to pronounce it \'kä-dər\ (KAH-dur)? Which one will transform me from a lumpen buffoon into a lithe and elegant viscountess? Help me, O Dictionaries!

But by modern standards, Johnson does diddly-squat to help those who want to help themselves. Johnson's discussion of pronunciation is nestled tightly into a treatise on orthography, not handled as a discipline all its own. In the grammar, he occasionally mentions the pronunciation of certain letters and how they have historically sounded, but he notes that "by writing in English I suppose my reader already acquainted with the English language, and consequently able to pronounce the letters, of which I teach the pronunciation; and because of sounds in general it may be observed, that words are unable to describe them." At individual entries in his *Dictionary,* he includes marks to tell the reader which syllable is accented, but there is no attempt to render any sort of transcription of what Johnson thinks a word's pronunciation should be.

But the fact remained: How were pupils of English going to learn how to say the words correctly? Pronouncing dictionaries were created to step into the breach. The first dictionary devoted primarily to pronunciation was James Buchanan's 1757 *Linguae Britannicae Vera Pronunciatio,* which he wrote specifically for educating youth. His dictionary is the first to include diacritical marks to help distinguish between long vowels and short ones, as well as accent marks to tell the reader which syllable was stressed.

Half a dozen more pronunciation dictionaries were published in the last half of the eighteenth century. Most were both prescriptive and aspirational; some intended to fix the defects of speech that had crept even into the upper echelons of society. So what was their model of elegance and propriety? Each claimed to represent the speech of the London gentry, and yet they offer vastly different pronunciations for the same word. One book's pronunciation of "fear" gives the digraph "ea" a long-*a* sound, \ā\, like in the English "day"; another's gives it a long-*e* sound, \ē\, like "meet" and "deceit"; another lexicographer notes it has the sound in "beer" and "field"—though "beer" and "field" use different vowel sounds (the short "ih" \i\ and the long-*e* \ē\, respectively). So whose standard is *the* standard?

There's a technical problem with these prescriptive pronouncing dictionaries. Each of their systems for rendering pronunciation relies on the reader's somehow intuiting what the vowel quality of their reference word is *supposed* to sound like, as opposed to what it *actually* sounds like in their dialect. To a Londoner, that \ā\ in "fear" sounds pretty Scottish; to a Scotsman, that \i\ or \ē\ sounds pretty southern. This really isn't that surprising. "It's not that there's written language and spoken language," says Josh. "There's language, and there's writing. You start with the phonetics, and you design a writing system based on the phonetics and phonology of the language. English just has a poorly matched system, but that's anomalous."

There have been attempts to remedy this. Buchanan, Benjamin Franklin, and Noah Webster all proposed, with varying degrees of success, alternate spellings and alternate spelling systems that would bring the orthography of English more in line with its pronunciation. Only Webster succeeded, and his success was very limited: while Americans do use some of his spelling reforms, like "plow" for "plough" and "honor" in place of "honour," his more extreme suggestions ("wimen" for "women" and "tung" for "tongue," both of which show up in his 1828 dictionary) never caught on.* Josh thinks these reformations are bound to fail. "Regularizing spelling

---

* Webster likely enjoyed some success with "honor," "center," and "plow" because they were spelling variants already in use; they just weren't as common as "honour" and "centre" and "plough."

to match phonology—you could, in theory, do that. *In theory.* It would be a hell of an undertaking, and you couldn't do it in practice. You'd have to get everyone to agree to the new system." He searches for a good analogy. "It's not herding cats. It's herding 500 million cats."

Mismatch between English's pronunciation and its orthography is something that everyone, native speaker and learner alike, harps on. It feels like a bait and switch: after all, we learned as children that if words have the same cluster of letters at the end, they rhyme: *hop* on *pop, cat* in the *hat.* And then we encounter "through," "though," "rough," "cough," and "bough"—five words that all end with "-ough" and not only don't rhyme but don't even have similar pronunciations. But "won" and "done" and "shun" rhyme? Are you telling me Dr. Seuss *lied* to me about English?

The two biggest complaints we tend to get at Merriam-Webster about English pronunciations are about that desire for regularity. The first is always a request to change the way we say something based on how it's spelled. This isn't a new concept; Johnson posited in the preface to his *Dictionary* that "for pronunciation the best general rule is, to consider those of the most elegant speakers who deviate least from the written word." But because English isn't phonetic, that's a ridiculous proposition. Josh gives an example: "What if we said, okay, from now on, we're going to count 'own, twoh, three, fowar, five, six, seeven.' Those are the most common numbers, and there's a big mismatch between spelling and pronunciation. You think we can just say, no, it's 'own,' not 'won'?"

The second complaint is that the pronunciation of a foreign borrowed term is too Englishy. The usual suspects are almost always French: "croissant," "chaise longue." This is one area of pedantry that merely serves to show off the peever's educational bona fides—by recognizing that a word is a French borrowing and knowing what its French pronunciation is. Unfortunately, when foreign words are snatched into English, they are often given pronunciations based on English, not the origin language.

Josh offers three reasons why French gets singled out as the subject: English has a lot of French borrowings; French has a set of sounds that we don't have in English, so any Anglicization will be off; and there is, for English speakers, a prestige association with French, which means we see French words as high-class. But he points out that most French words have been so Anglicized that we don't even think of them as French anymore: "clairvoyant," "bonbon," "champagne." Anglicization is the norm; in fact, it was prescribed in early twentieth-century usage guides like Fowler's *Dictionary of Modern English Usage.*

But sometimes the desire to sound smart gets the better of us. Look at "lingerie." When it first came into English, it was Anglicized to \lan-zhə-(ˌ)rē\ or \lan-zhrē\, which was as close to the proper French pronunciation as we could get. Three things conspired against keeping \lan-zhrē\: the way we think French should sound, the way that English works, and our desire to be fancy.

French has five nasal vowels (that is, vowels whose quality changes when followed by an *n*), but for whatever reason English speakers really have only latched onto one of those vowels as sounding authentically French—the "an" vowel, which we render as \än\. We throw it into a whole bunch of French words, even when it doesn't belong, because it makes us look like we know French and are therefore smart: \ˈän-və-ˌlōp\ is the textbook example, and so is \län-zhrē\. We also tend to think of French words as ending in \ā\—"café," "résumé"—so we subbed the long \ā\ in for the final \ē\, giving us \län-zhrā\.

Next, we had to assign stress to "lingerie." French is an unstressed language, by which I mean that the language itself doesn't use stressed syllables. English, however, is highly stressed; stress plays a part in distinguishing homographs and meaning, like "PRO-duce" and "pro-DUCE." Where do we put the stress in a word that's unstressed? Pretty much all over the place: English speakers have stressed the first and last syllables of "lingerie" in turns.

And then there is our desire to be fancy. The closest Francophone pronunciation that English provides, \lan-zhrē\, sounds . . . ordinary. "It sounds like an everyday word for something that is, after all, considered to be an exotic, fantasy thing," says Josh. We cannot fathom that something so full of allure and mystery, something so *French,* could have a pronunciation that rhymes with "can tree." It's an exotic thing, so it must have an exotic pronunciation.

This general confusion about "lingerie" means that we collected so many pronunciation variants of it that we listed thirty-six of them in the *Third* and sixteen in the *Collegiate.**

We get particularly snippy when words have one pronunciation that seems to match the spelling of the word and one that doesn't, especially when one of those pronunciations is considered nonstandard. Nonstandard pronunciations are like nonstandard words: they are used naturally but attract the wrong kind of attention for being "uneducated" or otherwise stigmatized. Many of these are, like nonstandard words, dialect pronunciations: "LIE-berry" for "library," common in some dialects of American English, is one of the best known (and excoriated) examples. Nonstandard pronunciations, like nonstandard words, get entered into some dictionaries, like ours, when they're remarkably common. But trying to figure out what's a nonstandard pronunciation and what's an acceptable variant is not easy. "Judging whether something is nonstandard is not something you can do objectively from the data in a recording," Josh says. "That's just something you have to feel."

Why bother entering the nonstandard pronunciations? Don't we want people to say things correctly? That question presumes that there are tons of nonstandard pronunciations out there, when, in fact, there aren't. "Take a look at the vast majority of the 100,000 words in the dictionary," Josh says, "and you'll find precious few of them." That's not to say there aren't lots of variant pronunciations,

---

* Josh says that the pronunciation seems to be regularizing to the \län-jə-rā\ and \län-zhə-rā\ variants. Nothing gold can stay.

but those are different from nonstandard pronunciations. You can say \də-ˈle-mə\ or \dī-ˈle-mə\ for "dilemma," and both are considered standard and correct. "The great majority of words have no particular prescription to them for the pronunciations," says Josh. "There is nothing to decide."

That's not to say that people don't attempt to prescribe. An alternate pronunciation of "nuclear"—\ˈnü-kyə-lər\, the pronunciation that often gets spelled phonetically as "nucular"—has had a very hard run of it. It is, in modern times, universally reviled; usage commentators have called it a "spectacular blunder," an "aberration," and "beastly," and our correspondence files are full of outrage over its very existence. In fact, we received so much e-mail about the pronunciation \ˈnü-kyə-lər\ that we devoted an entire page of our online FAQ to the issue so we wouldn't spend most of our time answering e-mail about it.

Much of the Sturm und Drang surrounding \ˈnü-kyə-lər\ is oxymoronic: \ˈnü-kyə-lər\ is at once lazy and uneducated and yet still spoken by some of the most prominent (and highly educated) people in our public lives. The former president George W. Bush is often blamed for somehow promulgating this pronunciation of "nuclear," and the people who write to us all in a froth about it often accuse us of political pandering by including this pronunciation in our dictionaries.

And that, ultimately, is why people write to us: we have included that pronunciation in our *Collegiate Dictionary*. We give four possible pronunciations of "nuclear" in the *Collegiate:* \ˈnü-klē-ər\ (NEW-klee-ur), \ˈnyü-klē-ər\ (NYOO-klee-ur), \ˈnü-kyə-lər\ (NOO-cue-lur), and \ˈnyü-kyə-lər\ (NYOO-cue-lur). Those last two—the shudder-inducing \-kyə-lər\ pronunciations—are preceded by an obelus (÷), which is our shorthand way of marking nonstandard but widely used pronunciations in our dictionaries. In the event that you don't know what the obelus is for,[*] we have a

---

[*] And you are not alone, though here I ask you, again and graciously, to read the goddamned front matter.

short usage paragraph at "nuclear" that tells you right away that the pronunciations that end in \-kyə-lər\ are disapproved of by many. Unfortunately, we don't stop there, which is why we receive so much hate mail regarding "nuclear":

> Though disapproved of by many, pronunciations ending in \-kyə-lər\ have been found in widespread use among educated speakers including scientists, lawyers, professors, congressmen, United States cabinet members, and at least two United States presidents and one vice president. While most common in the United States, these pronunciations have also been heard from British and Canadian speakers.

The paragraph is actually a little out of date as of this writing. The pronunciation \'nü-kyə-lər\ has now been used by four-ish U.S. presidents—Dwight Eisenhower, Gerald Ford, Jimmy Carter (who also used the pronunciation \'nü-kyir\),* George W. Bush, and sometimes Bill Clinton and George H. W. Bush. It has also been used by a number of international leaders, U.S. congresspeople and cabinet members, governors, weapons specialists, military person-nel, a Nobel Prize–winning theoretical physicist—people who are in a position to use the word almost daily and yet still say \'nü-kyə-lər\. And as the tip of the hat to Eisenhower shows, it's also not a recent invention: we have evidence of this use back to at least the 1940s.

The linguistic process by which "nuclear" became \'nü-kyə-lər\ is called "metathesis," where two phonemes within a word switch positions.† This is the process that gave us the standard pronuncia-

---

* Jimmy Carter spent his time in the U.S. Navy working on propulsion systems for nuclear submarines, acting as an engineering officer of a nuclear power plant, and actually being lowered into a nuclear reactor core that had melted down in order to dismantle it. To my mind, he has earned the right to pro-nounce "nuclear" however he damned well pleases.

† Ironically, I have, for years, been mispronouncing "metathesis" as "MEH-tuh-THEE-sus." It is "muh-TATH-uh-sus." I am reproved.

tions of "iron" ("EYE-urn" instead of "EYE-run") and "comfortable" ("KUMF-ter-bul" instead of "KUM-fert-uh-bul") and other nonstandard pronunciations like "PURR-tee" for "pretty." Some lexicographers and linguists posit that "nuclear" underwent metathesis because there are not any other common English words that end in \-klē-ər\ (just "cochlear"),* but there are a good number of words like "molecular" and "vascular" that end in \-kyə-lər\, and the gravitational pull of these words and this more common speech pattern dragged "nuclear" into \-kyə-lər\ orbit. But the "how" is not as interesting to people as the "why," and we don't have a compelling "why." Why do people who have gone through some of the most rigorous graduate programs in the world use a pronunciation that's just not right?

If it can be believed, linguists haven't undertaken a study of it. We know it's not a regionalism: though Carter, Bush, and Clinton all hail from the South, Eisenhower and Ford did not, nor did Walter Mondale, the vice president who said \'nü-kyə-lər\. Rose Kennedy corrected Ted Kennedy's pronunciation of it in a letter— "I wish you would check your pronunciation of the word nuclear"— and Ted Kennedy was most certainly not southern. Evidence of \'nü-kyə-lər\ appears nearly all over the English-speaking world: in Australia, Canada, England, California, Iowa, Utah, Indiana, Pennsylvania, Texas. It's not just that we have recordings of people from all over saying it. We also have unironic use of the spelling "nucular" in printed obituaries, restaurant reviews, and press releases

---

* The linguist Geoff Nunberg notes that "nuclear" is phonologically pretty similar to "likelier," and we don't have any problems saying that, but my completely half-informed opinion is that the first vowel in "likelier" is more frontal (that is, when you say that vowel, it happens near the front of your mouth) than the first vowel in "nuclear," and so it matches the frontal nature of that long *e* in \-klē-ər\ a whole lot better. The first vowel in "nuclear" is near back—that is, it happens in the middle of your mouth, maybe heading a little bit more toward your throat, like the vowel in "food." That matches up better with that final back vowel in the diphthong in \-kyə\: \'nü-kyə-lər\. Sometimes we are mush mouths because we like symmetry.

from biomedical companies, to name a handful of published and edited sources. In other words, that verbal tic is natural enough to some people that they automatically spell "nuclear" as "nucular."

The linguists Geoff Nunberg and Allan Metcalf suggest it might be military jargon. Nunberg has talked to some of these people, who all manage to say "\ˈnu-klē-ər\ family" and "\ˈnu-klē-ər\ medicine," but anything having to do with weaponry is \ˈnü-kyə-lər\. "I once asked a weapons specialist at a federal agency about this, and he told me, 'Oh, I only say "nucular" when I'm talking about nukes.'" Metcalf notes the same general pattern, though he gives no anecdata* to support his contention. Steven Pinker, another linguist who got in something of a mild slap fight with Nunberg over \ˈnü-kyə-lər\, drops that in 2008 he spoke to the Strategic Studies Group at the Naval War College in Newport, Rhode Island, and heard \ˈnü-kyə-lər\ from two senior analysts there. Interestingly, the earliest print instances we have of "nucular," the spelled-out variation of the pronunciation that everyone hates, are in stories about and bulletins from people in the military, government, or nuclear sciences.

Some linguists, including Josh, think that because this variant occurs primarily in contexts like "nuclear weapons" and "nuclear power," it "suggests that 'nucular' may not be an alteration of 'nuclear' but formed from adding the '-ular' suffix to the root 'nuke.'" If "nuke" started as military jargon, that accounts for the appearance of this pronunciation mostly among people who have spent a fair amount of time in the military or the federal government. But then we'd have to account for "nuke" or "nuc" showing up well after the spelled-out "nucular"; our first attested print use of "nuke," in the word "thermonukes," dates to 1955, while recorded spellings of "nucular" go back to 1943.

But, as Josh says, "this is all conjecture." We don't have much

---

* A newish portmanteau of "anecdote" and "data," "anecdata" refers to personal experiences or anecdotes that are treated like objectively collected and analyzed data.

information about the original \'nü-kyə-lər\ users, and we don't have much information about current \'nü-kyə-lər\ users—nothing on their native dialects, languages, ages, nada. That, of course, makes it much easier to jump to a few conclusions about the people who use \'nü-kyə-lər\:

> But which of these stories explains why [George W.] Bush says "nucular"? Most people seem to assume he's just one of those bub-bas who don't know any better. But that's hard to credit. After all, Bush didn't have to learn the word nuclear in middle age, the way Eisenhower did. He must have heard it said correctly thousands of times when he was growing up—not just at Andover, Yale, and Harvard, but from his own father, who never seems to have had any trouble with the word. [*Ed. note:* Not true. We have evidence in our files of Bush senior using \'nü-kyə-lər\.] But if Bush's "nucular" is a deliberate choice, is it something he picked up from the Pentagon wise guys? Or is it a faux-bubba pronunciation, the sort of thing he might have started doing at Yale by way of playing the Texas yahoo to all those earnest Eastern dweebs?

Love him or hate him, that's not very fair to Bush. It's true that people do sometimes intentionally take on an accent to appeal to a group somehow or to distance themselves from a stigmatized group. But more often it's the case that people unconsciously change the way they pronounce something through sustained con-tact with other speakers. This has happened to me: after years of living in Greater Philadelphia, I find that sly Philly *o*, which sounds like all the vowels smeared together, in alphabetical order, popping up occasionally in words like "hoagie" and names like "Sophie." I used to say "FOUN-tin" and "fill-uh-DELL-fee-uh," the standard pronunciations for "fountain" and "Philadelphia"; now, when I am in a hurry, I say "FAN(t)-in" and "fill-LELL-fee-uh," just as the old-timers here do. I can no longer remember if I am supposed to name my home state as "cah-loh-RA-doh," making "RA" sound like the beginning of the word "rad," or "cah-loh-RAH-do," making "RAH" rhyme with "ma" and "pa." I listen intently to my ma and pa say "Colorado" to see if this jogs any lingual muscle memory, and because I am listening intently, I find that they say it inconsistently as well. "This has happened to me," says Josh. "I'll call the Springfield Public Library, say. They answer, 'Sprungfeld Public Library.' I'll say, 'I'm trying to verify a pronunciation. The name of your town, how is it pronounced?' They say, 'Springfield.' 'Never "Sprungfeld"?' 'Nope, never "Sprungfeld."' 'Okay, thanks.' And then I wait a while and call back just to see if I caught them on an off day, and—'Sprungfeld Public Library.'"*

Consider this cautionary tale: I don't say \'nü-kyə-lər\; none of my family say it; none of my colleagues say it; I have no contact with any person who naturally says \'nü-kyə-lər\. But since having researched the pronunciations, and emphatically saying "new-kyoo-lur" and "new-klee-ur" aloud every time I've typed the pronunciations in throughout the writing of this chapter, I have caught myself saying \'nü-kyə-lər\ twice when telling people what I was writing on, like some lexical version of guilt by association. I know what the standard pronunciation is, but circumstance ties my tongue.

---

* It's worth noting that this is a joke from *The Simpsons* and isn't representative of how people in Springfield, Massachusetts, say "Springfield." It's also worth noting that I didn't catch the reference until Josh pointed it out to me.

Nude

On Correspondence

T he Friday lunch crew had chosen (via pink) the Indian place downtown, and I tagged along in an effort to get to know my co-workers. Because none of us talked to each other during the work-day, this was our only opportunity to mingle. Conversation came in bursts, punctuated with sudden silences and lots of staring down at our pappadum. Though it didn't look like it, we were all enjoying the opportunity to attempt small talk with other people who got us.

Someone asked what I had been doing most recently, and I said I had been going through the letters. Each month, the editorial secretaries passed out copies of the answers we sent to people who wrote in with questions. It's an old and helpful tradition: you get to see the kinds of questions people ask and how other editors answer. Steve had given me an assorted stack of correspondence from the last year or two to look through, to get a sense of tone. "They're interesting," I offered. "Some of them, whew."

Dan cocked an eyebrow. "What do you mean, 'whew'?"

Some of the responses had been very curt, I said, and others seemed to ramble on before getting to the point. I had just left a job where every piece of correspondence I sent out was orchestrated and edited into a shapeless, tasteless mash. Here, everyone's personalities, both writer and editor, shone, for better or worse.

Dan put his fork down and quickly swallowed his bite. "You know what? You need to see the best piece of correspondence we've ever gotten. It's in the file."

"Oh, yes," Karen Wilkinson, another editor, said, "I know exactly what Dan means. It's worth the time to find it."

Once back in the office, Karen sent me a pink with a name on it. "Check the correspondence file," she wrote. "Worth the time." I found the archive of incoming mail with a bit of sleuthing and then went through the alphabetical index to find the name. The folder had just one piece of mail in it: a short typewritten note on office-standard typewriter paper. There was no signature; nothing that marked this as standout correspondence. Then I read the letter. It was very simple and straightforward. The correspondent wanted to know how long love lasts.

As I mentioned earlier, editorial correspondence is one of the duties of the Merriam-Webster lexicographer. It's considered a service to our users: anyone can write to the company and ask any question at all about the English language and get a response from an expert.

Allow me to generously shower that statement with caveats. Editorial correspondence is indeed one of many duties that Merriam-Webster editors have to take on; that said, it is one of the lesser duties that can be set aside when the deadlines are not just looming but have begun climbing the building and pawing around inside for hostages. We call it the "press of editorial duties" in our correspondence; for a while, there was a physical Press of Editorial Duties in Gil's office, an old letterpress brought up from the depths of basement storage. Maybe it strikes you as a tired joke, but we are lexicographers, and tired jokes are our forte. The press of editorial duties is real.

It sounds risky, perhaps, to give agency over correspondence to people who would rather proofread than do customer service. But this is less about stretching the lexicographer and more about practicality: sometimes the "questions about the English language" we receive are not about the English language. Sometimes they aren't even *in* the English language.

•

Editorial correspondence at Merriam-Webster was originally a guerrilla marketing tactic. During the mid-nineteenth century, the G. & C. Merriam Company faced stiff competition from Joseph Worcester, Noah Webster's protégé/nemesis. Worcester's dictionaries were much more popular than Webster's dictionaries were, and the Merriam brothers, shrewd businessmen that they were, knew they needed some sort of angle to lure in buyers. They began running advertisements offering a free dictionary to any person who wrote in with evidence of a word that wasn't already entered in one of the Webster dictionaries. It worked: they gave away hundreds of dictionaries and gained some pen pals in the process.

In the 1980s, we formalized the process a bit and created the Language Research Service, which conjures images of tie-clad eggheads in their shirtsleeves, hordes of them, bustling around looking for the answer to "what's the word for when you have to explain what kind of a thing you're using when you didn't have to do that in the past, like now we have to say 'film camera'?"* The Language Research Service, or LRS for short, is a service offered by the editorial staff at Merriam-Webster and open to anyone with a copy of *Merriam-Webster's Collegiate Dictionary,* as the very last page of the book explains. It worked: we have, over the course of the LRS, answered hundreds of thousands of queries and gained hundreds and hundreds of pen pals.

It's a rare and charming thing, these days, to write to a company and get a response from a real person. The number of people who write back to us merely to say, "Wow! I didn't expect a person to reply!" is surprisingly high. It's an even rarer thing to love words and find a group of other people who not only love them as much as you do but also know a lot about them, so you can understand the impulse to keep the conversation going, to enmesh yourself

---

*   **ret·ro·nym** \'re-trō-ˌnim\ *n* : a term consisting of a noun and a modifier which specifies the original meaning of the noun <"film camera" is a *retronym*> (*MWC11*)

into this unique community. We've all had correspondents over the years who send question after question, some worth answering and some not.* Emily has a Japanese professor who writes to her and asks questions that are deceptively simple: Why do we say "he gave his grandma a kiss" and not "he gave a kiss to his grandma," or when do you use "how come" and when do you use "why"? The minute you begin digging for an answer, you turn up convoluted root system layered on convoluted root system, but because the lexicographer loves and respects English, we tease things apart as best we can. That sort of expertise is winning, and some of these correspondents hang on for a long time: we've had one correspondent who has asked these sorts of questions for almost twenty years. He began writing to us in high school, always asking us to explain the usage differences between two words—say, "continual" and "continuous." In time, he sent us his prom picture; later, articles he wrote for his college newspaper, as if we were distant but kindly relatives.

You can tell just from handling the letters that writing in to the dictionary involved pomp and ceremony for some. Letters are meticulously typewritten or very carefully scribed; questions are phrased very carefully, and the usual protocols of salutation and closing are observed. This is a question sent to the dictionary, after all: this is serious shit.

The correspondence was initially intended to alert Merriam-Webster to words missing from its dictionaries, but as its history has grown, so too have the questions. The amount of scrutiny some of our correspondents give the dictionary is dizzying. I once got an e-mail from someone who caught what's called a bad break in one of our dictionaries: the word "silence" was at the end of a line and was split into "sil-" and "-ence" instead of "si-" and "-lence," as the dots in the headword indicate.† This correspondent wondered if

---

* The referent of that phrase is intentionally vague.

† Here is the one thing that our pronunciation editor wishes everyone knew: those dots in the headwords, like at "co·per·nic·i·um," are not marking

we had ever consulted our own dictionary, because if we had, we would have seen that the word "silence" is split after the "-i-": "si / lence." When I finished reading the e-mail, I realized that my hands had floated, palms up, and were on either side of my head, while my mouth had fallen open and remained that way. I looked like an Edvard Munch painting. One bad break in a book that has literally tens of thousands of breaks in it, and this person *found it.* That is commitment to the dictionary that goes above and beyond.

Sometimes the questions are ones that we cannot possibly answer. "I remember when I was handling the earliest e-mail correspondence," Karen said. "Someone wrote to us and asked us where to buy beans." Some of the more notable queries I've received include the following: Why are manhole covers round? Do woodchucks actually chuck wood? Why is the rainbow divided into seven colors, and why we do start with red? What should you look for when purchasing an Alaskan malamute? If you sneeze with your eyes open, will your eyeballs fall out? Can dogs dive three hundred feet? Are babies natural?*

There are two phrases you see in editorial responses a lot: one you are already familiar with ("the press of editorial duties"); the other is "outside the scope of our knowledge." That's the hedge that enables us to do what we've promised—respond to queries that come in—while at the same time not giving any sort of substantial answer whatsoever. Because how can we? *Are babies natural?* I don't even know what that string of words *means,* and finding the meanings of words is my wheelhouse.

---

syllable breaks, as is evident by comparing the placement of the dots with the placement of the hyphens in the pronunciations. Those dots are called "end-of-line division dots," and they exist solely to tell beleaguered proofreaders where, if they have to split a word between lines, they can drop a hyphen.

* Easier to replace in a hurry because you don't have to square the corners; no, they merely chew wood, not throw it; probably because seven is a sacred or holy number, and we probably start with red because that's generally the color that is at the outermost edge of a rainbow; good yet varied breeding stock; no; probably not; definitely not.

•

Though the correspondence that we receive can be wide-ranging, most of it comes from well-meaning people who petition us to enter, remove, or change a word for them. We often have to tell these correspondents that lexicography doesn't function like reality TV: people don't get to vote words in or out of the language by contacting us. Of course, this being lexicography, there is always an exception. Sometimes correspondents let us know that there's a definition that is plain wrong or outdated that needs attending to.

In 2015, *BuzzFeed* put together a smart video featuring women of color trying on garments whose color is called "nude" by the manufacturer. Every item the women tried on was some variation on beige. The women in the video are laconic about the mismatch between dark skin and nude undergarments. One woman smirks that if she wanted nude pantyhose, she'd be better off wrapping her legs in plastic wrap.

The video heats up unexpectedly when each woman is asked to comment on the dictionary definition of the adjective "nude." The online entry from Merriam-Webster.com, which is the one the news site used, has a number of different definitions, including a set of definitions written in simpler language for people learning English as a foreign language. These are the definitions the women in the video read:

> : having no clothes on
> : of or involving people who have no clothes on
> : having the color of a white person's skin

The women are justifiably outraged. "These definitions don't make sense," says one participant. "'Having no clothes on'—me naked is not the same thing as me having the color of a white person's skin." At the end of the video, the same woman shakes her head at the printout with the definitions on it. "I still can't believe this is actually in the dictionary. It is?" She drops the paper and looks heavenward. "That is insane."

I didn't see the video the day it came out but the day after. I had just logged in and was scanning the editorial e-mail while sipping my coffee, when I saw I had been CC'd on an e-mail that we had four complaints about the definition of "nude."

People write in to the dictionary about all sorts of things, but it's very unusual for more than one person to write in to the dictionary about the same thing on the same day. As I scrolled through the editorial in-box, the cluster turned into a long smear of e-mails, all with the word "nude" in the subject line. On a hunch, I checked the spam folder, and yep: there were more letters, shunted into the junk drawer of our e-mail program. Evidently, our internal netminder decided that between the subject line of these e-mails—"nude"— and the content, which featured the word "fucking" a lot, these complaints were pornographic spam. I opened up my web browser and, now dyspeptic, began searching for the source of all the complaints.

My sour stomach was the result of some deep, burbling editorial angst. I don't mind when people have complaints about definitions; hell, there are definitions that I could complain about, and I've written some of them. More often than not, though, these complaints stem from misunderstandings that are (usually) easily cleared up. Someone doesn't know, for instance, that we list definitions in chronological order and so is upset that the "whorehouse" sense of "stew" shows up before the "thick soup" sense does. Or we might hear from a person who is upset that we have entered the word "impactful" even though it is jargon (true) and meaningless (not true) and ugly (amen). A short note will generally assuage any concerns people have about the entry.

This complaint, however, was an onion of suck, layer after layer of problems. The entry as it appeared online was presented poorly: without sense numbers, those separate definitions read like one long definition, and that's absolutely not the case. There were no example sentences to help orient the reader, nothing that ties a definition, which speaks in generalities, to a particular use, which grounds that generality in everyday life. Moreover, the contested sense is a color definition.

Color definitions are notoriously difficult for the lexicographer, who must accurately describe what the color "nude" is using only printed descriptions from catalogs that are usually no help whatsoever: "Ladies' S, M, L, available in Cranberry, Mauve, Holly, Navy, Nude, Ebony, Coral." The advertisement might as well be listing the Seven Dwarfs for all the lexicographer knows; there is nothing here to orient you as to what color "nude" actually is. The files are full of this: no color plates, no good images. Just lots of catalog copy.

Wrap those three things around the acrid heart of the complaint—that the differentia refers to "a white person's skin" and drags into that eight-word definition the weight of being a person of color navigating a white world—and no matter how you slice it, there will be indigestion and tears.

I put my head down on my desk and breathed a procession of "shits" into my mouse pad for good measure.

Whenever a sensitive topic is broached over e-mail, and especially when it is likely that more than one person will write in, it's normal form to consult with people who know more than you do in vetting your reply. I followed the chain of e-mails about this that had been started by one of the digital team members. How should we respond? Is the definition problematic? For my own part, I couldn't see how that definition *wasn't* problematic. This called for a quick review of the evidence. I pulled up the citations database and searched for "nude" near any word I could think of that would be paired with this particular sense. Eyes closed, fingers wiggling over the keyboard, I poked my sprachgefühl awake and started rummaging through my internal citation files. What things get called "nude"? Panty hose, bras, underwear for sure—I added those three to my search criteria. Keep digging, I urged. What else? I suppose any piece of clothing could be nude, though no one would call khakis "nude trousers." Ah, but nude dresses—yes, I know I had seen that phrase. I added it to the criteria, then closed my eyes again. A flash of catalog whizzed mentally by, a host of feet: nude pumps. The search engine began spitting out results. Yes, I thought, now we are most assuredly cooking with gas.

The evidence we had for the color sense of "nude" was, as I feared, completely useless without pictures. "A nude silk crepe dress with fringe," "almost all your bras should be nude," "shapely legs, covered by nude hose"—all completely idiomatic uses of "nude" that give me no information whatsoever about what color "nude" actually is.

Meanwhile, talk on the e-mail chain had turned philosophical. One editor defended the definition: defining colors by analogy to something in the real world is an established practice, and effective. You could say the word "nude" refers to a range of colors that are light yellow-brown or yellow-pink to dark tan, but that sort of abstraction leads you on a Technicolor romp through the dictionary without conveying useful information. His verdict: "It's a good definition."

I indulged in some audible groaning. In a theoretical world, it's a perfectly fine definition. But we weren't living in a theoretical world: we were living in this very real world, a world where everything from fashion to the way photography film captures color has been calibrated for whiteness. Referencing race in a color definition in this day and age was messy at best and stupid at worst. Against my better judgment, I put my oar in: you could make an argument, I wrote, that the definition as it stands needlessly racializes something that doesn't need to be racialized. Ah, another person chimed in, but what's actually telling the truth about this word: a definition that ignores the white-normative fashion industry that gave rise to the color name "nude," or a definition that tries, however poorly, to communicate something about the history of racism in America?

Regardless of the sociolinguistic implications of the word "nude," we now had, according to another editor on e-mail duty, a growing pile of angry correspondents who needed an answer. They wanted a change: Were we going to give it to them?

Lexicography, even in the digital age, is a slower process than most people want it to be. The citation files would have to be combed through to see if the definition merited revision. I did a bare search for "nude" in the database: over one thousand hits. That would take time to sift through. We'd likely have to do some Internet searches for images and then manually add those to the database, because our citation program only slurped text from the net. If the definition merited a revision, someone would have to come up with one, and then someone else would have to vet it, and then another editor would have to do the copyedit and cross-reference work on it. Then we would have to wait for the next data upload to the website to add it in. None of this was going to be accomplished in the next ten minutes.

Others came up with a response; I set my citation spelunking aside. The definition struck me as antiquated, and at the very least I thought it could be better worded, but I was under deadline, as were we all. We'd have to delve deeper when we had more time.

These things have a way of digging in and wriggling around your brainpan, though. A few weeks later, I was walking the aisles of a large department store with my fifteen-year-old daughter, trying to be a Good Mom who takes her child shopping, even though I would rather pull my own fingernails out with pliers than spend an afternoon wandering around the mall. We were ostensibly picking up a few things she needed for an after-school activity when, surprise, she also totally forgot to tell me earlier that she was completely out of foundation and mascara. "Forgot," I intoned, watching my afternoon stretch into an infinite hellscape of linoleum walkways and tinny pop music under fluorescent lights. She beamed brightly. "Might as well get them while we're here!"

While waiting for her to choose between Deep Black and Blackest Black mascara, I let my eyes wander over the racks of makeup, then started. I grabbed a box of makeup from the shelf, then awkwardly swished my free hand through my purse, trying to find my cellphone. My daughter narrowed her eyes. "What are you doing?"

In my hand was a set of eyeshadows ranging from white to dark brown. I held it at arm's length, then fumbled my cellphone camera into operation. Beep, *sh-shk:* now I had a good enough photograph for the cit files of the eyeshadows, lined up in order of hue, encased in a wrapper that read "NUDE palette." I put the makeup back, then turned to see my daughter staring at me. She looked world-weary, like a circus clown two shows away from retirement, dolefully waiting for the inevitable pie right in the smacker. "Are you taking pictures for work again?"

"Just one."

"Oh my God," she moaned, "can you ever just, like, live like a normal person?"

"Hey, I didn't choose the dictionary life—"

"Just stop—"

"—the dictionary life—"

"MOM—"

"—chose me," I finished, and she threw her head back and sighed in exasperation.

The next day at work, I did a series of Internet image searches for "nude lip," "nude eyeshadow," and "nude makeup," then remembered to turn on the "Safe for Work" filter after the IT administrator e-mailed to remind me that all Internet searches made using company property were logged and reviewed. I snagged picture after picture of brown, dark pink, and mauve lipstick all labeled "nude"; eyeshadows that ranged from black to white and every shade of brown and gray in between; makeup palettes called "nude" that contained muted shades of the rainbow, including what my makeup-dumb eyes would call "green" and "blue"—colors that certainly don't match a white person's skin.

I clicked one lipstick image to save it and gasped when I saw the name of the article it was attached to: "12 Nude Lipsticks That Are Actually Nude on Darker Skin." Though I had the picture proof that the word "nude" as used of colors didn't just refer to beige or tan, here was something I was used to dealing with: plain words. And it was the perfect use: the second instance of "nude" here, applied to darker skin, was an unglossed, completely idiomatic use. If I could have burst into song and triumphantly moonwalked in my cubicle without getting fired, I would have.

Instead, I sent off an e-mail to Steve. Whenever we get the chance, I said, we should revise "nude." He responded with a proposed revision. The definition as it was written erred in being too narrow, he said. His proposed revision was "having a color that matches a person's skin tones—used especially of a woman's undergarments." Certainly better, but I responded that the usage note, "used especially of a woman's undergarments," didn't encompass the other uses of "nude" that I had been scouting out recently, like "nude lip" and "nude makeup." He responded by saying that maybe we could drop the usage note and just insert some example sentences to orient the reader—say, "nude pantyhose" or "nude stockings."

The revision looked good, but we both let it simmer for a few days. A definition is a bit like stew (sense 4a):* the longer you let it sit, the better it ends up getting. Steve sent another revision: "having a color (typically a pale beige) that matches a person's skin tones <*nude* stockings>."

The minute it was on the page, we both began squirming. That "typically" didn't really sit right with either of us. "On the one hand," Steve wrote, "it seems accurate. On the other hand . . ." Was the word "nude" typically used to refer to a pale beige color? Our recent spelunking seemed to suggest not. Does the word "typically" imply that the word "nude" when used of a pale beige was "normal"? If so, this is just another way of implying that white skin was normative. I suggested we change it to "often"; Steve countered that maybe the best way to go was with the tried-and-true formulaic "such as": "having a color (such as a pale beige) that matches a person's skin tones."

I felt the scalp-prickling mental fission that comes when I'm getting closer to a good definition. When definers use "such as" in a parenthetical, it gives us the opportunity to use more than one

---

* ¹ **stew** *n* \'stü, 'styü\ . . . **1** *obsolete* : a utensil used for boiling **2** : a hot bath **3 a** : WHOREHOUSE **b** : a district of bordellos—usually used in plural **4 a** : fish or meat usually with vegetables prepared by stewing **b** (1) : a heterogeneous mixture (2) : a state of heat and congestion **5** : a state of excitement, worry, or confusion *(MWC11)*

modifier. What if, I suggested, we added "or tan" to the parenthetical to make it clear that "nude" actually represents a range of colors? Steve liked that addition. "I'm now also inclined to change 'a person's' to 'the wearer's,'" he said. I wasn't sure; after all, not all colors called "nude" end up matching the wearer's skin tone, right? I was, I assured him, happy to second-guess myself and would start doing so right now.

Steve explained that the advantage of "the wearer's" was that it subtly communicated that this sense was generally limited to things that you wore, rather than something like a bicycle or a loaf of bread. "Though," he said, "I suppose you could wear a loaf of bread if you really wanted to." No judgment, I replied.

The revision, "having a color (such as pale beige or tan) that matches the wearer's skin tones <*nude* pantyhose> <*nude* lipstick>," was entered into the data file with no fanfare or announcement. No matter how passionately our correspondents felt about the color "nude," it was just another definition at another entry to us. We made it better, and then we moved on.

It becomes startlingly clear when you begin answering letters from people that the way people use language is personal. The indignant looking for justice or justification in "misogyny" or "misandry"; the incarcerated asking us to explain the difference between "misdemeanor" and "felony"; the parents who have lost a child and write hoping that we know of a simple word, like "widow" or "orphan," that is a placeholder for their pain, some word that will spare them the inevitable and exhausting explication of their loss to a stranger. We don't just want our words to *have meaning,* we want them to *mean something,* and the difference is palpable.

Correspondence is not the primary job of a lexicographer, but it ends up being a way to make English—a difficult language that's got more twists and turns in it than the cumulative plotline of *Days of Our Lives*—human. It's an ironic thing that people who enjoy solitude and quiet, and have chosen to work in a place that rewards you for it, end up being the very human connection behind English for thousands of people.

•

We answered the question about how long love lasts. Of course we did. The blurb in the back of the dictionary promised we would:

> Dear [redacted]:
> We thank you for your letter, but your question about how long love lasts is not something we can answer. We lexicographers are good at defining words. Questions about the nature and permanence of deeply felt human emotions, though, are a little outside our field.
> We're sorry not to be more helpful.
> Sincerely,
>
> Stephen J. Perrault

Marriage

On Authority and the Dictionary

It was Friday, morning-break time, and I was not just tired; I was beat, wiped, whipped, laid out, done in, *dead*. Usually during morning break, I got up for a bit of a stretch, walked around, refilled my coffee. I was working from home at the time and sometimes indulged in a little wander around my yard—a hard reset before I got back to work. Today, however, I had ignored the nice weather and instead put my head on my desk, forehead pressed to the Formica and arms covering my skull. I had joked with one of my yoga-loving co-workers that I was developing a series of poses we could do at our desks—a head-in-hands slump over galleys called Drudge's Hunch, the arms-over-head seated stretch called Fluorescent Salutation, the hand-out position used to catch the fire door so it didn't slam and bother everyone was Worrier's Pose. My current pose was called Nuclear Fallout.

It had been two weeks of workplace hell. I was attempting some deep, yogic breaths (facedown on my desk—not the ideal position), intently listening to the sounds of my home office: the bone creak of the house corner being pushed by wind, the borborygmus* rumble of a delivery truck idling outside, that goddamned mockingbird that had built a nest in the eaves right outside my office and was currently doing the Top 40 Birdcalls of North America on repeat. In a

---

*   **bor·bo·ryg·mus** \ˌbȯr-bə-ˈrig-məs\ *n, pl* **bor·bo·ryg·mi** \-ˌmī\ **:** intestinal rumbling caused by moving gas *(MWCII)*

few minutes, I heard my e-mail program bing, then bing again. I turned my head and peeped out from under my arm; Peter had sent me a link to a video, followed by about fifteen exclamation points.

I ducked my head back under my arm and tried to be as Zen as possible, but curiosity got the better of me. I clicked the link and was taken to a clip from *The Colbert Report.* "Folks," Colbert began, "turns out my old nemesis is back." As he pulled a *Collegiate* up onto his desk, I maneuvered the mouse over to the pause button and jabbed violently. *Noooooope,* I thought, no, I can't watch this. Not after the last two weeks. But the screen had frozen at an odd point, and I felt slightly uncomfortable staring at a grimacing Stephen Colbert. I relented. I slid my glasses up to the top of my head and rubbed my face vigorously. My forehead throbbed where I had been pressing it to my desk.

Colbert was finishing up a joke about "zymosan" when I focused on the screen again. He was saying that we had changed the definition of "marriage," and added a new meaning: "the state of being united to a person of the same sex in a relationship like that of a traditional marriage." This was true. "That means, gay marriage," he explained. "I'm beginning to suspect that Merriam and Webster were conjugating more than just irregular verbs."

I snickered. It had been the first honest laugh I'd had in a while.

The segment was only three minutes long, but I devoted the rest of my break to it, then wandered—a changed woman—out of my office and into the house. My husband was sitting at the dining room table, headphones on, scribbling out a horn arrangement. I stood next to him until I had his attention. I smiled incandescently, radiant; my face was damp with tears; the world smelled beatifically of roses. He raised an eyebrow in expectation.

"Welp," I said, "I've made the big leagues. I've been parodied by Colbert."

Lexicographers like to justify our existence by saying that words matter to people, and that the meaning of words matter to people, therefore *lexicography matters*. This is only a bit of a lie: if a word matters to a person, it's most likely because of the thing that word describes and not because of the word itself. Sure, everyone has a word (or a handful of words) that they adore because they love the sound, the feel, the silliness or silkiness of the word; I defy anyone to say the word "hootamaganzy" aloud and not immediately fall in love with it, regardless of what it means.* But scanning through the top lookups on any dictionary website shows that most words that interest us do so because we are unclear about the thing to which they are applied or we want to use the definition to run a litmus test on the situation, person, event, thing, or idea that that word was used of.

We know this bit of behavioral trivia not because this is innate knowledge lexicographers have about how people interact with their dictionaries but because of Internet comments. As dictionaries have moved online, lexicographers have developed a direct connection with users that they've never had before. The one thing that is most striking about all these comments—good, bad, ugly, and uglier—is that lots of people are really interacting with language in the etymological sense, expecting a mutual and reciprocal discourse from the dictionary definition.

Lexicographers are the weirdos in the room: they'll rhapsodize about the word itself, talk endlessly about the etymology or history of usage, give you weird facts about how Shakespeare or David Foster Wallace used the word. But ask them to comment on the thing that word represents, and they fidget. Ask them to do that with a word whose use and meaning describe systems, beliefs, and attitudes that have shaped Western culture, and they will do their damnedest to leave the room as quickly and quietly as possible.

The problem is not so much that lexicographers are objectively

---

* It's another name for a hooded merganser. Don't worry if you don't know what a hooded merganser is, because that doesn't detract from the wonder of "hootamaganzy." Shout it out an open window; it's as good as Prozac and cheaper.

disordered when it comes to words (though they undeniably are). It is that the general public—particularly in America—has been trained to think of the dictionary as an authority, and so what "the dictionary" says matters. "The dictionary," in a bid for cultural relevance and market share, is the one who has trained the public to think this way, but what we hold ourselves to be authorities on has changed dramatically since we started this gambit.

This has bitten us in the ass a few times.

In the late 1990s, we undertook a revision of the *Collegiate Dictionary* in which we added about ten thousand new entries. The new edition, the *Eleventh,* was released in 2003, and in an attempt to get people actually to buy dictionaries and not just talk about them, we highlighted some of the new entries in a marketing campaign and handed out "New Words Samplers" like candy at a parade. People wrote in for a few weeks asking about the new entries, and we had lively e-mail discussions with correspondents about "phat" (which, contrary to widespread belief, is not an acronym of "pretty hips and thighs" or "pretty hot and tempting")[*] and "dead-cat bounce" (which despite looking like a phrase is actually considered a word for entry purposes).[†] But not all ten thousand new entries were highlighted; lots of new information lived in that dictionary for a long time before people found it.

One of the new additions was a second-level subsense—a sub-subsense—at the entry for "marriage" that was designed to cover uses of "marriage" that referred to same-sex marriage. We had hundreds of citations sitting in the files for this use, and more and more were coming in daily as states were debating the legality

---

[*] **phat** \ˈfat\ *adj* **phat·ter; phat·test** [probably alteration of ¹*fat*] (1963) *slang* : highly attractive or gratifying : EXCELLENT <a *phat* beat moving through my body—Tara Roberts> *(MWC11)*

[†] **dead-cat bounce** *n* [from the facetious notion that even a dead cat would bounce slightly if dropped from a sufficient height] (1985) : a brief and insignificant recovery (as of stock prices) after a steep decline *(MWC11)*

of gay marriage. The definition we settled on was "the state of being united to a person of the same sex in a relationship like that of a traditional marriage."

Given the nature of the thing being described, we were very careful with how we defined that use of the word. We felt, reading through the citational evidence at the turn of the millennium, that it would be best to cover gay marriage in a separate subsense instead of broadening the existing definition of "marriage" ("the state of being united to a person of the opposite sex as husband or wife in a consensual and contractual relationship recognized by law"). The reasons straddled that line between the thingness and the wordness of "marriage" in ways that make lexicographers sink into Drudge's Hunch. In 2000, while we were writing the *Collegiate,* the legality of same-sex marriage (the thing) was hotly debated; no state in the union had passed a law that allowed same-sex marriage, though several had challenged constitutional bans on same-sex marriage and one (Vermont) had passed a law allowing same-sex civil unions. Heterosexual marriage, however, was legal nationwide. So it's not surprising, then, that the vast majority of our citations for the "romantic partnership" uses of the word "marriage" touched on the legality of the thing "marriage." One *thing* being called "marriage" was legal, and another *thing* being called "marriage" was in a state of legal flux, but "marriage" was used to describe both things.

There was also a lexical marker that swayed us toward dividing this into two separate subsenses: "marriage" was increasingly used with modifiers to tell us what sort of marriage the writer was referring to. Prior to the 1990s, "marriage" was, relatively speaking, seldom modified by words like "gay," "straight," "heterosexual," "homosexual," or "same-sex." But by 2000, all these words were common modifiers of the word "marriage"; by 2003, when the *Eleventh Collegiate* was released, "gay" and "same-sex" were the top two most frequently used modifiers of the word "marriage." This signals two interesting (and seemingly contradictory) facts about the word "marriage": that it was being used of a union between gay people, which accounts for the modifiers "gay," "same-sex," and "homosexual," and that people were also seeking to differentiate between same-sex marriage and heterosexual marriage, which accounts for the use of modifiers like "heterosexual" and "straight." If we had seen more use of the unmodified "marriage" of any committed couple, regardless of their genders, that would signal to us that the "gay" marriage sense and the "heterosexual" marriage sense were merging into one. Modifiers mark a philosophical—and, in this case, lexical—divide.

We were one of the last major dictionary makers to make this change to our dictionaries: the vagaries of dictionary production cycles meant that *The American Heritage Dictionary* and the *Oxford English Dictionary* both entered definitions or usage notes that covered same-sex marriage in 2000. The *Oxford English Dictionary* went with a usage note at its existing definition ("The condition of being a husband or wife; the relation between persons married to each other; matrimony") that read, "The term is now sometimes used with reference to long-term relationships between partners of the same sex," with a cross-reference to the entries for "gay." *The American Heritage Dictionary* revised the first sense of its entry for "marriage" in 2000 to "A union between two persons having the customary but usually not the legal force of marriage," and then in 2009 to "The legal union of a man and woman as husband and wife, and in some jurisdictions, between two persons of the same sex, usually entailing legal obligations of each person to the other." Dictionary.com had also already entered a definition that covered the same-sex meaning: "a relationship in which two people have pledged themselves to each other in the manner of a husband and wife, without legal sanction: trial marriage; homosexual marriage."

Our decision was neither unique nor, in dictionary circles, controversial. It was boring, lexical. We gave it due thought, entered it, and moved on. The language is a big place: you can't stop in one spot for too long. We moved ahead into the second half of the alphabet. The world, meanwhile, was spinning circles in court.

You cannot look at the evolution of the word "marriage" without looking also at the evolution of the thing itself. Though words have a life of their own, they are tethered to real-world events. Throughout the late 1990s, states began passing amendments to their own constitutions limiting marriage to a union between one man and one woman. In 1993, the Hawaiian Supreme Court ruled that denying marriage licenses to same-sex couples violated the equal protection clause of the Hawaii Constitution, which became the trigger for H.R. 3396—the bill known as the Defense of Marriage Act. By the time the *Eleventh* came out in July 2003, two states had already passed domestic partnership and civil union legislation, with one more soon to do it (Merriam-Webster's home state, Massachusetts), and four states had, through judicial action or legislation, declared that marriage was restricted to one man and one woman. That left forty-three states on the table. The War on Marriage was in full swing.

Not that we saw much of it in the dictionary offices. "We never heard a peep," notes Steve Kleinedler. "Nothing. I kept expecting it, but . . ." He trails off, his hands opening into a shrug. A handful of questions about the new subsense began to trickle in to the Merriam-Webster editorial e-mail, but it was a literal handful, and they were mostly questions about when we updated the entry. A small grump of correspondents complained—but to be honest, fewer correspondents complained about the changes we made to the entry for "marriage" than complained about the inclusion of the word "phat" in the *Eleventh Collegiate*. The culture war seemed to have passed us by.

The operative word in that sentence is "seemed."

On the morning of March 18, 2009, I padded into my home office with a large cup of coffee and booted up my work e-mail. I blew on my coffee while the e-mail loaded, then blew again; the e-mail was taking a very long time to load. When the program crashed, I groaned and took a huge, scalding gulp of coffee. An e-mail program crash could mean only one of two things: (1) the servers and building were on fire or flooded, or (2) there was a write-in campaign afoot. I rebooted my computer and fervently prayed for number 1 to be the case. My computer dinged to life, and the e-mail began downloading again, which meant the building was not on fire; I covered my face and mooed in despair. The resident mockingbird heard me and answered with a litany of birdsong.

Write-in campaigns are the inevitable product of a strong conviction that someone or something is wrong, a woefully misguided sense of grassroots justice, and unfettered Internet access. A person discovers an entry they don't like in the dictionary, and they petition nine hundred of their closest friends to write to us and tell us to remove or revise that entry. Those nine hundred people then post the write-in request to their blogs or social media profiles, and then nine hundred of *their* closest friends write in about the word they want removed or revised. It's like a perverse, linguistic pyramid scheme: everyone pays in a little and gets nothing in return except for the person at the top (me). I get a ton of e-mail to answer.

When the morning e-mail loaded, I saw why my computer had balked: sitting in my in-box were hundreds of e-mails, most of them with subject lines like "Definition of marriage" and "OUTRAGED!" While I scanned the numbers, my e-mail program binged again: fifteen new e-mails in the last two minutes. I slunk into Drudge's Hunch and wished for a swift and painless death.

The first thing an editor must do in the face of a write-in campaign is figure out where the e-mail is coming from. Fortunately, one of the first people to write in, frothing with rage, handily linked to one source of their displeasure: a story published on the conservative news site *WorldNetDaily* titled "Webster's Dictionary Redefines 'Marriage.'" The article began, "One of the nation's most prominent dictionary companies has resolved the argument over whether the term 'marriage' should apply to same-sex duos or be reserved for the institution that has held families together for millennia: by simply writing a new definition."

I carefully scooted my keyboard and coffee cup to one side and then placed my head on my desk and groaned. *No, no, no:* we were not involved in this cultural argument. Leave the dictionary be.

The article included a one-minute video that, from the get-go, makes it clear that this was not just about recording a word's use for some folks. Over ominous music, the question appears: "What do you do if the dictionary does not support your definition of a word?" I knew where this was going—straight to Panictown. The video flashed some various definitions of "marriage" on-screen to make its point: that marriage has been described as "permanent" and between a man and a woman. Then it showed the new definition we had added in 2003, and suggested that we changed the definition of "marriage" because we didn't agree with what the *institution* of marriage was: permanent and between one man and one woman. The definition faded to black, and the video ended with a giant "WAKE UP!" which grew until it swallowed the screen.

Reluctantly, I clicked back to the article. It went on to note that a dictionary from 1913 made no mention of same-sex marriage and, in fact, offered biblical support for marriage. At this, I began cackling, desperately. Of *course* one of our dictionaries from 1913[*] didn't mention same-sex marriage: it wasn't a common use of the word "marriage" back then! And of *course* it offered example sentences from the Bible. If you were literate in the United States during that time period, you were likely familiar with the Bible, because it was one of the few books that even the poorest families had on their shelves, and so was used didactically in educational settings.

The article claimed we refused to comment—"Hey, that's a lie, I *have* to respond to everything that comes in!" I yelled at the

---

[*] This dictionary, *Webster's Revised Unabridged,* is actually a warmed-over version of *Webster's International Dictionary* from 1890. The *Revised Unabridged* doesn't cover a lot of modern linguistic territory, like "automobile" or "airplane," and its definition of "Republican" mentions slavery and Lincoln.

computer—but noted that an editor denied any agenda to a *World Net Daily* reader.

Upon reading this, my stomach slid into my shoes and tried to hide under the desk. I bet I knew that editor:

"We often hear from people who believe that we are promoting—or perhaps failing to promote—a particular social or political agenda when we make choices about what words to include in the dictionary and how those words should be defined," associate editor Kory Stamper wrote in response.

"We hear such criticism from all parts of the political spectrum. We're genuinely sorry when an entry in—or an omission from—one of our dictionaries is found to be offensive or upsetting, but we can't allow such considerations to deflect us from our primary job as lexicographers."

Stamper justified the redefinition, too. "In recent years, this new sense of 'marriage' has appeared frequently and consistently throughout a broad spectrum of carefully edited publications, and is often used in phrases such as 'same-sex marriage' and 'gay marriage' by proponents and opponents alike. Its inclusion was a simple matter of providing our readers with accurate information about all of the word's current uses," Stamper wrote.

I took a deep breath, and began searching through my e-mail replies while half of my brain ran circles around my head, screaming in terror. I found the very lengthy response I had sent months earlier to a reader and compared it with what had been quoted in the article. Yes, that was exactly what I had written. They had quoted a big middle chunk of my reply without altering it. I exhaled, and only then did I realize I had been holding my breath.

I looked at the very first e-mail that came in after the article ran. It began, "Sirs: Your company decision to change the definition of the word 'marriage' to include same-sex perversion is an utter disgrace."

In the meantime, while I had been reading the article and watching the video, fifty more e-mails had come in. With an acid pit opening in my stomach, I decided to see who else was calling for God's judgment on the dictionary. Time to go googling for controversy.

One of the first hits I turned up was from a web forum that quoted my very first correspondent, Hal Turner. He had a blog, where he had posted his response to us and encouraged all his listeners and readers to share their upset with us. Something scratched deep in my brain; I *knew* that name, where had I heard that name? I opened up a new browser window and searched for Hal Turner and discovered where I had heard that name before: I had read and marked an article in *The Nation* about him:

> In 2003 Turner said US District Judge Joan Humphrey Lefkow was "worthy of being killed" for ruling against white supremacist leader Matthew Hale in a trademark dispute. The day after Lefkow's husband and mother were found murdered on February 28, Turner penned an article for the far-right chat room Liberty Forum outlining tips to help white supremacists avoid scrutiny from federal agents. "So what can we, as White Nationalists (WN), expect as a result [of the killings]?" Turner wrote. "Frankly, a SHIT STORM!"

The rationalizing nerd part of my brain spoke up. But look, it reasoned, at least he didn't advocate violence against dictionary editors, right?

I went back to the original browser window and clicked a link to the forum that had re-posted his blog post. There was a short inscription to introduce the re-post and set the tone for readers: "fucken [*sic*] gay homosexual pervert pedophile sodomizing faggot shit-eaters." I shoved the keyboard aside and slid into Nuclear Fallout position.

After a few deep breaths, and bolstered by the decision that, come hell or high water, I was absolutely going to have *two* beers tonight, I closed out the hate forum and went back to the *WND* article to scan for comments. I caught the author's last name and the silken thread of my sanity snapped cleanly. It was "Unruh," which means "smooth" in Old English. *Mr. Smooth.*

I cackled for a long enough time that my husband set aside his work, came downstairs, and poked his head into my office. "Are you okay?"

"No," I laughed, "no, I am not, and I will not be so for—" Here I looked at my e-mail and made a quick calculation on how long it would take me to answer all 500, nope, now 513 complaints about "marriage." "I will not be okay for at least three days. Assuming nothing else comes in." Two beats, then my e-mail binged obligingly, notifying me of new mail. Only the universe could have such impeccable comedic timing. I redoubled my laughter.

My husband furrowed his brow. "Hon . . ."

"Hey," I said, suddenly serious, "you didn't drink the last two beers in the fridge, did you?"

The complaints about this subsense of "marriage" came down ultimately to one common sore spot: gay marriage (the thing) was not legal or moral, and so our revisions to "marriage" (the word) were also not legal or moral. Enough people felt passionately about this that the defining batch I had been working on prior to March 18, 2009, ended up being three weeks late.

There's certainly nothing wrong with feeling passionately about language; hell, if lexicographers feel passionate about anything, it is most certainly language. But people who start up and perpetuate write-in campaigns to the dictionary are usually grossly mistaken about what a change to the dictionary will actually accomplish. They believe that if we make a change to the dictionary, then we have made a change to the language, and if we make a change to the language, then we also make a change to the culture around that language. We see this most poignantly in requests to remove slurs of various kinds from our dictionaries. If you remove "retarded" from the dictionary, people tell us, then no one will smear someone as "retarded" ever again, because that word is no longer a word. I am the unfortunate drudge who must inform them that we cannot miraculously wipe out centuries of a word's use merely by removing it from the dictionary.

To letter this sign with a slightly larger brush: removing a word from the dictionary doesn't do away with the thing that word refers to specifically, or even tangentially. Removing racial slurs from the dictionary will not eliminate racism; removing "injustice" from the dictionary will not bring about justice. If it were really as easy as that, don't you think we would have removed words like "murder" and "genocide" from the dictionary already? Jerkery, like stupidity and death, is an ontological constant in our universe.

It's easy to scoff at that notion, but before you do, consider this: dictionary makers themselves are the ones who have created this monster.

The prevailing attitude toward words in the nineteenth century, you will remember, was that right thinking led to right usage, and right usage was a hallmark of right thinking. American lexicographers had, to a certain extent, bought into this notion. Even Uncle Noah gets into the act: he makes it clear in the preface to his 1828 dictionary that his work is a natural extension of American exceptionalism, the same doctrine by which the nation "commenced with civilization, with learning, with science, with constitutions of free government, and with that best gift of God to man, the christian religion."* But in the end, it wasn't American exceptionalism that gave rise to the notion that the dictionary was an authority on language and life: it was marketing.

It begins, for Noah Webster and the American dictionary as an institution, with Joseph Worcester. Joseph Worcester was an American lexicographer and, to Noah's mind, Webster's protégé. He was

---

* The word "Christian" never appears with an initial capital in the entirety of the 1828. This is likely a holdover from Johnson's styling of the word "Christian" in his dictionary (from which Webster "borrowed" liberally, ahem). Worcester capitalized "Christian" in his 1830 *Comprehensive Pronouncing and Explanatory Dictionary of the English Language*.

one of the nameless assistants to Webster during the compilation
of the 1828 and also produced his own abridgment of Johnson's
dictionary, supplemented with a popular pronouncing dictionary of
the day. Webster hired Worcester to help him complete an abridgment of the 1828, knowing that he had to find a way to make money
off his magnum opus. Worcester assisted him and then promptly
released his own dictionary in 1830, *A Comprehensive Pronouncing and Explanatory Dictionary of the English Language*. Webster was livid—hadn't he given Worcester his start?—and more to
the point Worcester's dictionary was suddenly in direct competition with Webster's dictionaries to capture the hearts, minds, and
(most important) extra cash of America's schoolchildren and their
families. Worcester's more conservative approach to the language,
which preserved more of the British spellings and pronunciations of
words, earned him a number of fans.

And thus begins the Dictionary Wars of the nineteenth century.
Webster went on the offensive with the best tool in the nineteenth-
century marketer's arsenal: the scalding anonymous letter to the
editor. Webster (or someone representing his interests) started the
volley with an anonymous letter published in the Worcester, Massachusetts, *Palladium,* in November 1834, accusing Worcester of plagiarism and implying that those who bought his dictionaries were
not only getting an unoriginal work but also supporting a common
thief and materially injuring an American patriot:

> [Worcester] has since published a dictionary, which is a very close
> imitation of Webster's; and which, we regret to learn, has been
> introduced into many of the primary schools of the country. We
> regret this, because the public, inadvertently, do an act of great
> injustice to a man who has rendered the country an invaluable ser-
> vice, and ought to recieve [*sic*] the full benefit of his labors.

Worcester defended himself, and the hostilities were on.

When George and Charles Merriam bought the rights to Webster's dictionaries in 1844, they knew that they couldn't continue

to sell the dictionary at the price that Webster himself had sold it—twenty dollars, exorbitant for the age.* Their first order of business was to revise the 1841 edition of Noah's *American Dictionary* into a single-volume dictionary that could be sold for six dollars—a sum that, while still a bit steep, was much more in line with what the average consumer could afford in the mid-nineteenth century. The whole point of doing so was to keep up with Worcester. The sale of Webster's work had been on the decline since Worcester had published his 1830 dictionary, and when Worcester came out with another dictionary in 1846, *A Universal and Critical Dictionary of the English Language,* all hope seemed lost.

The Merriams didn't care about the Webster legacy. Market share was at stake, and so they resorted to the marketing tactics of the nineteenth century: hyperbole and smear.

The hyperbole begins as soon as the 1847 edition of *An American Dictionary of the English Language* is published. Advertisements placed in the *Evening Post* of New York give an extensive list of the new *American Dictionary*'s merits but end with this:

> The work contains a larger amount of matter than any other volume ever published before in the country, and being the result of more than *thirty years'* labor, by the author and editors, at the low price of $6, it is believed to be the *largest,* CHEAPEST, and BEST work of the kind ever published.

By contrast, ads for Worcester's 1846 *Universal* were staid and stately. No typography tricks, no bluster: just a lengthy explication on the goals and methods of the lexicographer, followed by a few encomiums and testimonials that appealed to the taste and

---

* To give you a sense of how much money twenty dollars was in New England at that time, here is an ad from the January 11, 1829, *Fitchburg (Mass.) Sentinel* for W. M. Gray, a grocer on Main Street: "One Dollar will Buy 25 lbs. Rolled Oats or 10 Packages Rolled Avena, or 14 lbs. Nice Rice, or 25 Cakes Good Laundry Soap, or 12 lbs. Pure Lard, or 12 lbs. Salt Pork, or 15 lbs. Muscatel Raisins, or 30 lbs. Best Flour, or 2 gallons Best Molasses."

judgment of the discerning reader. But these ads were few and far between. Most mentions of Worcester's *Universal* in the papers of 1846–1848 were in ads placed by booksellers that often contain no more information than the title of the dictionary itself.

The Merriams, on the other hand, continued their lexicographical putsch. Ads full of interesting typography blared, "The largest, best, and cheapest DICTIONARY in the English language is, confessedly, WEBSTER'S." Worcester's publishers steadfastly refused to bow to the vulgarity of cheap advertising, while the Merriam brothers went bonkers for it. "Get the best!" ads in 1849 proclaimed and never really stopped.

Meanwhile, the race was afoot: Worcester was working on a new dictionary, and one of the higher-level editorial staff at the G. & C. Merriam Company heard it was going to have illustrations in it. The Merriams went into action: they slapped some illustrations in a slightly expanded reprint of the 1847, called it a "New Revised Edition" of Webster's *American Dictionary,* and started the campaign blitz for its 1859 release all over again. Worcester released his massive dictionary, *A Dictionary of the English Language,*[*] in 1860 to great acclaim, and his publishers had, in the years leading up to its release, tried to hop on the tagline train with "Wait, and get the best." But by then, the Merriams had plastered their ads with interesting typography and illustrations all over the papers. "Get the best" was expanded to "Get the best. Get the handsomest. Get the cheapest. Get Webster." And, as advertising is designed to do, vast claims were made about what owning one of these dictionaries would do for you: "A man who would know everything, or anything, as he ought to know, must own Webster's large dictionary. It is a great light, and he that will not avail himself of it must walk in darkness."

Combine all these things—the mudslinging and character assas-

---

[*] It goes without saying that Worcester's dictionary name was in homage to Johnson's dictionary and a direct refutation of Webster's *American Dictionary of the English Language*—the name of the latter being equal parts homage and repudiation. Johnson fetishism runs deep in lexicography.

246 . *Word by Word*

sination, the outsized commendations of each book, the claims
about what owning one of these tomes will do for you—and you
can see why the dictionary is considered not just an educational
but a moral book in many people's minds. Later dictionary marketing campaigns did nothing to discourage people from thinking
this way. "The last twenty-five years have witnessed an amazing
evolution in Man's practical and cultural knowledge," an ad for
Webster's Second New International claims in 1934. "No one can
know, understand, and take part in the life of this new era without a
source of information that is always ready to tell him what he needs
to know." Sales pamphlets for the *Third* didn't tone down the gran-
diloquence, either: "Hold the English language in your two hands
and you possess the proven key to knowledge, enjoyment, and success!" In 1961, Mario Pei, in reviewing the *Third* for *The New York
Times Book Review,* finishes his review with "It is the closest we
can get, in America, to the Voice of Authority." A new marketing
tagline was born: Merriam-Webster used "The Voice of Authority"
in its marketing materials well into the 1990s.

It was the marketing and sale of the *Third* that made the connection between the dictionary, usage, and morality crystal clear.[*]
Reviewers of the *Third* threw up their hands in horror (often over
things that were imagined) and declared that the English language
as we knew it was *finito*. Critics called it "a scandal and a disaster"
and "big, expensive, and ugly" and said that it was indicative of
"a trend toward permissiveness, in the name of democracy, that is
debasing our language."[†] But the criticism wasn't just bell tolling
for English: it was a warning that the *Third* marked a change in our
way of living.

---

[*]   There are far better writers who have undertaken a full study of the production, sale, and fallout from the *Third,* and if the subject interests you, I would
recommend you read those books (particularly Morton's *Story of "Webster's
Third"* and Skinner's *Story of Ain't*) in addition to this one. Alas, I have but
one book to write, and that book ain't it.

[†]   Gil claims that no editors gave much credence to all this critical foofaraw.
"Our problem was getting a *Collegiate* out, not worrying what some ignorant
journalists thought."

Jacques Barzun, a well-known writer and historian, ripped into the *Third* as a culture changer in his review of it for *The American Scholar*. "It is undoubtedly the longest political pamphlet ever put together by a party. Its 2662 large pages embody—and often preach by suggestion—a dogma that far transcends the limits of lexicography. I have called it a political dogma because it makes assumptions about the people and because it implies a particular view of social intercourse." Evidence of that dogma? Entries that note that "disinterested" and "uninterested" are sometimes used synonymously, regardless of what usage commentators think. "The book is a faithful record of our emotional weaknesses and intellectual disarray," Barzun concludes.

Pei began to have second thoughts about the *Third* in the summer of 1962 and wrote a piece for the *Saturday Review* in 1964 that was the culmination of those thoughts. It is a circumspect diatribe on Anglicized pronunciations, the peculiarities of in-house style sheets regarding punctuation and spelling, and the usual faffing about the labels "standard," "nonstandard," and "substandard." But he frames the issue about a third of the way into his article: "There was far more to the controversy than met the eye, for the battle was not merely over language. It was over a whole philosophy of life." The creation of *The American Heritage Dictionary* in the 1960s wasn't just a linguistic response to the *Third* but a calculated cultural response to it. One ad for the first edition of *The American Heritage Dictionary* showed a long-haired young hippie; the ad copy read, "He doesn't like your politics. Why should he like your dictionary?"

It is human nature to want to justify your own opinions by appealing to an external authority, and I can back that assertion up by eavesdropping: "my dad says," "my priest told me," "it's the law," "I read an article that says," "doctors claim," to infinity and beyond. It's why advertisements tell you to "ask your doctor if" their drug is right for you; it's why teachers make students cite their sources when they write.

Dictionary companies had no problem setting themselves up as an authority on life, the universe, and everything throughout most of their history, because doing so ultimately *sold books.* Actual human lexicographers, on the other hand, would rather hide under their desks than be reckoned culture makers. In fact, and in spite of their publishing house's own marketing copy, they have been deliberately avoiding the cultural fray since at least the mid-nineteenth century. Noah Porter, the editor in chief for Webster's 1864 *American Dictionary of the English Language,* sent notes to the staff warning against using quotations from antislavery sermons in the dictionary, because a reference book was not the place for them. Nonetheless, people still assumed that the dictionary was a cultural and political tool: an 1872 article in the McArthur, Ohio, *Democratic Enquirer* that compares the 1864 with previous editions actually asks, "Why does Dr. Porter ignore the Constitution of the United States?" Dr. Porter, it must be said, was merely writing a dictionary.

When I scanned the e-mail that had come in about the word "marriage," it seemed like not much had changed in 137 years. We were accused of partisanship, of bowing to the "gay agenda," of giving in to pressure to be politically correct instead of just plain correct, of abandoning common sense and Christian tradition. Noah Webster was turning in his grave with shame, I was told. People weren't just angry; they were frothing mad. "You have crossed the line where you are irresponsible and attempting to pollute the minds of MY CHILDREN . . . BACK OFF!" one woman warned. I was invited to personally rot in hell no fewer than thirteen times. I was told to get a life, get a *fucking* life, to fuck off and die, and also to swallow shards of glass mixed in acid. The e-mails were, almost to the letter, uninterested in actually knowing *why* we entered this new subsense of "marriage." They didn't care about the mechanics of language change; they cared about the mechanics of culture change. The existence of this definition was not merely recording a common use of "marriage" (the word); it was a declaration that same-sex marriage (the thing) was possible, and an engine by which same-sex marriage (the thing) would be firmly cemented in our society. Comments on Internet forums echoed the same thought. Jim Daly, the president of the Christian organization Focus on the Family, wrote a blog post highlighting the change to the definition. "The majority of voters in states across the U.S. have consistently rejected the idea of same-sex 'marriage,'" Daly notes in a comment on the post. "As such, it could be argued that Merriam-Webster is shaping culture through their online dictionary."

Our marketing director sent me a very quick note on the first day of the onslaught: set aside any e-mails that make actual threats against the company or my person. "Just in case," she said. I forwarded her e-mail along to our senior publicist, Arthur Bicknell. "I've got a guy in here who is calling us all faggots and telling us we deserve to die. Is that actionable? And does this mean I finally qualify for hazard pay?"

Arthur and I had endured a number of write-in campaigns together—he called us Brother Perpetual Spin and Sister Accidental Scapegoat—but this one was particularly difficult. Every bit of spittle-flecked vitriol that he and I received on a daily basis was horrifying; we both felt dehumanized by it. The hateful comments weren't just directed toward gay people. One e-mailer asked if the next thing we were going to legislate was letting different races marry (sorry, the Supreme Court actually beat us to that one, thanks for writing), and another's e-mail handle was like a glossary of white nationalist tropes.

When you deal with that level of hatred and anger for weeks at a time, there are two paths of sanity open to you: quit your job, or crack jokes. I needed the money, so humor it was. I forwarded one e-mail to Arthur that read, in part, "Marriage is the union of one man and one woman. They are made to fit together and can serve no purpose other than to bring about Aids and spiritual death." "And this is why you proofread your hate speech," I commented. "REPENT OF YOUR HOMOSEXUAL MARRIAGE!" one e-mailer bellowed, and I forwarded it to my husband: "This is news to me, but okay: I repent."

But the animosity and personal attacks meant the har-dee-har facade I had put up was prone to crumbling. The Sunday after the write-in campaign started, I was milling around after church when a friend approached to tell me she had seen my name in the news. I didn't respond at all but tried to look nonchalant; I am sure that I looked ready to kick off my shoes and sprint away at the first sign of torches and pitchforks. The first day of the write-in campaign, my mother-in-law sent me an e-mail that began, "I was casually listening to the 700 Club," and before I read any further, I closed out the e-mail, then the e-mail program, then my browser, and then stabbed at the computer's power button until the screen went dark, just for good measure.*

Fortunately, it seemed like most of my correspondents were less interested in scaring the shit out of me and more interested in maintaining the sanctity of marriage. A large number of the correspondents in my in-box also mentioned that same-sex marriage (the thing) wasn't legal in most states, and by entering this definition of "marriage" (the word), we were influencing the legality of same-sex marriage. It was clear that same-sex marriage cases were going to appear before the Supreme Court of the United States at some point in the future, and everyone knows that the members of the Court look at dictionaries when deciding a case.

They do, in fact—a study has shown that their use of dictionaries in deciding cases has increased through the Rehnquist and Roberts courts—but their use is inconsistent, prone to personal whims, and, most important, always secondary. A 2013 study analyzing the Court's dictionary use in criminal, civil, and corporate law cases found that the justices tended to use dictionaries to bolster an opinion that was already held, rather than confirming the objective meaning of a word. The justices also tend to prefer certain dictio-

---

* It turns out that she had heard a report about Finland and thought of me.

naries, some of which have been arguably out of date since 1934 and inarguably out of print since 1961:

> During our twenty-five year period, the heaviest dictionary users in our dataset include Justices Scalia, Thomas, Breyer, Souter, and Alito. The dictionary profiles for these justices are individualized and distinctive. Justice Scalia opts more heavily for *Webster's Second New International* and the *American Heritage Dictionary*, general dictionaries that have been characterized as prescriptive in the lexicographic literature.[*] Justice Thomas relies disproportionately on *Black's Law Dictionary*. Justice Alito is partial to *Webster's Third New International* and the *Random House Dictionary*, both regarded as descriptive. Justices Breyer and Souter are more eclectic: each is a frequent user of *Black's* but Breyer also invokes *Webster's Third* and the *Oxford English Dictionary* (*OED*) with some regularity while Souter turns more often to *Webster's Second*. Indeed, even the justices who make disproportionate use of one or two dictionaries are eclectic in that they frequently cite other dictionaries in particular cases. This pattern is consistent with a practice of seeking out definitions that fit a justice's conception of what a word should mean rather than using dictionaries to determine that meaning.

The justices even joke about dictionaries while in session. In the oral argument for *Taniguchi v. Kan Pacific Saipan Ltd.,* counsel for the petitioner notes that the defendant only appeals to one dictionary for a definition of "interpreter"—*Webster's Third:*

> JUSTICE SCALIA: Webster's Third, as I recall, is the dictionary that defines "imply" to mean "infer"—
> MR. FRIED: It does, Your Honor.

---

[*] It makes perfect sense that Justice Scalia would have preferred *The American Heritage Dictionary,* because he was a member of its Usage Panel.

JUSTICE SCALIA:—and "infer" to mean "imply." It's not a very good dictionary. (Laughter)[*]

There are a number of pivotal court decisions regarding same-sex marriage in America, but four Supreme Court cases take center stage: *Lawrence v. Texas* (2003), which, while not ruling directly on gay marriage, set the stage by overturning state laws prohibiting sodomy in Texas (and, by extension, thirteen other states); *Hollingsworth v. Perry* (2013), which upheld the Ninth Circuit Court of Appeals ruling that overturned Proposition 8 (a California ballot measure and state amendment banning same-sex marriage); *United States v. Windsor* (2013), which held that the part of the Defense of Marriage Act that restricted "marriage" and "spouse" to heterosexual couples was unconstitutional under the due process clause of the Fifth Amendment; and *Obergefell v. Hodges* (2015), in which the Court decided that the fundamental right to marriage for same-sex couples was guaranteed by both the due process clause and the equal protection clause of the Fourteenth Amendment. All four cases were heard after changes to the definition of "marriage" were made to every major dictionary in use. In all four of the cases, in both oral arguments and written decisions (and dissents), a dictionary definition of "marriage" was cited only twice, in *Obergefell v. Hodges*. They appear in Chief Justice Roberts's dissent in support of a restrictive definition of marriage (the thing, not the word); he cites Webster's 1828 and *Black's Law Dictionary* from 1891. Also cited are James Q. Wilson's *Marriage Problem*, John Locke's *Second Treatise of Civil Government*, William Blackstone's *Commentaries*, David Forte's *Framers' Idea of Marriage and Family*,

---

[*] Not quite: The *Third* doesn't say that "imply" and "infer" mean the same thing, though it does use the word "implication" in one definition of "infer" and "inference" at one definition of "imply." The firewall between "imply" and "infer" is a fairly recent invention; the two words have had close meanings since at least the seventeenth century, when that slacker Shakespeare used "infer" to mean "imply" and vice versa.

Joel Bishop's *Commentaries on the Law of Marriage and Divorce,*
G. Robina Quale's *History of Marriage Systems,* and Cicero's *De
Officiis* (in translation). There are four written dissents; only Justice
Roberts's calls upon dictionary definitions.

If legislatures and courts are looking at dictionary definitions,
it's not the definitions that are swaying their opinions. To quote the
2013 study again, "The image of dictionary usage as heuristic and
authoritative is little more than a mirage." But try convincing people upset over the Court's decision to redefine marriage that that's
the case.

Two weeks after the kerfuffle began, I sat at my desk, wheezing
with much-needed laughter, as Stephen Colbert deftly skewered the
whole write-in campaign. Every joke and punch line landed like
a water balloon on a hot day. "The most sinister part is," he continued, "Merriam-Webster made this change back in 2003." Here
I hollered at the screen—"Oh God, yes! *Thank you!*"—while he
continued. "Which means that for the past six years of my marriage,
I may have been gay-married and *not known it.*"

The floodgates opened and I sobbed with laughter, delighted that
someone else was open throatedly mocking the whole situation.
The little bits that I heard between my braying—calling us "same-
sexicographers" who might "engayify" other straight words—were
a balm unto Gilead, just the right response to two weeks of being
told I was single-handedly bringing judgment down upon this great
nation because I happened to answer an e-mail about the word
"marriage."

We continue to get a handful of e-mails complaining about the
definition for "marriage" in the *Collegiate,* but around 2012 the
substance of the complaints changed. Now we get just as many
complaints that the two subsenses aren't combined into one gender-
neutral sense as we do that gay marriage is ruining America.

The definition, as of this writing, is still divided into those two subsenses. Language always lags behind life. Even after *Oberge-fell v. Hodges,* people still debate the dictionary definition of "marriage," waiting for the Voice of Authority to prove them right once and for all.

Us "same-sexicographers," however, have moved on. We're well into the letter *N* at this point.

Epilogue

The Damnedest Thing

If people think at all about lexicography, they think of it as a scientific enterprise. Go to the web, type in "define insouciance," and you assume that the magic algorithms that buzz around Google's servers like bees will do their secret dance and produce a definition for you. Most modern books on lexicography—and there are some, if you can believe it—are scholarly, and therefore make defining sound more like coding: IF ["general" = gradable,comparable,+copula,+very] THEN echo "adjective" ELSE echo "adverb." The exactness of defining, the logic conditions put in place during parsing, the clinical approach that lexicographers take when analyzing words, even the language we use when talking of lexicography ("analyze," "parse," "clinical," "objective"), are borrowed from the realms of lab coats and test tubes.

In the end, however, lexicography is as much a creative process as it is a scientific one, which means that good lexicography relies on the craft of the drudges at their desks. Lexicographers will frame their work as "an art and a science," though we only throw that tired old coat over the bones of our work because it's recognizable shorthand for saying that this thing—the act of creating a definition, sifting through pronunciations, conjuring Proto-Indo-European roots, ferreting out dates of first written use, rassling with the language—isn't just a matter of following a set of rules.

I call it "craft" and not "art" for connotative reasons. "Art" conjures an image of the lexicographer as medium or conduit—a live

255

wire that merely transmits something unkenned, alien. But "craft" implies care, repetitive work, apprenticeship, and practice. It is something that is within most people's reach, but few people devote themselves to it long enough and with enough intensity to do it well. That sort of dedication to words comes across as batty, so we speak in metaphor. Defining is the mental equivalent of free throws in basketball: anyone can stand at the free-throw line and sink one occasionally; everyone gets lucky. But the pro is the person who stands at the free-throw line for hours, months, years, perfecting that one motion until it is as fail-safe as humanly possible, until it looks so much like second nature that an uncoordinated clod like me can watch them lob a rare miss at the net during a game and say, "Are you *kidding*? How easy is it to shoot a free throw?"

"The analogy I use," says Steve Perrault, "is the carpenter. When you first start a project, you're hesitant: you miss the nail, you don't know what you're doing. When you hire a professional, he or she will come in, and what seems like an insurmountable problem to you, they've done it before. It's the same thing for a definer."

"I think everything about defining is easier the longer that you've been doing it," says Joan Narmontas, one of Merriam-Webster's science editors, echoing a sentiment I have heard from everyone who has done practical lexicography for any length of time. "Someone might ask me for a definition, and I can just"—she snaps, a simple, practiced motion—"there it is. It's out." "Experience has a great deal to do with competence," Steve says.

Our modern conception of art happens in a flash; we speak of the lightning striking, the lightbulb going on, the inspiration hitting. Craft takes time, both internal and external. You need patience to hone your skill; you need a society willing to wait (and pay) for that skill.

Unfortunately, time is one thing everyone's short on.

Though this book has been a nitty-gritty, down-and-dirty, worm's-eye view of lexicography, one cannot ignore that dictionary making and reference publishing are commercial enterprises. American dictionaries, in particular, are a slave to the dollar: they are not magnanimously sponsored by academic institutions, as many people believe. Most of the innovations in American dictionaries have been driven by a desire to gain market share and outcompete other publishers, and it's been that way since Noah Webster. The difference between then and now is in how people consume and use dictionaries.

Nineteenth-century lexicographers produced books, and their audience had fixed expectations of what those books were: static things that were the culmination of years of research. If you wanted a dictionary, you scrimped and saved for it, and if you couldn't afford one, then you went to your local public library and used the one copy it had on that rickety maple stand. This was the mode of consumption until the 1990s, when a slow shift from print to digital books began. When I graduated from high school in the early 1990s, I was given a print dictionary as a graduation gift.* It got plenty of use during my college years, but by 2000 it was another doorstop collecting dust. I no longer used print dictionaries; I used online ones.

The Internet is our double-edged sword. Lexicographers have access to new materials for free (or close to it), a better sense of what the user is doing with the entries they create, and a flexible way to organize and present dictionary information that is more intuitive and less fusty and esoteric. We suddenly have unlimited space: we can expand abbreviations that were opaque, stretch our legs a little bit in defining, indulge in some extra example sentences and etymology notes. Gone are the business concerns that if we turn a line here, we will turn a page, and if we turn a page here, we'll end up with six more pages than we have room for, and if we do that, then we need to append a new thirty-two-page folio to

---

* My shameful confession: it was a *Webster's New World Dictionary,* and I loved it. I still love it.

the book, and if we append a new folio to the book, we will have to increase the price of the dictionary by a dollar, and studies have shown that while people will buy a twenty-six-dollar dictionary, they will not buy a twenty-seven-dollar dictionary. But the Internet, keen and fast, is also a knife's edge publishers have to dance along: slow down too much and you'll feel the blade bite into your feet.

People expect information on the Internet to be comprehensive, free, and up to date, which puts reference publishers in a pretty pickle. No information is ever fully free: dictionaries are written by slobs like me, and even slobs need a paycheck. And, as mentioned, it takes time to write a good definition. Assume that a lexicographer can handle one word per workday, on average. That means that doing nothing but defining, one lexicographer can churn out 250 entries a year. Do you spend that editorial time adding new words to be comprehensive or revising out-of-date entries so you're up to date? It's not like this is a new consideration for the lexicographer— we've never had enough time to do everything we want—but the Internet magnifies that time crunch. Dictionaries move online and they are no longer fixed objects, revered books kept on the family shelf, but malleable, ever-changing works that mirror the quicksilver nature of our language.

There's another cutting edge to the Internet: it has made it easier to find an answer to your question, but it's also given us a surfeit of information to sift through. The lexicographer feels this keenly: Joanne Despres when searching data sources for dating, Emily Brewster when searching for the perfect quotation for an entry, Neil Serven when looking through hundreds of thousands of citation hits for a simple word, Dan and Joan and Christopher when trying to collate information for science entries. No one has time to go through six pages of search engine results to weigh which of those results best suits their needs or is most trustworthy, so they rely on the search engine to do that for them. This is the new way of finding information, and it privileges the sources that play the game of search engine optimization.

Of course, all publishers have had to rely on others to ply their wares for them. It used to be that bookstores were the middlemen that sold our products; now it's mostly Google and other search providers. But as Neil pointed out, it's hard to draw an analogy between the two. Bookstores shared "a cultivative interest" with publishers: more book buyers were good for both of them. But search engines and Internet ad providers don't share that interest, or at least not in the same way. They truck in a type of user engagement that dictionaries are historically not good at. As Emily said, people now pay with their eyes, not with their wallets, which means that an online dictionary that runs ads needs to keep eyeballs on its pages longer. The craft of writing a good definition isn't important in the click economy: what is important is being agile enough to do what it takes to get to the top of an Internet search results page. It's a very sudden shift for the staid lexicographer who likes to keep low to the ground.

Like everyone else, lexicographers need to move faster. This is, to be frank, nothing new: we have always felt the heavy thumb of business concerns whenever we define. And while defining gets easier with experience, and the easier it is to do something, the faster you can do it, there is a terminal velocity in lexicography. After a certain point, you simply can't go any faster; to do so compromises the quality of what you're doing. "The job is to get it right," says Neil. "But I do aspire to go faster," answers Emily. Craft takes time, but time is money, and that is another thing that reference publishers are not particularly swimming in.

As I was wrapping up the writing of this book, Merriam-Webster had its first large-scale layoff in decades. I got the news via phone call, and though I had a defining batch open on my desktop and feebly poked at it throughout the day, most of that Tuesday was spent sending everyone else in the office e-mails. "Are you okay?" I asked, and in return I got an echo: "Are *you* okay?" I was not sure if I was okay. None of us were sure if we were okay.

The story of Merriam-Webster's layoff itself isn't interesting or unique. It played out the same way at Merriam-Webster that it has in every other industry in the world; in reference publishing itself, it was just par for the course. The language is booming, but lexicography is a shrinking industry: Funk & Wagnalls, Random House, Encarta, and Century are just a few of the dictionary publishers who have ceased operations in recent history. This is the reality of a commercial enterprise: some will flourish and others will not. Them's the breaks.

But for those of us left trying to ply our trade, we feel each reduction's loss in triplicate. It isn't just that we lose friends; it isn't just that we lose colleagues; it's that we lose *craftspeople*. Most of the editors who are let go when a dictionary publisher shutters have decades of experience writing and editing dictionaries, and the craft that represents is irreplaceable.

"The real strength of a dictionary that is written by skilled lexicographers is sadly perhaps in the entries that are not so commonly examined," Emily says. "If you want to know what 'FTW' means, you can find that in any number of online acronym glossaries. But if you want to know what 'disposition' means, you really need a competently written definition." She thinks for a moment. "I worked really, really hard on the definition of 'build-out,' but I'm sure no one has ever really looked at it."

"I sometimes find it frustrating," Steve says. "I don't think people appreciate all the thought that has to go into the creation of a dictionary, and of a particular dictionary entry. Everything behind it—it's kind of invisible. I feel like people take the dictionary for granted to a large extent. They don't think of it as having been written by anybody, and they don't appreciate all the decisions that had to be made for everything in it. They'll notice errors, but you can't notice excellence in a dictionary, for the most part, because it consists of a lack of errors." He continues. "When was the last time anybody was looking up something in the dictionary and they were so struck by the excellence of it that they had to read it aloud to somebody—'I mean, isn't this wonderful?'"

Madeline nods. "The expectation is that it's going to be right on the money."

Drudges learn to find the good even in complaints. "Even that kind of correspondence is really a genuflection to the entity that is the dictionary," says Emily, and she is right. "The concept of a dictionary—the dictionary as an object—will be useful for a long time." The business of lexicography is in flux, but the work of lexicography is unbowed. Merriam-Webster's staff is small, and we're all sore and still tasting blood, but like all other lexicographers huddled in our hobbit holes, we're moving forward.

Over dinner with Madeline* and me, Steve tells me about how he ended up at Merriam-Webster. He's the type of guy who seems as permanent a Merriam-Webster fixture as the high-gloss conference room tables or the citation files, but the first time he applied for a job at Merriam-Webster, he didn't get it. Another editor was hired, and he went back to looking through newspaper want ads for work. Six months later, an editor left, and Merriam called Steve back and hired him.

"I wasn't working at the time. It was Halloween Day, and I was sitting at home, watching *As the World Turns* in the afternoon, just me and the dog. The phone rang, and I answered it: it was Fred Mish, offering me the job. The salary was nothing; it was laughable. But I knew this was the biggest thing that had ever happened to me, getting the job. I felt that my life had just changed. It was an amazing moment. I told him I'd take the job, and I walked down to the wharf, sat there, and looked at the ocean, just feeling like my life was about to begin. It was the damnedest thing."

Business considerations aside, it *is* the damnedest thing to spend your career in the company of this gorgeous, lascivious language. We don't do the work for the money or prestige; we do it because English deserves careful attention and care. After a time, he sums

---

* Steve and Madeline married a few years after Madeline began at Merriam-Webster. Their desks were near each other's, and they used to bounce definitions off each other. They are just one of a few editorial couples at Merriam-Webster. Like calls unto like, deep unto deep.

up the cri de coeur of every harmless drudge who has ever spent a solitary Thursday hunched over their desk, sifting the grist of "but" or "surfboard" or "bitch" or "marriage" through their fingertips. "That's what I do," he says simply. "This is my own little contribution to the world." English bounds onward, and we drudges will continue our chase after it, a little ragged for the rough terrain, perhaps, but ever tracking, eyes wide with quiet and reverence.

Author's Note

If language is like a river, always moving and changing, then any written chronicle of it is like a snapshot of that river. No matter how artfully the picture is composed or how much detail is captured or how often you stick it in a tub of water and shimmy it around to make it look and feel more realistic, that snapshot is not the river.

The point here is, some of the information given in this book has changed since *Word by Word* was first released in 2017. The English language and the dictionaries that document it have kept changing. Don't panic: this is the nature of the beast.

Two of the biggest changes that have occurred since initial publication of this book have to do with two of the most contentious words discussed here: "marriage" and "bitch." Both words came up for review between the time that the manuscript for *Word by Word* was finished and when it was published, and the revisions made to each provide interesting footnotes to those chapters here.

For "marriage," the change hinted at in the end of the chapter has come to pass. The two subsenses at the entry, one which described straight marriage and one which described same-sex marriage, were combined into one genderless definition ("the state of being united as spouses in a consensual and contractual relationship recognized by law"), which was posted to our online dictionary in late 2016. This was not a fawning pander to The Mighty Gay Agenda, but rather a correction. After *Obergefell v. Hodges* in 2015, our definition that covered uses like "same-sex marriage" or "gay marriage" was inaccurate. It had read "the state of being united to a person of the same sex in a relationship like that of a traditional marriage," but once the legal barrier that differentiated same-sex marriage from straight marriage was removed by the Supreme Court, that "like that of a traditional marriage" was kaput. Legally, same-sex marriage wasn't *an analog* to straight marriage anymore; it was all just "marriage" now. The revision reflects the current legal status of gay marriage in the United States.

The revision also conveniently does away with that tricky phrase, "like that of a traditional marriage." What, exactly, is a traditional marriage? That depends on what the dictionary user thinks is traditional. I recently took a cab ride with an Egyptian Muslim man who talked with me about his two wives and in the middle of his story quickly interjected, "Men can marry up to four women, you know, in my tradition." This is probably not the same sort of traditional marriage that, say, Focus on the Family has in mind. But it is, for this particular gentleman, traditional. And what do we do with all the people who assume that traditional marriage isn't just a legal arrangement, but a social one as well? I'm in a heterosexual marriage, but it is not what I would consider "traditional" by any stretch: my husband and I have taken turns being the breadwinner or the primary caregiver of our kids or the cook or the one who clears out the mousetraps under the kitchen cabinets. (I am currently the one in a squeamish phase vis-à-vis the mousetraps; we trade off.) Maybe this is traditional to other people, but it's not the archetype that pops into my head when I think of a "traditional marriage." And that's the problem: "traditional marriage" is a moving target, and so can be interpreted differently. What the definer really meant was "like that of a legally sanctioned heterosexual marriage," though that is much longer than "like that of a traditional marriage" and so probably would have been edited down anyway.

But we're not insensitive to the fact that this meaning of "marriage" is still contentious for some. There's now also a new usage paragraph at the online entry that explains this and ends with: "The definition of marriage shown here is intentionally broad enough to encompass the different types of marriage that are currently recognized in varying cultures, places, religions, and systems of law." To date, we have not gotten any rabid hate mail about these changes.

Regarding the entry for "bitch," senses 2a and 2b, the ones I focus on here and that have historically been labeled as "opprobrious" or not at all, were given a usage warning: both are now labeled "often offensive" in our online dictionary. That's not to say, however, that we've sorted it. There are still pinks in the file suggesting that we do a full overhaul of the entry. Should sense 2a ("a lewd and immoral woman") get a "dated" label? Do we have enough evidence of the reclaimed "a strong woman" sense to include it? If so, should we write a usage paragraph to explain the process of linguistic reclamation? What about the uses of "bitch" for men; are we going to enter those? The latest comment on one pink sums up the current editorial workload: "deferred until we have more time."

That, at least, hasn't changed too much. We're still lolloping clumsily after English, our quicksilver darling, but the pursuit is no longer as linear as it was even two years ago. The possibilities that the Internet provides mean that the very idea of *what a dictionary is* is in flux—which means that the work that a lexicographer does is also in flux. It's not all definitions and hate mail these days: we also write content for partner websites or articles for our own; we research and write the extra usage paragraphs that appear in the online dictionary; we spend time debugging and proofreading data structures and tagging schemes; we take to social media, God help us, to explain that no, it is not a political statement when we tweet that millions of people are looking up a word because Donald Trump (mis)used it, or yes, you're right that a manhole cover is actually round because a circle is the only shape that can't mistakenly be rotated in such a way that it could accidentally drop through the manhole.[*] Our feelings about this shift are complicated: on the one hand, it's a lexicographer's dream to be able to share more in-depth and real-time information about a word's use, history, and

---

[*] Many thanks to all fifty-four of you who took the time to write, e-mail, or tweet to let me know that my conjecture regarding the real reason that manhole covers were round, found in the chapter titled "Nude," was, in fact, wrong.

problems without worrying about space; on the other, editorial time is a finite resource, and the eight hours I spend researching and writing about the history of "throw shade" is eight hours I can't spend revising the entry for "bitch." The proverbial press of editorial duties has gotten bigger and heavier.

But regardless of the slow yet tectonic upheaval our industry is going through, the core work of lexicography—the painstaking untangling of a word's uses, the orderly construction of a definition, the weighing of connotation and denotation—is still worth something to people. If it weren't, no one would bother visiting our website or writing in to tell us where they saw a word used or bothering to complain that we haven't entered "urban planner" yet (I promise, I'm going just as lickety-goddamned-split as I can). We're in a cultural moment where words and their meanings matter to people more than ever, which is why the work of we harmless drudges continues apace. Change is gonna come, to quote Sam Cooke. But in the meantime, if you need me, I'll be knee-deep in the middle of the letter *S*.

Acknowledgments (in alphabetical order)

agent \ˈā-jənt\ *n* -**s** : a person who acts as a representative for someone (such as an artist, writer, or athlete) and encourages, protects, advises, or kicks the ass of their client <Without my *agent,* Heather Schroder of Compass Talent, this book would never have gotten off the ground.>

col·league \ˈkä-(ˌ)lēg\ *n* -**s** : an associate in a profession; *specifically* : any of several people who share work experience, knowledge, a preference for silence, and sometimes chocolate <My *colleagues* who graciously agreed to speak to me about lexicography—E. Ward Gilman, Emily Vezina, Emily Brewster, Peter Sokolowski, Daniel Brandon, Karen Wilkinson, Joshua Guenter, James Rader, Joanne Despres, Neil Serven, Stephen Perrault, Madeline Novak, Steve Kleinedler, and Jane Solomon—deserve to be left alone for a very long time.> <All my *colleagues* at Merriam-Webster, American Heritage Dictionaries, Oxford University Press, and Dictionary.com were invaluable assistants in jogging my memory, filling in gaps, and providing some much-needed sanity throughout the writing of this book.>—see FRIEND

ed·i·tor \ˈe-də-tər\ *n* -**s** : a person who prepares something (such as books or other printed materials) for publication; *especially* : one who reads, alters, adapts, and corrects a written work a great number of times while simultaneously convincing the writer that the written work is good, though not yet *good* <Andrew Miller, my steadfast and patient *editor* at Pantheon, has earned his weight in gold.> <Emma Dries, another Pantheon *editor,* asked just the right questions in going through this work.> <Many thanks to Laura M. Browning, who acted as first-line *editor* on some particularly nasty and rambly bits of this work.>—called also *miracle worker*

fam·i·ly \ˈfam-lē\ *n* -**lies 1 a** : a group of people sharing common ancestors <I'm grateful for the support of my *families,* Stamper and Behny alike.> **b** : a group of people related to one another and living together in one very messy household <The cheerleading from my *family*—Ansa, Hilja, and Josh—was sometimes the only thing that kept me writing.> <I am sorry that my *family* lived on pizza and chips and salsa for a year while I wrote this book.> **2** : a group of people united by common affiliation with and love for each other <The *family* of City Church Philadelphia kept me buoyed up

with encouragement and wouldn't let me whine about how hard writing a book is.>

friend \'frend\ *n* **-s** : one who favors or promotes something (such as the writing of a book) especially by providing emotional, physical, spiritual, or gastronomic support <This book has been brought to you by the quiet patience and gentle encouragement of a number of *friends,* including especially Katy Rawdon, Abby Breitstein, Matt Dube, Billie Faircloth, the praying ladies, and the Dorset 5 + 1 crew.>

men·tor \'men-ˌtȯr, -tər\ *n* **-s** : a trusted counselor or guide; *especially* : a person with greater experience and wisdom who teaches and guides a younger or inexperienced person no matter how irritating that inexperienced person may be <I am lucky to count Madeline Novak, Stephen Perrault, and E. Ward Gilman as my lexicographical *mentors.*>—see FRIEND

re·treat \ri-'trēt\ *n* **-s** : a place of privacy away from one's normal surroundings; *especially* : a place of quiet for a particular purpose (such as writing a book or eating one's host out of house and home) <Many thanks to Alison Pacuska and James Mathieson for providing me with a *retreat* where I could write and talk, and to the Brewster-Janke household for same.>

won·der \'wən-dər\ *n* **-s 1** : a cause of astonishment or admiration : MAR-VEL **2** : MIRACLE <I can never say enough about Josh Stamper, my husband, friend, and co-laborer in creative endeavors, who is for me a daily *wonder.*>

Notes

All entries cited in the footnotes come from either *Merriam-Webster's Collegiate Dictionary, Eleventh Edition* (2014) or *Merriam-Webster's Unabridged Dictionary* (2015).

HRAFNKELL: *On Falling in Love*

7   "Hē is his brōðor": Cassidy and Ringler, *Bright's Old English Grammar*, 24.

9   It's more American than football: See "For to Make Tartys in Applis," in *The Forme of Cury, a Roll of Ancient English Cookery, Compiled, About A.D. 1390, by the Master-Cooks of King Richard II, Presented Afterwards to Queen Elizabeth, by Edward Lord Stafford, and Now in the Possession of Gustavus Brander, Esq.* . . . (London: J. Nichols, 1770), 119, for a delightful apple tart recipe, and *Oxford English Dictionary*, 3rd ed., s.v. "football" (2015), which makes it plain the game originated in Warwickshire.

13   "When P* is less than P": Fitch, *Dictionary of Banking Terms*, 449.

21   "I knew that the work": Johnson, *Plan of a Dictionary*, 1.

21   "It is the fate of those who toil": Johnson, preface to *Dictionary of the English Language*.

BUT: *On Grammar*

26   "gradience": Quirk et al., *Comprehensive Grammar of the English Language*, 90.

27   In the West, they were first hinted at: Plato, *Cratylus* 392a–399b.

27   "a sound without meaning": Aristotle, *Poetics* 1456b.

27   The parts of speech we use today: Thrax, *Grammar of Dionysius Thrax*.

27   This system has been futzed with: For more information, see ibid.; Priscian, *Institutitones grammaticae* (ca. 500); and Redinger, *Comeniana grammatica*.

28   "4.2 Article. There are three:": Merriam-Webster, "Quirky Little Grammar," 7.

37   "I have been sympathetic": White to J. G. Case, Dec. 17, 1958, quoted in Elledge, *E. B. White,* 331.

IT'S: *On "Grammar"*

39   That meant that while Medieval Latin: The Latin is taken from Latham et al., *Dictionary of Medieval Latin from British Sources;* the Old French from Kelham, *Dictionary of the Norman or Old French Language,* 74–75; and the Middle English from *Oxford English Dictionary,* 3rd ed., s.v. "right, adj" (2010).

39   "English now had to serve the functions": Merriam-Webster, *Merriam-Webster's Concise Dictionary of English Usage,* xiii.

40   "our naturall tong is rude": Skelton, *Boke of Phyllyp Sparowe.*

41   In 1586, William Bullokar: See Bullokar, *Bref Grammar for English,* and Cawdrey, *Table Alphabeticall.*

41   "to encourage Polite Learning": Defoe, *Essay upon Projects,* 233.

41   "By such a society I daresay": Ibid., 233–34.

42   "I cannot allow any pleasures": Defoe, *Complete English Tradesman,* 118–19.

43   "It is with reason expected": Lowth, *Short Introduction to English Grammar,* vii.

44   "The confusion of the possessive 'its'": Truss, *Eats, Shoots & Leaves,* 44.

44   "I proudly consider myself a punctuation martyr": "Nataliya's Reviews: Eats, Shoots and Leaves," Goodreads.com, June 11, 2014, accessed April 23, 2016, http://www.goodreads.com/review/show /177243634?book_show_action=true.

44   "In summary of the proof": Gwynne, *Gwynne's Grammar,* 6.

45   At one point in time, "it" was its own possessive: Both the King James Bible and *King Lear* cited in Merriam-Webster, *Concise Dictionary of English Usage,* 442–44.

46   "I cast my eyes": Dryden, *Defense of the Epilogue,* 217.

47   Later editions of his work: Lynch, *Lexicographer's Dilemma,* 30–31.

48   "really extreme usage fanatic": Wallace, "Tense Present," 41.

48   he used "nauseated" instead of "nauseous": Wallace, "Broom of the System," 29, as well as Wallace, "English 183A," 633.

48   Bryan Garner, one of Wallace's prescriptivist heroes: Garner, *Garner's Modern American Usage,* 560–61.

48   "The moment hung there": Wallace, "Compliance Branch," 19.

49   "the deplorable Ignorance": Swift to Isaac Bickerstaff, Esq., in *Works,* 268.

49   E. B. White says in *The Elements of Style:* Strunk and White, *Elements of Style,* 35; and White, "Some Remarks on Humor," 174.

49   "eloquently speaks to the value": Joanne Wilkinson, review of *Eats, Shoots & Leaves,* by Lynne Truss, *Booklist,* June 1, 2004.

51   "If the changes that we fear": Johnson, preface to *Dictionary of the English Language.*

IRREGARDLESS: *On Wrong Words*

57   "I remembered the magnitude of his problems": Walker, "Old Artist," 39.

58   "The language of the people": "The Seer's Latest Warning," *Albany Evening Herald,* April 5, 1911, 2.

58   "If the Board sees proper": "Another Gripe," *Weekly Kansas Chief* (Troy, Kans.), Feb. 2, 1888, 2.

59   "Parson Twine has a new word": *Atchison Daily Globe,* Jan. 30, 1882, 4.

59   "The REPORTER has been given a copy": "A Star Specimen," *Logansport (Ind.) Reporter,* March 24, 1893, 2.

65   even in the oral arguments: *Obergefell v. Hodges.* The counsel who used "irregardless" in oral arguments got his undergraduate degree from DePauw University, which is in Indiana, where we have lots of evidence of the use of "irregardless."

66   This particular construction: Fruehwald and Myler, "I'm Done My Homework."

67   "When another linguist and I": Marguerite Rigoglioso, "Stanford Linguist Says Prejudice Toward African American Dialect Can Result in Unfair Rulings," *Stanford Report,* Dec. 2, 2014.

CORPUS: *On Collecting the Bones*

70   The letter's a marvel: "Nowe if the word, which thou art desirous to finde, begin with (a) then looke in the beginning of this Table, but if with (v) looke towards the end" and following quotation both from Cawdrey, *Table Alphabeticall.*

73   "a man of bizarre appearance": Lynch, *Lexicographer's Dilemma,* 74.

74   "the business of a lexicographer": Webster to John Pickering, in Morton, *Story of "Webster's Third,"* 205.

75 "Mansplain" stuttered into existence: Zimmer and Carson, "Among the New Words," 200–203.

76 This trend has been much more common in the U.K.: "Bored by, of, or with?," *Oxford Dictionaries* (blog), April 24, 2016, www.oxforddictionaries.com.

79 "trying to chisel in on the beer racket": *Merriam-Webster Unabridged,* s.v. "chisel, verb."

80 And now we see the word "muggle": "The Supreme Court's reading and defense of Obamacare meant to him that 'words no longer have meaning' and he decried his fellow justices for their 'interpretive jiggery-pokery.' That last insult was an unusual one, and it led the muggles of the Internet to wonder where they'd heard it before." Marina Koren, "Antonin Scalia and the Supreme Court of Jiggery-Pokery," *National Journal,* June 25, 2015.

80 He has made—by hand: Andrew McMillan, "One Man's Quest to Rid Wikipedia of Exactly One Grammatical Mistake," *Backchannel,* Feb. 3, 2015, www.backchannel.com.

82 "We can actually measure": Manuel Ebert, quoted in Natasha Singer, "Scouring the Web to Make New Words 'Lookupable,'" *New York Times,* Oct. 3, 2015.

85 In November, just five months: "On fleek," Google Trends, 2014.

85 My colleague Emily interviewed Monroee: Emily Brewster, "Raising an Eyebrow on 'Fleek': PART TWO," *Merriam-Webster Unabridged* (blog), Feb. 12, 2015.

87 "At the Barbra Streisand $5000-a-head Demo fund-raiser": Herb Caen, *San Francisco Chronicle,* Sept. 12, 1986, 43.

SURFBOARD: *On Defining*

95 "L ong O vercoming V alues E ffect ~ love ?": Comments on the entry for "love," Merriam-Webster.com.

98 "hella": Nancy Friedman, tweet, "Hella t-shirt!," Oct. 23, 2015.

101 In fact, it appears to have been coined: Chris Cole, "The Biggest Hoax," *Word Ways* (1989), accessed April 24, 2016, http://www.wordways.com/biggest.htm.

101 "It was concluded": Stoliker and Lafreniere, "Influence of Perceived Stress," 148.

104 "This memo is concerned primarily": Gove, "Punctuation and Typography of Vocabulary Entries," 390.

110   "Wherfore incontinent I caused the printes to cesse": Elyot, dedication in *The Dictionary of Syr Thomas Eliot Knyght.*

120   There's an awful lot of chatter: "The demand for Hobie's surfboards grew faster than they could even get balsa wood, so Alter started developing and mass producing foam and fiberglass surfboards. That changed everything." Nathan Rott, "Hobie Alter, the Henry Ford of Surfboards, Dies at 80," *All Things Considered,* NPR, March 31, 2014.

PRAGMATIC: *On Examples*

127   "Aren't politicians supposed": Joe Klein, "In the Arena," *Time,* June 2, 2011, 23.

130   huge *tracts* of land: King of Swamp Castle (on his son's imminent marriage to Princess Lucky): We live in a bloody swamp. We need all the land we can get.
Prince Herbert: But I don't like her.
King of Swamp Castle: Don't like her? What's wrong with her? She's beautiful, she's rich, she's got huge . . . tracts of land. (*Monty Python and the Holy Grail,* directed by Terry Jones and Terry Gilliam, 1975)

TAKE: *On Small Words*

140   "With the Angels dispatched": Tom Verducci, "They're At It Again," *Sports Illustrated,* Oct. 18, 2004, 51.

140   "Whether or not": Starr, excerpt, *Starr Report.*

BITCH: *On Bad Words*

149   Taboo language of all sorts: Florio, *Worlde of Words,* 137.

152   "þou bycche blak as kole": *Castle of Perseverance,* 2117, a1450, in *Middle English Dictionary,* s.v. "bicche."

152   By the time Shakespeare: "A blind bitch's puppies, fifteen i' the litter." Shakespeare, *Merry Wives of Windsor,* 3.5.10.

154   He was an English Baptist minister: Ash, *New and Complete Dictionary of the English Language.*

154   "those Burlesque Phrases, Quaint Allusions": Grose, *Classical Dictionary of the Vulgar Tongue,* iii.

155   "There were 8 or 9 of them": Trial of Thomas Wright, April 1726, *Old Bailey Proceedings Online,* Ref. No. t17260420-67.

156 "Be God, he ys a schrewd byche": *The Friar and the Boy,* 54, a1475, in *Middle English Dictionary,* s.v. "bicche."

156 Henry Fielding uses it: All attestations in this paragraph are given in *Green's Dictionary of Slang Online,* s.v. "bitch, n.1."

158 "A woman should be proud": Joreen [Jo Freeman], *The BITCH Manifesto* (1968), 1970.

159 "I think queer harkens back": Kichi, in Susan Donaldson James, "Gay Man Says Millennial Term 'Queer' Is Like the 'N' Word," *ABC News,* Nov. 12, 2013.

159 "As feminism taught us long ago": Kleinman, Ezzell, and Frost, "Reclaiming Critical Analysis," 61.

162 "In the specific applications the term": John Bethel, in-house pink, Merriam-Webster, May 29, 1947.

164 Susan Brady, one of our associate editors: Susan Brady, in-house pink, Merriam-Webster, May 1, 1992.

166 "an actress recently described": Wayne Warga, "Lee Grant," *Cosmopolitan,* Dec. 1977, 72.

166 "It contains his two most": Edmund Wilson, "Books," *New Yorker,* Sept. 18, 1971, 134.

166 ". . . was a hard *bitch*": Peter Evans, "Bernadette Devlin," *Cosmopolitan,* Nov. 1972, 207.

166 "'So someone calls you a *bitch*'": Meg Cox, "Female Rappers Sing of Smut and Spice and Nothing Nice—They Make It in Men's World by Being Rude and Nasty," *Wall Street Journal,* April 11, 1991, A9.

POSH: *On Etymology and Linguistic Originalism*

172 "We read, in the Scriptures": Webster, introduction to *American Dictionary of the English Language.*

173 "Everything in etymology is conjecture": Liberman, "Occam's Razor and Etymology," DSNA-20 & SHEL-9.

173 "He had the notion": Quoted in Micklethwait, *Noah Webster and the American Dictionary,* 170.

177 "The cavalryman, far more than the infantryman": Vivian, *British Army from Within,* 86.

178 "Sir,—In the Oxford New English Dictionary": T. D. Atkinson, letter to the editor, *Times Literary Supplement,* Oct. 17, 1935, 625.

180 The account also mentions: Pierre-Jean Grosley, *Londres* (1770), 1:626.

183   "to use decimation": White, *Words and Their Uses,* 106.

183   "How often does one really": Shea, *Bad English,* 16.

185   "twou'd be as Criminal": Defoe, *Essay upon Projects,* 237.

185   "not arrived to such a Degree": Swift, *Proposal,* 15.

186   "passel of double-domes": editorial, *The New York Times,* October 12, 1961, 21.

186   "badly needs new guidance": *Springfield Union,* Feb. 19, 1962, quoted in Morton, *Story of "Webster's Third,"* 223.

186   "an affront": John G. Rodgers, *New York Herald-Tribune,* Feb. 20, 1962, quoted in Morton, *Story of "Webster's Third,"* 224.

186   "take the Third out of print!": "Dictionaries: The Most Unique," *Newsweek,* March 12, 1962, 105, quoted in Morton, *Story of "Webster's Third,"* 224.

186   The authority upon which: Morton, *Story of "Webster's Third,"* 229; "The Panelists," *American Heritage Dictionary* (blog), accessed April 24, 2016, https://ahdictionary.com/word/usagepanel.html.

186   The December 1964 ballot: *American Heritage Dictionary* Usage Panel, "Letter A" in-house balloting summary, *American Heritage Dictionary*/Houghton Mifflin Harcourt archives, Dec. 1964.

187   "There is always the danger": Cowley, Asimov, and Tuchman, quoted in Steinway, "Archivist Mines the Usage Ballots."

187   in the early years of the twenty-first century: *American Heritage Dictionary,* 5th ed., s.v. "dilemma," usage note.

188   Interestingly enough, only 90 percent: Ibid., s.v. "irregardless," usage note.

188   Eighty-one percent of them: Ibid., s.v. "decimate," usage note.

AMERICAN DREAM: *On Dates*

192   Tacitus did mention brothels: Tacitus, *Annales* 15.37.

193   "These Safari are neither starved": Burton, *The Lake Regions of Central Equatorial Africa* (1859), 410, quoted in *Oxford English Dictionary,* 3rd ed., s.v. "safari."

193   "kind of a quick slap": Britt Peterson, "'Car Talk' Lives On—in the Dictionary," *Boston Globe,* April 26, 2015.

193   "Well, the first thing I'd do": Tom Magliozzi and Ray Magliozzi, "When the Oil Light Comes On, Stop the Engine Immediately," *Car Talk* (blog), March 1, 1992.

195   "The arrangements for shopping": Smith, *Essays on Questions,* 55.

196   "Every republic": *Nation,* Nov. 8, 1900, 362.

196   The linguist Arnold Zwicky: Arnold Zwicky, "Why Are We So Illuded?" (abstract for conference paper, Stanford University, 2006).

196   John Gower used "hap": Gower, *Confessio Amantis,* 43.

197   Or that "OMG" goes back to 1917: John Arbuthnot Fisher to Churchill, Sept. 7, 1917, in *Memories and Records by Admiral of the Fleet Lord Fisher* (New York: George H. Doran, 1920), 87.

NUCLEAR: *On Pronunciation*

204   "A Besides this generall note": Mulcaster, *Elementarie,* 111.

204   "Pronunciation . . . is an apte orderinge": Wilson, quoted in Johnson, *Dictionary of the English Language.*

204   "established the jargon": Johnson, preface to ibid.

206   One book's pronunciation: see Buchanan, *Linguae Britannicae;* Kenrick, *New Dictionary of the English Language;* and Sheridan, *Complete Dictionary of the English Language.*

210   "spectacular blunder": Robert Burchfield, quoted in Elster, *Big Book of Beastly Mispronunciations,* 347.

210   "aberration": Richard Lederer, quoted in ibid., 349.

210   "beastly": Right there in the title, Elster, *Big Book of Beastly Mispronunciations.*

211   "Though disapproved of by many": *Merriam-Webster's Collegiate Dictionary,* s.v. "nuclear," usage note.

211   a Nobel Prize–winning theoretical physicist: The physicist in question is Julian Schwinger: "Schwinger also had some speech mannerisms, which many of the students began unconsciously to imitate. I don't know how many of the Ph.D.s he had produced—there was [*sic*] sixty-eight by the time he left Harvard, an incredible number for a theorist, since each Ph.D. represents at least one publishable research idea—began to say 'nucular' and 'We can effectively regard,' two of the Schwinger standards." Jeremy Bernstein, "Personal History," *New Yorker,* Jan. 26, 1987.

212   "I wish you would": Quoted in transcripts from Charles Gibson, "Kennedy Letters: Insight into History," *ABC World News* transcripts, Sept. 28, 2006.

213   "I once asked a weapons specialist": Geoffrey Nunberg, "Going Nucular," *Fresh Air,* NPR, Oct. 2, 2002.

213   Metcalf notes: Metcalf, *Presidential Voices,* 108.

213 Steven Pinker, another linguist: Steven Pinker, "Pinker Contra Nunberg re Nuclear/Nucular," *Language Log,* Oct. 17, 2008.

213 But then we'd have to account: *Oxford English Dictionary,* 3rd ed., s.v. "thermonukes" and "nuclear."

214 "But which of these stories explains": Nunberg, "Going Nucular."

NUDE: *On Correspondence*

221 In 2015, *BuzzFeed:* "Black Women Try 'Nude' Fashion," *BuzzFeed,* May 20, 2015.

226 I clicked one lipstick image: Ashley Reese, "12 Nude Lipsticks That Are Actually Nude on Darker Skin," Gurl.com, June 5, 2014.

MARRIAGE: *On Authority and the Dictionary*

231 I clicked the link: "Merriam-Webster's Word's Worth," *The Colbert Report,* Comedy Central, April 2, 2009.

234 by 2003, when the *Eleventh Collegiate* was released: Brigham Young University, *Corpus of Contemporary American English,* s.v. "marriage."

235 *Oxford English Dictionary:* Oxford English Dictionary, 3rd ed., s.v. "marriage" (Dec. 2000).

235 *The American Heritage Dictionary:* American Heritage Dictionary, 4th ed., s.v. "marriage," (2000, 2009). The definition has been revised several times since 2009.

235 Dictionary.com had also: Dictionary.com, s.v. "marriage" (2009). The definition has since been revised.

237 "One of the nation's most prominent": Bob Unruh, "Webster's Dictionary Redefines 'Marriage,'" *WorldNetDaily,* March 17, 2009.

239 "We often hear": Ibid.

240 "In 2003 Turner said": Max Blumenthal, "Hannity's Soul-Mate of Hate," *Nation,* June 3, 2005.

240 "fucken [*sic*] gay": "Webster's Dictionary Re-defines 'Marriage' to Include Same-Sex Perversion," alt.conspiracy, March 18, 2009.

242 "commenced with civilization": Webster, preface to *American Dictionary of the English Language.*

243 "[Worcester] has since published": Quoted in Micklethwait, *Noah Webster and the American Dictionary,* 225.

244 "The work contains": Advertisement, *Evening Post,* Oct. 20, 1847, 2.

245 "Get the best!": Advertisements with exclamation point ran in the

North Carolina Argus, June 19, 1849, 3; and *Lewisburg (Pa.) Chronicle,* Nov. 28, 1849, 4. There were other ads that ran in various papers in 1849 that merely stated, "Get the best."

245   "Wait, and get the best": Advertisement in *Times-Picayune,* Feb. 13, 1857, 5.

245   "Get the best. Get the handsomest": Advertisement in *Pittston (Pa.) Gazette,* June 14, 1860, 3.

245   "A man who would know everything": Advertisement in *Lewisburg (Pa.) Chronicle,* March 14, 1856, 2.

246   "The last twenty-five years": Advertisement for *Webster's New International Dictionary, Second Edition,* in-house archive, Merriam-Webster.

246   "Hold the English language": Advertisement for *Webster's Third New International Dictionary,* in-house archive, Merriam-Webster.

246   "It is the closest we can get": Mario Pei, "'Ain't' Is In, 'Ravolis' Ain't," *New York Times,* Oct. 22, 1961, BR6.

246   "a scandal and a disaster": Wilson Follett, "Sabotage in Springfield," *Atlantic Monthly,* Jan. 1962, 74.

246   "big, expensive, and ugly": Garry Wills, "Madness in Their Method," *National Review,* Feb. 13, 1962, 98.

246   "a trend toward permissiveness": Dwight Macdonald, "The String Untuned," *New Yorker,* March 10, 1962, 166.

247   "It is undoubtedly the longest political pamphlet": Barzun, "Scholar Cornered," 176.

247   "There was far more to the controversy": Mario Pei, "A Loss for Words," *Saturday Review,* Nov. 14, 1964, 82.

247   "He doesn't like your politics": Quoted in Skinner, *Story of Ain't,* 296.

248   "Why does Dr. Porter ignore": "Falsifying Partisanship of Webster's Dictionary," *McArthur Democratic Enquirer,* April 3, 1872, 1.

249   "The majority of voters in states": Daly, comment on "Webster redefines marriage."

251   "During our twenty-five year period": Brudney and Baum, *Oasis or Mirage,* 3–4.

251   "JUSTICE SCALIA": Oral arguments, *Taniguchi v. Kan Pacific Saipan Ltd.,* 18–25.

252   They appear in Chief Justice Roberts's dissent: Roberts, dissent in *Obergefell v. Hodges,* 1–29.

253   "The image of dictionary usage": Brudney and Baum, *Oasis or Mirage,* 6.

Bibliography

Abbott, Karen. "The House That Polly Adler Built." *SmithsonianMag.com*, April 12, 2012.

American Heritage Dictionaries. *The American Heritage Dictionary of the English Language*. 4th ed. 2000. Boston: Houghton Mifflin, 2009.

———. *The American Heritage Dictionary of the English Language*. 5th ed. Boston: Houghton Mifflin Harcourt, 2014.

Aristotle. *Poetics*. Vol. 23 of *Aristotle in 23 Volumes*. Translated by W. H. Fyfe. Cambridge, Mass.: Harvard University Press, 1932.

Ash, John. *The New and Complete Dictionary of the English Language*. Vol. 1. London, 1775.

Bailey, Nathan. *An Universal Etymological Dictionary of English*. 1721. London, 1763.

Barzun, Jacques. "The Scholar Cornered: What Is a Dictionary?" *American Scholar* (Spring 1963): 176–81.

Brigham Young University. *Corpus of Contemporary American English*. 2015. Accessed Aug. 11, 2015. http://corpus.byu.edu/coca/.

Brudney, James J., and Lawrence Baum. *Oasis or Mirage: The Supreme Court's Thirst for Dictionaries in the Rehnquist and Roberts Eras*. Fordham Law Legal Studies research paper No. 2195644, Jan. 2, 2013.

Buchanan, James. *Linguae Britannicae Vera Pronunciatio: or, A New English Dictionary*. London: A. Millar, 1757.

Bullokar, William. *Bref Grammar for English*. In *Booke at Large* (1580) *and Bref Grammar for English* (1586): *Facsimile Reproductions*. 1586. Delmar, NY: Scholars' Facsimiles and Reprints, 1977.

Cartigny, Jean de. *The Voyage of the Wandering Knight. Deuised by Iohn Carthenie, a Frenchman: And Translated out of French into English, by VVilliam Goodyear of South-hampton Merchant. A Vvorke Vvorthie of Reading, and Dedicated to the Right Worshipfull Sir Frauncis Drake*. London, 1581.

Cassidy, Frederic G., and Richard N. Ringler, eds. *Bright's Old English Grammar & Reader*. 1891. 3rd ed. Fort Worth, Tex.: Harcourt Brace Jovanovich, 1971.

Cawdrey, Robert. *A Table Alphabeticall.* London: I.R., 1604.

Coote, Edmund. *The English Schoole-Master Teaching All His Schollers....* 1596. London: B. Alsop and T. Fawcet, and George Purslowe, 1630.

Crystal, David. *The Fight for English: How Language Pundits Ate, Shot, and Left.* Oxford: Oxford University Press, 2006.

Defoe, Daniel. *The Complete English Tradesman in Familiar Letters.* Vol. 1. London, 1726.

———. *An Essay upon Projects.* London: R.R., 1697.

Dryden, John. *Defence of the Epilogue; or, An Essay on the Dramatic Poetry of the Last Age.* 1672. Vol. 4 of *The Works of John Dryden.* Edited by Sir Walter Scott. London: William Miller, 1808.

Elledge, Scott. *E. B. White: A Biography.* New York: W. W. Norton, 1985.

Elster, Charles Harrington. *The Big Book of Beastly Mispronunciations: The Complete Opinionated Guide for the Careful Speaker.* 2nd ed. New York: Houghton Mifflin, 2005.

Elyot, Thomas. *The Dictionary of Syr Thomas Eliot Knyght.* London, 1538.

Fitch, Thomas P. *Dictionary of Banking Terms.* New York: Barron's, 1990.

Florio, John. *A Worlde of Wordes; or, Most Copious, and Exact Dictionarie in Italian and English.* London, 1598.

Fruehwald, Josef, and Neil Myler. "I'm Done My Homework—Case Assignment in a Stative Passive." *Linguistic Variation* 15, no. 2 (2015): 141–68.

G. & C. Merriam Company. *Webster's Collegiate Dictionary.* Springfield, Mass.: G. &. C. Merriam, 1898.

———. *Webster's New International Dictionary.* Springfield, Mass.: G. & C. Merriam, 1909.

———. *Webster's New International Dictionary, Second Edition.* Springfield, Mass.: G. & C. Merriam, 1934.

———. *Webster's Seventh New Collegiate Dictionary.* 7th ed. Springfield, Mass.: G. & C. Merriam, 1963.

Garner, Bryan A. *Garner's Modern American Usage.* 3rd ed. New York: Oxford University Press, 2009.

Gove, Philip Babcock. "Marking Instructions." In Black Books. Merriam-Webster, July 13, 1953.

———. "Punctuation and Typography of Vocabulary Entries." In Black Books. Merriam-Webster, Jan. 31, 1956.

Gower, John. *Confessio Amantis of John Gower.* a1393. Edited by Reinhold Pauli. Vol. 1. London: Bell and Daldy, 1857.

Gowers, Ernest. *The Complete Plain Words.* Edited by Sidney Greenbaum and Janet Whitcut. Boston: David R. Godine, 1988.

Grose, Francis. *A Classical Dictionary of the Vulgar Tongue.* London, 1785.

Gwynne, N. M. *Gwynne's Grammar: The Ultimate Introduction to Grammar and the Writing of Good English.* London: Ebury Press, 2013.

Huddleston, Rodney, and Geoffrey K. Pullum. *The Cambridge Grammar of the English Language.* Cambridge, U.K.: Cambridge University Press, 2002.

Johnson, Samuel. *A Dictionary of the English Language.* London, 1755.

———. *The Plan of a Dictionary of the English Language Addressed to the Right Honorable Philip Dormer, Earl of Chesterfield, One of His Majesty's Principal Secretaries of State.* London: J. and P. Knapton, T. Longman and T. Shewell, C. Hitch, A. Millar, and R. Dodsley, 1747.

Kelham, Robert. *A Dictionary of the Norman or Old French Language.* London: Edward Brooke, 1779.

Kendall, Joshua. *The Forgotten Founding Father: Noah Webster's Obsession and the Creation of an American Culture.* New York: Berkley Books, 2010.

Kenrick, William. *A New Dictionary of the English Language.* London, 1773.

Kleinman, Sherryl, Matthew B. Ezzell, and A. Corey Frost. "Reclaiming Critical Analysis: The Social Harms of 'Bitch.'" *Sociological Anaylsis* 3, no. 1 (Spring 2009): 47–68.

Kurath, Hans, et al. *Middle English Dictionary.* 2001. Ann Arbor: University of Michigan Press. Accessed August 11, 2015. http://quod.lib.umich.edu /m/med/.

Latham, R. E., D. R. Howlett, and R. K. Ashdowne. *Dictionary of Medieval Latin from British Sources.* Oxford: British Academy, 2013.

Liberman, Anatoly. "Occam's Razor and Etymology." Paper presented at the DSNA-20 & SHEL-9 Conference, Vancouver, B.C., June 7, 2015.

Lowth, Robert. *A Short Introduction to English Grammar with Critical Notes.* 2nd ed. London: A. Millar, R. Dodsley, J. Dodsley, 1763.

Lynch, Jack. *The Lexicographer's Dilemma: The Evolution of "Proper" English, from Shakespeare to "South Park."* New York: Walker, 2009.

Merriam-Webster. *Merriam-Webster's Collegiate Dictionary.* 11th ed. 2003. Springfield, Mass.: Merriam-Webster, 2014.

———. *Merriam-Webster's Collegiate Dictionary.* 10th ed. Springfield, Mass.: Merriam-Webster, 1993.

———. *Merriam-Webster's Concise Dictionary of English Usage.* Springfield, Mass.: Merriam-Webster, 2002.

———. *Merriam-Webster's Intermediate Dictionary.* 1998. Springfield, Mass.: Merriam-Webster, 2011.

————. *Merriam-Webster's School Dictionary.* Springfield, Mass.: Merriam-Webster, 1994.

————. *Merriam-Webster Unabridged.* 2015. Accessed April 24, 2016. unabridged.merriam-webster.com.

————. "Quirkly Little Grammar." In In-House Training Materials. 1998.

————. *Webster's Third New International Dictionary of the English Language, Unabridged.* 1961. Springfield, Mass.: Merriam-Webster, 2002.

Metcalf, Allan. *Presidential Voices: Speaking Styles from George Washington to George W. Bush.* New York: Houghton Mifflin Harcourt, 2004.

Micklethwait, David. *Noah Webster and the American Dictionary.* Jefferson, N.C.: McFarland, 2000.

Morton, Herbert C. *The Story of "Webster's Third": Philip Gove's Controversial Dictionary and Its Critics.* Cambridge, U.K.: Cambridge University Press, 1994.

Mulcaster, Richard. *The First Part of the Elementarie Which Entreateth Chefelie of the Right Writing of Our English Tung.* London: Thomas Vautroullier, 1582.

Murray, James. *An Appeal to the English-Speaking and English-Reading Public to Read Books and Make Extracts for the Philological Society's New English Dictionary.* Privately printed, 1879.

Obergefell v. Hodges. 576 U.S. ___ (2015).

Orm. *Ormulum, with the Notes and Glossary of Dr. R. M. White.* Edited by Robert Holt. Oxford: Clarendon Press, 1878.

Oxford English Dictionary. "History of the OED: Reading Programme." *Oxford English Dictionary* (blog). 2013. Accessed Aug. 11, 2015. http://public.oed.com/history-of-the-oed/reading-programme/.

————. *Oxford English Dictionary.* 3rd ed. Oxford: Oxford University Press, 2011.

Phone Call. Performed by Key and Peele. Comedy Central, 2011.

Plato. *Cratylus.* Vol. 12 of *Plato in Twelve Volumes.* Translated by Harold N. Fowler. Cambridge, Mass.: Harvard University Press, 1921.

Queer Nation. "Queers Read This." New York, 1990.

Quirk, Randolph, Sidney Greenbaum, Geoffrey Leech, and Jan Svartvik. *A Comprehensive Grammar of the English Language.* London: Longman, 1985.

Redinger, Johann Jakob. *Comeniana grammatica: Primae classi Frankenthalensis Latinae scholae destinata. . . .* Hanau, 1659.

Select Trials in the Sessions House at the Old-Bailey for Murders, Robberies, Rapes, Sodomy, Coining, Fraud, Bigamy, and Other Offences. London, 1743.

Shakespeare, William. *Love's Labour's Lost.* In *The Complete Works of William Shakespeare.* New York: Dorset Press, 1984.

Shea, Ammon. *Bad English: A History of Linguistic Aggravation.* New York: Perigee, 2014.

Sheridan, Thomas. *A Complete Dictionary of the English Language.* London, 1780.

Skelton, John. *The Boke of Phyllyp Sparowe.* c. 1500. London: Rychard Kele, 1545.

Skinner, David. *The Story of Ain't: America, Its Language, and the Most Controversial Dictionary Ever Published.* New York: HarperCollins, 2012.

Smith, Goldwin. *Essays on Questions of the Day Political and Social.* New York: Macmillan, 1893.

Solomon, Jane, and Orion Montoya. "How Do People Use Cross-References in Online Dictionaries?" Paper presented at the DSNA-20 & SHEL-9 Conference, Vancouver, B.C., June 6, 2015.

Starr, Kenneth, comp. "Referral to the United States House of Representatives Pursuant to Title 28, United States Code, § 595(c)." In *Starr Report.* U.S. Government Printing Office, Sept. 9, 1998.

Steinway, Susan. "An Archivist Mines the Usage Ballots." *American Heritage* (blog), Jan. 28, 2014. Accessed Sept. 28, 2015. http://ahdictionary.tumblr.com/post/74834243179/an-archivist-mines-the-usage-ballots.

Stoliker, Bryce E., and Kathryn D. Lafreniere. "The Influence of Perceived Stress, Loneliness, and Learning Burnout on University Students' Educational Experience." *College Student Journal* 49, no. 1 (Spring 2015): 146–60.

Strunk, William, Jr., and E. B. White. *The Elements of Style.* New York: Macmillan, 1959.

Swift, Jonathan. *A Proposal for Correcting, Improving, and Ascertaining the English Tongue; in a Letter to the Most Honorable Robert Earl of Oxford and Mortimer, Lord High Treasurer of Great Britain.* 2nd ed. London, 1712.

———. *The Works of Jonathan Swift, Containing Interesting and Valuable Papers Hitherto Not Published.* Edited by Thomas Roscoe. London, 1841.

Taniguchi v. Kan Pacific Saipan Ltd. 566 U.S. ___ (2012).

Thrax, Dionysius. *The Grammar of Dionysius Thrax.* Translated by Thomas Davidson. St. Louis: R. P. Studley, 1874.

Truss, Lynne. *Eats, Shoots & Leaves: The Zero Tolerance Approach to Punctuation.* New York: Gotham Books, 2004.

Vivian, Evelyn Charles. *The British Army from Within.* New York, 1914.

Walker, Alice. "The Old Artist: Notes on Mr. Sweet." In *Living by the Word.* San Diego: Harcourt Brace Jovanovich, 1988.

Wallace, David Foster. "The Broom of the System." In *The David Foster Wallace Reader.* New York: Little, Brown, 2014.

———. "The Compliance Branch." *Harper's Magazine,* Feb. 2008, 17–19.

———. "English 183A—13 Nov. 2002—Your Liberal-Arts $ at Work." In *The David Foster Wallace Reader.* New York: Little, Brown, 2014.

———. "Tense Present: Democracy, English, and the Wars over Usage." *Harper's Magazine,* April 2001, 39–58.

Webster, Noah. *An American Dictionary of the English Language.* New York, 1828.

———. *A Letter to Dr. Ramsay of Charleston, (S.C.) Respecting the Errors in Johnson's Dictionary, and Other Lexicons.* New Haven: Oliver Steele & Company, 1807.

Webster, Noah, Chauncey A. Goodrich, and Noah Porter. *An American Dictionary of the English Language.* Springfield, Mass.: G. & C. Merriam, 1864.

White, E. B. "Some Remarks on Humor." In *The Second Tree from the Corner.* New York: HarperCollins, 1941.

White, Richard Grant. *Words and Their Uses, Past and Present.* New York: Sheldon, 1870.

Wilson, Tracy V. "How Surfing Works." HowStuffWorks.com, June 11, 2007.

Winchester, Simon. *The Professor and the Madman: A Tale of Murder, Insanity, and the Making of the Oxford English Dictionary.* New York: HarperCollins, 1998.

Worcester, Joseph. *A Comprehensive Pronouncing and Explanatory English Dictionary with Pronouncing Vocabularies.* Burlington, Vt., 1830.

———. *A Dictionary of the English Language.* Boston: Hickling, Swan, and Brewer, 1860.

———. *A Universal and Critical Dictionary of the English Language.* Boston: Wilkins, Carter, 1846.

———, ed. *Johnson's English Dictionary, as Improved by Todd, and Abridged by Chalmers; with Walker's Pronouncing Dictionary, Combined.* Boston, 1828.

Zimmer, Benjamin, and Charles E. Carson. "Among the New Words." *American Speech* 88, no. 2 (Summer 2013): 196–214.

Index

A (dictionary section), reasons for
  not starting with, 109–10
"a," 139–40
AAVE, *see* African-American
  Vernacular English
"abecedarian," 77–8
Abzug, Bella, 157
accent marks, 205
acronyms, 178–9
  initialisms vs., 179
"actress," 191–2
adjectives, 34
Adler, Polly, 79
adverbs, 29, 34
African-American Vernacular
  English (AAVE), 61, 62, 63,
  67
"ain't," 36, 50, 187–8
Akkadian language, 171
Albanian language, 171
Alito, Samuel, 251
alphabets
  phonemic vs. phonetic, 202
  proprietary, 201–2
*American Dictionary of the English
  Language, An* (Webster), 73–4,
  164, 172, 242, 245*n*, 252
  1847 edition of, 244
  1864 edition of, 248
"American dream," 195–6
American exceptionalism, 242

American Heritage Dictionary, The,
  31, 139, 171, 186, 200, 203,
  235, 247, 251
  Usage Panel of, 185–8
American Scholar, 247
Anabaptists, 77–8
analytical definitions, 114–15
Anglo-Saxon, 8
Annales (Tacitus), 192
"antidisestablishmentarianism," 101
Aristotle, 27
articles, 28, 32
Art of Grammar, The, 27
Ash, John, 154
Asimov, Isaac, 187
"asshat," 176
Atchison Daily Globe, 59
Austen, Jane, 45, 190–1
authorial quotations, 126–8
authority
  appeals to, 247
  dictionary as, 232–54

Bad English (Shea), 183
bad words, 73, 142, 149–68
  context and, 151–2, 165–6
  inclusion vs. exclusion of,
    149–50
  labels for, 150–1, 156–7
  reclamation of, *see* reclamation,
    linguistic

Bailey, Nathaniel, 72–3, 154
Barzun, Jacques, 247
Beastie Boys, 175
"beck," 172–3
"bent," 26–7
Bethel, John, 162
biases, *see* prejudices, linguistic
Bicknell, Arthur, 249
"bitch," 150–3, 154–8, 159–60, 264
BITCH Manifesto, The (Freeman),
    157–8
Black Books (Merriam-Webster
    style guides), 103–5, 106,
    150*n*, 151
Black's Law Dictionary, 251
bookstores, dictionaries and,
    259
"bored of," 76–7
Bostonians, The (James), 192
"Boston marriage," 192
Brady, Susan, 164
Brandon, Dan, 53, 169, 216–17,
    258
Bref Grammar for English
    (Bullokar), 41
Brewster, Emily, 17, 30–1, 85, 119,
    124, 128, 139–40, 156–7, 169,
    205, 219, 258, 259, 260, 261
Breyer, Stephen, 251
Bright's Old English Grammar, 7
broadcast media, as pronunciation
    sources, 200
"broadly," 121
"brothel," 192
Buchanan, James, 205, 206
Bullokar, William, 41
Burns, Robert, 156
Burnside, Ambrose, 171
Bush, George H. W., 211, 214

Bush, George W., 210, 211, 212,
    214
"but," 29–31
BuzzFeed, 221–2

cant, 71, 153–4
Car and Driver, 89
Car Talk (radio show), 193
Carter, Jimmy, 211, 212
Cassidy, Frederic, 7*n*
Cawdrey, Robert, 41, 70–1
Caxton, William, 40
Century Company, 260
Chaldee, 172
Chancery English (Chancery
    Standard), 39–40
Charles II, King of England, 153*n*
Chaucer, Geoffrey, 38
"chaus," 176
Chesterfield, Earl of, 21
Chicano English, 61, 62
Chippendale, H. A., 151
Churchill, Winston, 197, 198
citations, citation files, 18, 56–7
    emphasis on written vs. spoken
        language in, 83–4
    Internet and, 80, 257
    Johnson's use of, 73
    new vs. common words in, 88
    for pronunciation, 200
    sorting of, 138, 141–2, 144, 145,
        146
    as source of authorial quotations,
        126
    sources of, 85–6
    stamping of, 146
*Classical Dictionary of the Vulgar
    Tongue, A* (Grose), 154–5
Clinton, Bill, 140, 211, 212

clipping slang, 196
Cocking, Tom, 154
code-switching, 64*n*, 66
coinages, 50, 75–6
first print usage vs., 190–1
glosses of, 82–3
personal claims for, 197–8
recency illusion and, 197
Colbert, Stephen, 231, 253
Colbert Report, The (TV show), 231, 253
colors, defining of, 222–3, 224
communication, as inborn human desire, xi
Compendious Dictionary of the English Language, A (Webster), 9
Complete English Tradesman in Familiar Letters, The (Defoe), 42
Comprehensive Grammar of the English Language, A (Quirk et al.), 26, 29–30
Comprehensive Pronouncing and Explanatory Dictionary of the English Language (Worcester), 155, 242*n*
Confessio Amantis (Gower), 196
conjunctions, 29–30
Connor, Christopher, 75, 258
connotation, denotation vs., 165
context, defining and, 101–2
contractions, 49
Cook, Daniel, 162, 163, 167
Coote, Edmund, 70
copyediting, copy editors, 20, 117–18

corpus, corpora, 80–1, 88
dialects, regionalisms and, 81
limitations of, 82
correspondence, between users and lexicographers, 52–6, 216–29, 261
as duty of Merriam-Webster editors, 52–3, 216–17
humanization of language in, 228
as marketing tactic, 218
"outside the scope of our knowledge" questions in, 217, 220
relationships developed through, 218–19
cot-caught merger, 202–3
Cowley, Malcolm, 187
craft, lexicography as, 255–6, 259, 260
Cratylus (Plato), 27
cross-reference editors, 117
cubicles, of lexicographers, 169–70
"cunt," 154
"cynical," 101–2

Daly, Jim, 249
dates, in entries, 189
in *Collegiate* vs. *Unabridged*, 191–2
popular misconceptions about, 190–3
sources for, 190, 191, 194–5
dating editors, 117
"day hike," 194–5
"dead-cat bounce," 233
"decimate," 182–4, 188
Defense of Marriage Act (H.R. 3396), 236, 252

definiendum, definienda, 114
  see also entries
defining, lexical, 94–124
  analytical, 114–15
  biases in, 131–2
  citations in, 56–7
  of colors, 222–3
  context and, 101–2
  differentiae in, 115–16, 119,
    120–4
  editorialization in, 107–8
  entries in, *see* entries
  exactness and, 17, 19–20
  formulaic definition in, 102–3
  genus in, 114–15
  headword in, 96–7
  house style and, 103–10
  lexicographer's experience and,
    256, 259
  lexicographer's prejudices in,
    108–9
  linguistic reclamation and, 166–8
  lumpers vs. splitters in, 119–20
  ostensive, 112–13
  parenthetical adjuncts in, 120–1
  parts of speech in, 99, 102–3
  practice sessions in, 105–9
  real defining vs., 94–6
  risk of outdatedness in, 120–1
  senses and subsenses in, 96–7,
    107, 140–8, 162
  substitutability in, 103
  synonymous, 113–14, 150*n*
  see also entries
defining, real, 94–6
  in language acquisition, xi–xii
Defoe, Daniel, 41, 42
Democratic Enquirer, 248
denotation, connotation vs., 165

descriptivism, 35–7
Despres, Joanne, 190, 191, 194–6,
    197, 198, 258
diacritical marks, 205
dialects and regionalisms, 60–4
  author's personal experience of,
    61–3, 65
  corpora and, 81
  grammar of, 63
  marginalization of, 66–7
  as sign of linguistic growth, 63
  stereotyping and, 60–2, 63, 66
dictionaries
  as aspirational texts, 205
  authority of, 232–54
  bilingual, 69
  bookstores and, 259
  breadth and depth in, 75–80
  of cant, 153–4
  changing use and expectations
    of, 257
  as commercial enterprises,
    256–8, 259–60
  common words ignored by, 71
  correspondence with users of, *see*
    correspondence, between users
    and lexicographers
  entries in, *see* entries
  general view of, xii, 11–12
  hard words as focus of, 70–1
  historical, 189, 190
  history of, 69–74, 152–6, 203–4
  house style of, 103–10, 150–1
  as human documents, 12
  illustrations in, 113
  letter sections of, 109–11
  linguistic reclamation and, 167
  marketing of, 218, 233, 242,
    244–6, 248, 257

merchant class and, 69

misunderstandings about role of, 237–9

morality and, 245–6, 248–50

online and electronic, 97–8, 126, 203, 232, 257–8, 259, 265

open-source, 98

prescriptive vs. descriptive view of, 35–7, 52

production schedules for, 117–18

pronouncing, 205–6

proprietary alphabets of, 201–2

public readers employed by, 75

as records of language in actual use, 35–6, 54, 69

risk of outdatedness in, 20, 120–1, 258

small words in, 136

space limitation of, 257–8

specialized, 190

Supreme Court and, 250–3

of thieves' cant, 71

timelines for new editions of, 20

unabridged, 119

viewed as cultural and political tools, 236, 238, 241–2, 247–50

see also lexicography

Dictionary.com, 167, 235

Dictionary of Modern English Usage (Fowler), 208

Dictionary of the English Language (Johnson), 21, 73–4, 153, 155, 243, 245*n*

pronunciation guides in, 204, 205, 207

Dictionary Society of North America, 147–8

Dictionary Wars, 243–6

differentiae, 120–4

in definitions, 115–16, 119

"dilemma," 187

"dope slap," 193

double negatives, 50, 53, 54, 59–60

Dryden, John, 41, 46–7, 48

due process clause, 252

Early Modern English, 39–40, 174

Eats, Shoots & Leaves (Truss), 43–4

Ebonics, 61

editorialization, in definitions, 107–8

Eisenhower, Dwight, 211, 212

Elementarie (Mulcaster), 69–70, 204

Elements of Style, The (Strunk and White), 37, 49

Elyot, Thomas, 110

Encarta, 260

England, 40

English language

author's love of, 4, 9, 12, 86

flexibility and adaptability of, 25–6, 184, 187, 188

fluidity of, 8

foreign borrowings in, 40–1, 71, 207–8

as illogical, vii, 8, 53, 54–5, 60, 64, 182

invention and coinages in, 75–6

as language of record, 38–9

as literary language, 40–1

native speakers of, 13, 14–15

proposed academy for, 41, 185

rate of growth of, 100

redundancy in, 53, 54

spelling vs. pronunciation in, 201, 206–7

English language *(cont.)*
    spoken, *see* language, spoken
    variability of, 51
    written, *see* language, written
English Schoole-Maister, The
    (Coote), 70
Enlightenment, 72
Entertainment Weekly, 88
entries
    dates in, *see* dates, in entries
    example sentences in, *see*
        example sentences
    history of, 160–4
    inclusion vs. exclusion of, 97–8,
        149–50
    labels in, 150–1, 156–7, 164–5,
        186
    long shelf life as criterion for, 100
    meaningful use as criterion for,
        101
    pronunciations in, *see*
        pronunciation
    reviewing and revision of,
        117–18, 136, 138, 140–8
    substitutes in, 96–7
    usage notes in, 104*n*, 125, 157,
        163, 164, 189–90
    widespread use as criterion for,
        99–100
    write-in campaigns on, 236–7,
        249–50
    see also defining, lexical
equal protection clause, 252
"especially," 121
etymological fallacy, 182–5
etymology, 117, 169–88
    of acronyms, 178–9
    as based on conjecture and
        reconstruction, 173, 174
    erroneous, 176–82
    stories and, 179–80
    Webster and, 172–3
Evening Post (New York), 244
exactness, lexical defining and, 17,
    19–20
example sentences, 125–35
    authorial quotations as, 126–8
    function of, 134–5
    unattributed, *see* verbal
        illustrations

feminism, language and, 157–8,
    159
Fielding, Henry, 156
Fifth Amendment, 252
"figuratively"/"literally," 48–9
Finnish language, 170
"fishstick," 118–19, 120
Florio, John, 149, 153*n*
Focus on the Family, 249
food words, 198
Ford, Gerald, 211, 212
Fourteenth Amendment, 252
Fowler, Henry, 208
Franklin, Benjamin, 206
Freeman, Jo, 157–8
French language, 174–5, 185
    English borrowings from, 207–8
    as language of record, 38–9
    nasal vowels in, 208
Friedman, Nancy, 98
"fuck," 149–50, 154
Funk & Wagnalls, 260

G. & C. Merriam Company, 186,
    218
    see also Merriam-Webster
Garner, Bryan, 48

Garner's Modern American Usage (Garner), 48

gay marriage, *see* same-sex marriage

General Western American dialect, 61

genus, in definitions, 114–15

Germanic languages, 174

German language, 8

Gilliver, Peter, 148

Gilman, E. Ward "Gil," 16–17, 24–5, 28, 29, 32, 34–5, 50, 86, 94, 106, 107, 108, 109, 115, 128, 164, 217

glosses, of words, 82–3

"good"/"well," 34–5

Gove, Philip Babcock, vii, 103–4, 105, 129, 132

Gower, John, 196

gradience, 26

grammar
    of dialects, 63
    and flexibility of English, 25–6
    "good vs. bad" view of, 32–3, 36, 38, 41–2
    language acquisition and, 33–4
    of Latin vs. English languages, 47
    lexicographers and, 23–37
    morality and, 36, 42, 43, 50–1
    in Sanskrit, 27*n*
    usage distinguished from, 43, 48

grammar books, 36, 42–3, 49
    faulty logic in, 44–5
    merchant class and, 42
    usage rules in, 43–6

Greek, 28

Grose, Francis, 154–5

Guenter, Josh, 199, 200–1, 202, 206–10, 213–14, 215

Gwynne, N. M., 44

Gwynne's Grammar (Gwynne), 44

Haitian Creole, 67

Hamp, Eric, 171

Harper's, 48

Harry Potter books (Rowling), 80

headword, 96–7
    function of dots in, 219–20

"hella," 98–9, 103

Henderson, Bryan, 80

Henry V, King of England, 38

Henry VII, King of England, 38*n*

Henry VIII (Shakespeare), 45

Historia naturalis (Pliny the Elder), 176

historical dictionaries, 189, 190

Hockey: A Brutal Game (film), 193

Hollingsworth v. Perry, 252

"hotel," 119–20, 123–4

House Is Not a Home, A (Adler), 79

house style, 103–10, 150–1

Hrafnkell, 6

hyphens, use of, 15

Icelandic sagas, 5–6

identity, language and, 157–9, 165, 167–8

idioms, 142, 147
    familiarity with, 14

illustrations, in dictionaries, 113

immigrants, food words and, 198

"imply," 251–2

index cards, color-coding of, 18

"infer," 251–2

initialisms, 196–7
    acronyms vs., 179

intensive forms, 56, 64–5
International Phonetic Alphabet, 202*n*
Internet, 85
   citations and, 80, 257
   corpora and, *see* corpus, corpora
   definition searches on, 139, 232
   as double-edged sword for
      lexicographers, 257–8, 265
   free information as expectation
      on, 258
   as pronunciation sources, 200
   risk of outdatedness and, 258
   surfeit of information on, 258
"irregardless," 36, 53–60, 64–5,
   187–8, 271*n*
"is," 140
Italic languages, 174
"its/it's," 43–6

James, Henry, 192
Japanese language, 173–4
jargon and specialized vocabulary,
   83, 90
   of lexicography, 96, 255
Jeantel, Rachel, 66–7
Jefferson, Thomas, 45
Johnson, Samuel, 51, 79, 149–50,
   153, 155, 204, 205, 207, 242*n*,
   243, 245*n*
   dictionary of, *see Dictionary
      of the English Language*
      (Johnson)
   lexicographers as defined by,
      20–1
   on lexicography, 21
Journal to Stella (Swift), 49

Kay, Mairé Weir, 162–3
Kennedy, Rose, 212

Kennedy, Ted, 212
Key and Peele, 64*n*
Kichi, John, 158–9
King Lear (Shakespeare), 45
Kleinedler, Steve, 31, 139, 171,
   187, 200–1, 236
KLF, 95
Kurmanji, 171

labels, in entries, 150–1, 156–7,
   164–5, 186
language
   feminism and, 157–8, 159
   identity and, 157–9, 165, 167–8
   as personal, 167–8, 228, 231–2,
      237, 241
   see also specific languages
language, spoken
   citation and, 83–4
   as primary means of language
      acquisition, 84
   variability of, 39
language, written
   citation and, 83–4
   standardization of, 39
language acquisition
   defining in, xi–xii
   grammar and, 33–4
   sentences in, 134
   speech as primary means of,
      84
Language Research Service, 218
Latin language, 8, 28, 184
   as language of record, 38–9
   as ne plus ultra of elegant style,
      47
Lawrence v. Texas, 252
Lefkow, Joan Humphrey, 240
Letter to Dr. Ramsay . . . Respecting

the *Errors in Johnson's
Dictionary, A* (Webster), 79n
letter-writing guides, 42
lexicographers, 12
  as compulsive readers, 91
  correspondence between users
    and, *see* correspondence,
    between users and
    lexicographers
  cubicles of, 169–70
  as dying breed, 98, 260
  grammar and, 23–37
  human limitations on, 84–5, 167
  individual experiences and
    assumptions of, 159–60
  Internet as double-edged sword
    for, 257–8
  Johnson's definition of, 20–1
  lack of appreciation for, 260
  as linguistic bystanders, 166, 167
  as lumpers vs. splitters, 119–20
  Merriam-Webster's requirements
    for, 13–15
  misperception of, 68–9
  as native English speakers, 13,
    14–15
  parts of speech and, 34
  as plagiarists, 71, 155
  prejudices of, xii–xiii, 20, 34,
    50, 53, 54, 56, 108–9, 159–60,
    164–5, 167
  production schedules and,
    117–18
  reading as primary job of, 68–9,
    73
  role of, Webster on, 74
  search engines and, 258–9
  silence and solitude of, 11,
    15–17, 20, 199–200

source lists of, 78–80
specialist vs. generalist, 13–14,
  74–5, 117–18
sprachgefühl of, 15, 30, 56, 58,
  82, 117, 129, 142, 143, 223
time crunch and, 258, 259
tools of, 17–18
unique idiolects of, 89
usage rules and, 50
lexicography, 255
  as calling, 21–2, 256, 261–2
  as craft, 255–6, 259, 260
  jargon of, 96, 255
  Johnson on, 21
  as linguistic surgery, 160
  as mattering, 232
  as mix of science and art, 17, 255
  repetitive nature of, 20, 256
  as shrinking industry, 98, 260
  see also dictionaries
LGBTQIA movement, 158
Liberman, Anatoly, 173
Liberty Forum, 240
Lincoln, Abraham, 45
"lingerie," 208–9
*Linguae Britannicae Vera
  Pronunciatio* (Buchanan), 205
linguists, 32
literacy
  eighteenth-century boom in, 42,
    72
  Protestant Reformation and,
    71–2
"literally"/"figuratively," 48–9
Llewellyn, Bill, 189–90
Logansport Reporter, 60
logophiles, 170
Long, Percy, 161–2
"love," 95–6, 132n

Love's Labour's Lost
  (Shakespeare), 40*n*
Lowth, Robert, 42
lumpers, in definition writing,
  119–20
Lutheran Church, 158

Magliozzi, Ray, 193
Magliozzi, Tom, 193
"mansplain," 75–6, 165
marketing, of dictionaries, 218,
  233, 242, 244–6, 248, 257
"marriage," 231, 233–4, 248–50,
  253–4, 263–4
Martin, Trayvon, 66–7
Mary-merry-marry merger, 202–3
MDMA, 175–6
"measly," 17, 20
Meiji dynasty, 174
merchant class
  dictionaries and, 69
  grammar books and, 42
mergers, in pronunciation, 202–3
Merriam, George and Charles, 9,
  218, 243–5
Merriam-Webster
  author's job interview at, 3, 9, 16
  citation files at, 57
  correspondence between public
    and, *see* correspondence,
    between users and
    lexicographers
  dating project of, 189
  history of, 9
  holiday parties at, 19
  house style guides (Black Books)
    of, 103–5, 106
  Language Research Service of,
    218

layoffs at, 259–60
marketing by, 218, 233, 244, 246
offices of, 10–11
staff of, 261
Style and Defining classes at,
  24–5, 34, 50
see also G. & C. Merriam
  Company
*Merriam-Webster's Collegiate
  Dictionary,* 9, 20, 100, 117,
  148, 150, 191–2, 199, 203,
  209, 210
  Eleventh Edition of, 118, 136,
    139, 148, 233, 234, 236, 253
  first edition of, 164
  Ninth Edition of, 190
  Seventh Edition of, 164
  Tenth Edition of, 164
*Merriam-Webster's Concise
  Dictionary of English Usage,*
  24, 39
Merry Wives of Windsor, The
  (Shakespeare), 152
"metathesis," 211–12
Metcalf, Allan, 213
"microaggression," 165
Middle Chinese, 171
Middle English, 8, 39
Minor, William Chester, 74*n*
Mish, Fred, 16, 164, 167, 261
Modern English, 174
"molly," 175–6
Mondale, Walter, 212
Monroee, Peaches, 85
Monty Python and the Holy Grail
  (film), 130, 273*n*
morality, 56
  dictionaries and, 245–6, 248–50
  grammar and, 42, 43

Morton, Herbert C., 246*n*
"muggle," 80, 272*n*
Mulcaster, Richard, 69–70, 204
"mullet," 175
Murray, James, 74*n*, 173

Narmontas, Joan, 108, 256, 258
nasal vowels, 208
Nation, 240
New York Times, 82
New York Times Book Review, 246
"nigger," 168
North Inland dialect, 61
nouns, 29
Novak, Madeline, 85–6, 102, 169, 261
"nuclear," 210–15, 276*n*
"nude," 221–8
Nunberg, Geoff, 212*n*, 213

obelus, 210–11
Obergefell v. Hodges, 252, 254, 263, 271*n*
"obscene," 151
"OK," 188
Old Bailey, 155–6, 163
Old English, 7, 8
Old Frisian Etymological Dictionary, 170, 175
Old Norse, 173
   pronunciation of, 6–7
"OMG," 178, 196–7
"on fleek," 85
"origin unknown," 176
orthography, *see* spelling
ostensive defining, 112–13
Ottawa Citizen, 193–4
"outershell," 108–9, 115
overmarking, 89–90

Oxford English Dictionary, 148, 173, 189, 190, 191*n*, 235, 251
   public reading program of, 74

Palladium, 243
parenthetical adjuncts, 120–1
Parton, James, 186
parts of speech
   as based on Greek and Latin concepts, 27–8
   in definitions, 99, 102–3
   and flexibility of English, 25–6, 187
   gradience and, 26
   lexicographers and, 34
   sorting citations by, 138
"pasha," 181
"pedophile," 199
peeves, peevers, 32, 35–6, 56, 132, 182–3, 196–7, 207–8, 210
   etymological fallacy and, 182–5
   usage rules and, 46, 48–9, 50
   see also "irregardless"; prejudices, linguistic
Pei, Mario, 246, 247
Peninsular and Oriental Company, 177, 181
Perrault, Steve, 3, 9, 16, 34, 86–7, 88, 106, 109–10, 119, 124, 147, 164, 169, 189–90, 216, 227, 229, 256, 260, 261
Perry, Matthew, 174
"phat," 233, 236
"phlegmatic," 172
phonemic alphabets, 202
phonetic alphabets, 202
phrasal verbs, 143
Pinker, Steven, 213

"pinks" (Merriam-Webster interoffice communications), 17–18
pin-pen merger, 202
plagiarism, by lexicographers, 71, 155
Plato, 27
Pliny the Elder, 176
"pneumonoultramicroscopic-silicovolcanoconiosis," 101
Poetics (Aristotle), 27
Polish language, 173–4
political correctness, 248
Porter, Noah, 248
"posh," 177–8, 180–1
possessive forms, 43–6
"pragmatic," 127–8
prejudices, linguistic, xii–xiii, 20, 34, 50, 53, 54, 56, 108–9, 131–2, 164–5, 167–8
    see also peeves, peevers
prepositions, 29, 30
    ending sentences with, 46–7
prescriptivism, 35–7, 52, 251
printing press, standardization of English and, 40
profanity, *see* bad words
pronouncing dictionaries, 205–6
pronunciation, 199–215
    citations for, 200
    in early dictionaries, 203–4
    of foreign borrowings, 207–8
    mergers in, 202–3
    metathesis in, 211–12
    nonstandard, 209–10
    sources for, 200
    spelling vs., 201, 206–7
    standard variants in, 209–10
    stress in, 205, 208

transcription of, 201–2, 205–6
pronunciation editors, 117, 199, 200, 203
proofreaders, proofreading, 20, 118
Proposition 8 (California), 252
Protestant Reformation, 71–2
publications, list of, *see* Reading and Marking list
"pumpernickel," 182
Puritans, 153*n*
Pynson, Richard, 40

"queer," 158
Queer Nation, 158
Quirk, Randolph, 26
"Quirky Little Grammar for Definers, A," 25, 28

Rader, Jim, 169–71, 173, 175–6, 188
Random House, 260
Random House Dictionary, 251
reading, as lexicographer's primary job, 68–9, 73
reading and marking
    as compulsive activity, 91–3
    as core lexicographic skill
    lexicographer's unique idiolects and, 89
    overmarking in, 89–90
    practice sessions for, 86–8
    reading for comfort vs., 87
    skimming vs., 87
    specialized vocabulary and, 90
Reading and Marking list, 85–6
    multiple editors and, 89–91
recency illusion, 196, 197
reclamation, linguistic, 157–9, 165–6
    definitions and, 166–8

redundancy, 53, 54
Rehnquist, William, 250
retronyms, 218*n*
Richard I, King of England, 38*n*
Rickford, John, 66–7
Roberts, John, 250, 252–3
Rochester, John Wilmot, Earl of,
    153*n*
rogue literature, 71
Rule of Silence, 16

S (dictionary section), length of,
    111
"safari," 192–3
Safire, William, 24, 48
same-sex marriage, 233–4, 248–50,
    252–4, 263
"sandwich," 179–80
Sandwich, John Montagu, fourth
    Earl of, 179–80
Sanskrit, grammar in, 27*n*
Saturday Review, 247
Scalia, Antonin, 251–2, 272*n*
Scandinavian languages, 171
Schwinger, Julian, 276*n*
search engines, lexicographers and,
    258–9
Second Tree from the Corner, The
    (White), 49
senses, in definitions, 96–7, 107,
    140–8, 162
Serven, Neil, 13, 119, 124, 128,
    258, 259
sexism, 157, 159
Shakespeare, William, 8, 40, 45,
    79*n*, 152, 252*n*
"shaving glass," 190–1
Shea, Ammon, 183
"shoe-rose," 190–1

*Short Introduction to English
    Grammar, A* (Lowth), 42–3
"sideburns," 171
silence, lexicographers and, 11,
    15–17, 199–200
Simpsons, The (TV show), 215*n*
Skelton, John, 40
skimming, dangers of, 87
Skinner, David, 246*n*
slang, 71, 73, 153–4
    clipping, 196
slurs, 158
    microaggression in, 165
    see also "bitch"
small words, 136–48
    difficulty in defining, 137
    multiple senses of, 142–3
    slow rate of semantic shifts in, 139
"snollygoster," 100
Sokolowski, Peter, 27, 203
solitude, of lexicographers, 11,
    15–17, 20
Solomon, Jane, 164–5
source lists, 78–80
Souter, David, 251
Spanish language, 185
"specifically," 121
"specter," 174–5
speech, *see* language, spoken
spelling
    pronunciation vs., 201, 206–7
    reforms of, 206–7
splitters, in definition writing,
    119–20
sprachgefühl, 15, 30, 56, 58, 82,
    117, 129, 142, 143, 223
    pronunciation of, 201–2, 203
Stamper, Kory
    college studies of, 5–9

Stamper, Kory *(cont.)*
  customer service experience of,
    52
  dialects and, 61–3, 65–6
  English language as love of, 4, 9,
    12, 86
  Merriam-Webster job interview
    of, 3, 9, 16
  threatening e-mails to, 248,
    249–50
  as voracious reader, 3–4
Standard English, 36, 64, 66
  as dialect, 50, 60, 63
  as Platonic ideal, 50–1
"stew," 8–9, 222, 227*n*
Story of Ain't, The (Skinner),
    246*n*
Story of "Webster's Third," The
    (Morton), 246*n*
stress, in pronunciation, 205
Style and Defining classes, 24–5,
    34, 50
subsenses, 96–7
  in definitions, 140–1
substitutability, of definitions,
    103
substitutes, in entries, 96–7
superlatives, 55–6
Supreme Court, Hawaiian, 236
Supreme Court, U.S.
  dictionaries and, 250–3
  same-sex marriage decision of,
    250, 252–3, 254
"surfboard," 114–17, 120–1, 122
"sushi," 173–4
Swahili, 192–3
Swift, Jonathan, 41, 49
synonymous definitions, 113–14,
    150*n*

Table Alphabeticall . . . , A
    (Cawdrey), 41, 70–1
"taboo," 151
taboo words, *see* bad words
Tacitus, 192
"take," 136, 138, 140–8
*Taniguchi v. Kan Pacific Saipan
    Ltd.,* 251
Taylor, Patrick, 171
thieves' cant, 71, 153
Thomas, Clarence, 251
Time, 90
Times Literary Supplement,
    178
Tom Jones (Fielding), 156
Transitivity Tester, 27
translation, 7–8
Truss, Lynne, 43, 49
Tuchman, Barbara, 187*n*
Turner, Hal, 240
"twerking," 175
Twitter, 193–4

United States v. Windsor, 252
*Universal and Critical Dictionary
    of the English Language, A*
    (Worcester), 244–5
*Universal Etymological English
    Dictionary, An* (Bailey),
    72–3
Urdu, 181
usage
  familiarity with, 14
  grammar distinguished from,
    43, 48
usage notes, in entries, 104*n*, 125,
    157, 163, 164, 189–90
usage rules, 43–6
  lexicographers and, 50

morality and, 56
peeves and, 46, 48–9, 50

verbal illustrations, 126
    avoiding jokes and double
        entendres in, 130–1
    avoiding names in, 131
    avoiding perceived bias in,
        132
    lexicographer's assumptions
        in writing of, 129
    loaded language in, 133–4
    overwritten, 128–9
    use of pronouns in, 131–2
    verbal fatigue in writing of,
        129–30
Vezina, Emily, 19, 88
"virulent," 171
"vitiate," 204
voiceless alveolar lateral fricative,
    6–7
vowels, long vs. short, 205
"vulgar," 151

Wallace, David Foster, 48
Webster, Noah, 9, 73–4, 79, 97,
    149–50, 155, 242
    etymology and, 172–3
    role of lexicographers as viewed
        by, 74
    spelling reforms of, 206
    Worcester's rivalry with, 242–3
"Webster's," public-domain status
    of, 12
*Webster's New International
    Dictionary, Unabridged*
    first edition of, 161
    Second Edition of, 161–2, 186,
        246, 251

Webster's New World Dictionary,
    257n
*Webster's Revised Unabridged
    Dictionary,* 238n
*Webster's Third New International
    Dictionary, Unabridged,* 16,
        20, 32, 79, 103, 118–19, 132,
        151, 162–3, 175, 176, 190,
        191–2, 195, 209, 251–2
    criticisms of, 185–6, 246–7
    front matter of, 85
    marketing of, 246
Weekly Kansas Chief, 58–9
"well"/"good," 34–5
White, E. B., 37, 49
White, Richard Grant, 183
Wilkinson, Karen, 217, 220
Worcester, Joseph, 155, 218
    Webster's rivalry with, 242–3
"word," definition of, 54
word lists, 69–70
Wordnik, 82
words
    as able to cause pain, 168
    bad, *see* bad words
    denotation vs. connotation of,
        165
    for food, 198
    glosses of, 82–3
    "made-up," 65
    medium-length, as top lookups in
        online dictionaries, 139
    morality and, 56, 149–50, 196,
        241
    new, *see* coinages
    new uses of, 76–7, 187
    as personally important, 167–8,
        228, 231–2, 237, 241
    small, *see* small words

words (*cont.*)
    specialized, 83, 90
    things vs., 242, 248–9, 250
    see also entries
Worlde of Wordes, A (Florio),
    153*n*
WorldNetDaily, 237–9, 240–1
World War II, acronyms in, 179

"worth their salt," 172
write-in campaigns, on entries,
    236–7, 249–50

YouTube, 200

Zimmerman, George, 66–7
Zwicky, Arnold, 196

Permissions Acknowledgments

Grateful acknowledgment is made to the following for permission to reprint previously published material:

Houghton Mifflin Harcourt: Excerpt of "An Archivist Mines the Usage Ballots," published on the *American Heritage® Dictionary* blog, "The American Heritage® Dictionary of the English Language" (http://ahdictionary.tumblr.com/) on January 28, 2014; excerpt of entry for "marriage," from *The American Heritage Dictionary of the English Language, Fourth Edition*, copyright © 2000 by Houghton Mifflin Company; and excerpt of entry for "marriage," from *The American Heritage Dictionary of the English Language, Fourth Edition*, copyright © 2009 by Houghton Mifflin Harcourt Publishing Company. Summarization of "ain't" from the Houghton Mifflin Harcourt archives, in-house balloting summary, Usage Panel (December 1964); summarizations of usage notes for "dilemma," "irregardless," and "decimate" from *The American Heritage® Dictionary of the English Language, Fifth Edition*, copyright © 2016 by Houghton Mifflin Harcourt Publishing Company. Reprinted and summarized by permission from Houghton Mifflin Harcourt.

Merriam-Webster: Merriam-Webster definitions, correspondence, and in-house material including notes. Reprinted by permission of Merriam-Webster.

Public Affairs: Excerpt from "Going Nucular" by Geoff Nunberg, copyright © 2002 by Geoff Nunberg. Reprinted by permission of Public Affairs, a member of the Perseus Books Group.

Portions of this book originally appeared on the author's blog, "Harmless Drudgery" (www.korystamper.com).